Capitalist
Industrialization
in Korea

Westview Special Studies

The concept of Westview Special Studies is a response to the continuing crisis in academic and informational publishing. Library budgets are being diverted from the purchase of books and used for data banks, computers, micromedia, and other methods of information retrieval. Interlibrary loan structures further reduce the edition sizes required to satisfy the needs of the scholarly community. Economic pressures on university presses and the few private scholarly publishing companies have greatly limited the capacity of the industry to properly serve the academic and research communities. As a result, many manuscripts dealing with important subjects, often representing the highest level of scholarship, are no longer economically viable publishing projects—or, if accepted for publication, are typically subject to lead times ranging from one to three years.

Westview Special Studies are our practical solution to the problem. As always, the selection criteria include the importance of the subject, the work's contribution to scholarship, and its insight, originality of thought, and excellence of exposition. We accept manuscripts in camera-ready form, typed, set, or word processed according to specifications laid out in our comprehensive manual, which contains straightforward instructions and sample pages. The responsibility for editing and proofreading lies with the author or sponsoring institution, but our editorial staff is always available to answer questions and provide guidance.

The result is a book printed on acid-free paper and bound in sturdy library-quality soft covers. We manufacture these books ourselves using equipment that does not require a lengthy make-ready process and that allows us to publish first editions of 300 to 1000 copies and to reprint even smaller quantities as needed. Thus, we can produce Special Studies quickly and can keep even very specialized books in print as long as there is a demand for them.

About the Book and Author

South Korea's rapid industrialization has often been cited as a development success story, but there is strong disagreement and controversy over the factors and policies that lie behind that spectacular growth. In order to explain how industrial capital became the dominant economic and social force in South Korea, Dr. Hamilton assesses the effects of Japanese colonialism on an economic system that was based primarily on tenant agriculture. He then traces the impact of government policies implemented by the strong centralized Korean state that, bolstered by U.S. aid, emerged after World War II. Using a computable general equilibrium model, he analyzes the relation between structural change and accumulation in the Korean economy in the 1960s and 1970s. Because the full empirical application of the model, which is derived from East European planning techniques, has not been attempted before, Dr. Hamilton also examines the model's usefulness, its drawbacks, and its applicability to market economies.

He finds that several factors were critical for sustained growth—the transfer of surplus from the agricultural and service sectors to manufacturing; technical innovations; and especially imports. Exporting, claims Dr. Hamilton, was not an end in itself and in fact was often unprofitable. However, the Korean government strongly encouraged the export sector in order to gain the foreign exchange needed to buy the imports on which growth depended. The state used the price system to validate investment decisions based on criteria other than private profitability. The book concludes with an evaluation of the implications of the Korean experience for other developing nations.

Dr. Clive Hamilton is a teaching Fellow at the Development Studies Centre, Australian National University.

Capitalist Industrialization in Korea

Clive Hamilton

Westview Press / Boulder and London

Westview Special Studies on East Asia

Copyright © 1986 by Westview Press, Inc.

Published in 1986 in the United States of America by Westview Press, Inc.; Frederick A. Praeger, Publisher; 5500 Central Avenue, Boulder, Colorado 80301

Library of Congress Cataloging in Publication Data
Hamilton, Clive.
  Capitalist industrialization in Korea.
  (Westview special studies on East Asia)
  Bibliography: p.
  Includes index.
  1. Saving and investment—Korea (South)—Mathematical models. 2. Korea (South)—Industries—1960— .
3. Korea (South)—Economic policy. I. Title.
HC470.C3H33 1985   338.09519'5   85-8997
ISBN 0-8133-7069-8

Printed and bound in the United States of America

The paper used in this publication meets the minimum requirements of the American National Standard for Permanence of Paper for Printed Library Materials Z39.48-1984.

6   5   4   3   2   1

Contents

List of Tables

List of Figures

Acknowledgements

Acknowledgements of help are made with gratitude to the following people: Jon Halliday, Rob Eastwood, Gordon White, Hans Singer, Tony Michell, Parvin Alizadeh and Manfred Bienefeld. Sometimes their interventions have come at critical times. While always willing to assist me, all of these people would disagree with parts or even most of this book, and so none should be implicated in its conclusions. I must also thank the ever-helpful staff of the library of the Institute of Development Studies (IDS), University of Sussex.

Three people deserve special thanks for their contributions to this work. Henry Lucas wrote the programmes and was always unselfish with his time when I needed help with computing and statistical problems; without his generosity and great skills it would all have been much harder. Richard Luedde-Neurath was not only unhesitating in his offers of assistance when he travelled to Korea but was also a constant source of good ideas, detailed knowledge of Korea's trade regime and constructive criticism. Finally, I must thank David Evans of the IDS who contributed time and patience in abundant measure. His intellectual influence has been very strong, especially, but by no means exclusively, on the modelling side of this work.

The book is dedicated to Janenne Hamilton who provided the most essential ingredient of all.

Clive Hamilton

CHAPTER 1
Introduction

Initially, this was to have been a study of the international division of labour and the laws which govern it. In the spirit of radical development theory, this would attempt to explain underdevelopment by the way in which Third World countries fit into the world capitalist system and become subject to economic forces controlled by the advanced countries. But it became apparent that the 'laws' of the international division of labour could not be used to make general statements about the development and underdevelopment of the Third World. This was not an easy break since it goes against the tenor of the whole Marxist-dependency line of analysis and the various shades of opinion within the radical persective. Whether discussing the influence of imperialism in promoting capital accumulation in the Third World (Lenin, Warren), or its creation of a structure of dependency and underdevelopment (Frank, Amin, Cardoso, Emmanuel); whether studying the influence of the 'internationalization of capital' on development (Hymer, Murray, Froebel et al.) or the imperatives of the 'world system' (Wallerstein, dependency theory's *reductio ad absurdum*); all of these attribute the development or underdevelopment of the Third World to forces which arise in the industrial centres of the West and which are imposed on the periphery. This attribution of development to global forces is not confined to radical analyses but lies at the heart of orthodox trade theory - if Third World countries specialize and trade they will be blessed with the riches of the West.

The questioning of the whole approach was not due simply to the fact that there are a few countries of the Third World - the newly industrialized countries (NICs) - which appear to have broken out of the trap of dependency and underdevelopment, nor indeed, with Warren in mind, that most countries have failed to so break out. The real question revolved around how those international forces controlled by capital in the centre - trade, investment, technology - actually impinge on countries of the periphery. The countries of the Third World do not form an undifferentiated mass; about the only thing they have in common is their poverty, and that in many different forms. International forces affect Third World countries according to their internal economic structures. Increased foreign investment will have quite a different impact on development in a Third World country which has a big home market, a diverse manufacturing base and a strong state than on another country which is small, dependent on a single export crop and politically weak.

The level of abstraction on which current theories are based lies at the heart of the problem. (This will be discussed in more detail in the final chapter.) International laws and interpretation of trends are developed at a high level of abstraction, but they need to be brought down to a lower level in order to be applied to the study of particular countries and thus the Third World as a whole. This is in no way meant to imply that one should abandon the practice of

1

abstraction and insist that every country has its own story (as in the facile agnosticism of the ultra-Althusserians), for we take as a starting point the concepts and categories of capitalism. This is so simply because (outside socialism) growth and development are the growth and development of capitalism. But capital and wage-labour, private property and accumulation all occur within a particular and historically-specific structure of class relations, and it is the development of that structure which forms the locus of the explanation of the poverty and wealth of nations.

Instead of trying to determine directly the forces which impose obstacles to development (the notion of 'obstacles to development' is itself suspect since it implies that there is some natural process that is being obstructed) it was decided to study some of those countries which had apparently overcome those obstacles and had taken the road (if not the turnpike) of capitalist industrial expansion. Their growth and development is interpreted in the context of the accumulation of industrial capital. This is Marx's primitive accumulation, but whereas Marx saw capitalism and growth occurring in an industrial setting, we know today from Third World experience in particular that capitalism can take root and flourish within agriculture, or trade, without ensuing industrial growth. But it is industry that is the bearer of sustained development and wealth. One is led, then, to ask specifically about the conditions necessary for primitive accumulation of industrial capital. Of all economic processes this latter most decidedly grows out of particular social conditions and does not lend itself to general law-making. The social and economic conditions which prevailed in, say, Hong Kong and Taiwan in the fifties were disparate in the extreme, and it is only the categories of capitalism which allow us sensibly to discuss them together. The reason for this (reasoning which dependency theory cannot grasp) is that primitive accumulation, as a process of class formation, is equally a political and an economic process. Here is the specificity of development. Because of this the role of the state in the process has been everywhere central. On the one hand it has been the failure of dependency and related theories to recognize the particularity of these social and political conditions which has led it to an impasse. On the other hand, in the light of the central role of the state, neoclassical accounts which set out to prove that the success of the NICs has been due to the operation of free markets appear tendentious indeed.

It had become clear, then, that the question of industrial development in the Third World needed to be answered in a particular historical context, and we initially set out to look at the diverse experiences of the four East Asian NICs - Hong Kong, Singapore, Taiwan and South Korea (Hamilton, 1983). However, the forms of accumulation were quite different - for instance, in Taiwan industry was almost wholly home-owned while in Singapore it was almost wholly foreign-owned - so that any review could not go into much depth. It was decided to focus attention on South Korea, largely because there is a mass of material available which is ripe for reinterpretation. The interpretation of the recent economic history of South Korea has been the almost exclusive preserve of orthodox, conservative analysis. The selection of South Korea was reinforced by the decision to examine empirically the relationship between accumulation and structural change, for, as one of the 'Third World' countries most intensively studied in the West, the data on South Korea are well-developed and extensive. US involvement in the financing and planning of the development of this strategically important country gave data-gathering a high priority from the early sixties. South Korea presented itself as a good choice for other reasons; it has a history of intense colonial exploitation, in the fifties it was an essentially agricultural country marked by great poverty and inequality, and rapid industrial growth took place in the sixties and seventies. In a sense it is a classic case, but this is not meant to imply that it is in some way typical of the Third World; in fact its recent history shows it to be aberrant.

The explanation of the causes in South Korea of the hegemony of private industrial capital in the sixties cannot be found in the sixties. The failure of orthodox work on the country to ask the important questions about its development is evident from the exclusive attention paid to the sixties and seventies, except for the usual, brief 'historical' chapter at the beginning to prove that they can 'put it into context'. It will be shown in Chapter 2 that the transition to the dominance of industrial capital grew out of changes in the fifties and this requires an understanding of the class structure and political developments after the civil war in Korea, including the role of the USA. But in order to explain changes in the class structure - for instance and in particular, why the traditional landlord class was too weak to prevent the land reforms which stripped it of economic power, and why subsequently merchant capital became the centre of accumulation - it was necessary to revert to the period of Japanese colonial rule (1910-1945) and indeed (very briefly) to the pre-colonial period in order to provide a sufficiently stable social bedrock on which to construct an explanation.

Lest this appears to portend another 'historical review', let it be clear that in what follows the history of Korea (South Korea after 1945) is interpreted from a very particular perspective - that of the development of the structure of classes. The single aim of the analysis is to explain how it was that industrial capital became the dominant economic force in the sixties. That is the purpose of Chapter 2; it forms the core of the explanation of industrial development in South Korea, and has the most significant implications for Third World development in general. In no sense should it be considered to be a 'background chapter'.

It might be appropriate to say here that it is not intended to argue that industrial growth is directly caused by changes in the class structure in a unilateral manner. Class changes are also responses to economic developments; for instance, the emergence of a class of merchants in response to state policies with respect to foreign aid and trade, or the transformation of merchant into industrial capital in response to social conditions or the constraints of international trade. In other words, changes in the class structure have causes too. The question should not be posed in terms of linear cause and effect, for Third World industrialization is examined *through* the development of the class structure. The same approach is adopted with respect to the state. On the one hand we want to avoid characterizing state policy as a mere reflection of the class structure and the dominance of a particular class (determinism); on the other hand we want to discount the notion, which lies behind orthodox thinking, that state policies are adopted on their own merits, with their own rationality, that people act on the basis of 'free will', that state policies have no social context (voluntarism). The central question of development economics, viz. which policies should be pursued by a Third World country in order to industrialize and grow, is meaningless unless the state is put into its social context, and recommendations are useless unless either the structure of classes is already conducive to industrial development or the state has the will and the ability to undertake a thoroughgoing social transformation. In most Third World countries the class structure is not so conducive and the state, because of this, has neither the will nor the strength. The conceptualization of the state in the development process will be taken up again in the last chapter.

While the question of the process whereby industrial capital becomes the dominant social and economic force is the critical one, alone it is inadequate if we wish to understand the process of industrial development in South Korea. For although the detailed answer to this fundamental question can explain why industrial development came about, it cannot reveal very much about the particular form of industrial development, the nature of capital and the rate of accumulation. In particular, we are interested in looking at the industrial structure of South Korean development and how it changed over the period of industrialization. This would reveal a great deal about the accumulation process: in what ways South Korean industrialization was tied into the world economy, how interindustry relations influenced the growth rate, how state policy affected industrial structure and the allocation of investible surplus, how technical change has affected growth and structural change, and how wage levels have influenced growth. These questions are fundamental to understanding the progress of industrial development and can be answered empirically.

There are many empirical techniques available which can specify or approximate these variables related to structural change and growth. Mostly they are variations on input-output analysis, varying in complexity from simple multiplier analysis to computable general equilibrium model-building. The technique adopted here is expounded in Chapter 3 and the results are presented and interpreted in Chapter 4. It has not been used before to study a Third World country, nor even to study an advanced capitalist country. In fact, the only empirical applications have been in Eastern Europe where one aspect of the many aspects of the model has been worked on. Of course, the model and its results have a very different interpretation when applied to centrally planned economies and these latter studies were of very little help. We were left with the bare theoretical outline of the model worked out by András Bródy (1970). In applying this model to South Korea we interpreted it as a kind of computable general equilibrium model, but one quite different to others which have been constructed. It is not interpreted as a planning model but as a technique of analysis designed to reveal relationships of the past. This will become much clearer in Chapter 3. The results which emerge are used in Chapter 4 to reinterpret South Korean industrialization.

The empirical side of this study has three strands. Firstly, it was necessary to comprehend the theoretical structure of the model. This process continued through to the end and included: i) the interpretation of the model as a near-linear form of a more general model, ii) understanding how it relates to the more usual general equilibrium models which have been constructed, and iii) extending it from the basic form of Bródy so that it can be used to conduct counterfactual experiments (to enable us to ask, for example, what the effect of technical change has been on growth and structure). All of this appears in Chapter 3.

The second task was to interpret the theoretical structure in empirical terms and to compile the data. Fortunately, the important sources of statistics on South Korea, including input-output tables, are available in English. Although work on the data took a long time, this particular model is not as data-intensive as other general equilibrium models. All of the data except the input-output tables appear in Appendixes A, B and C.

Thirdly, there was the process of interpreting the solutions. Given the lack of previous applications, interpretation was by far the most difficult part of the modelling process, and this is perhaps reflected in Chapter 4. The reason is closely related to the notion employed in the model of maximal growth involving optimal output proportions and relative prices. The hypothetical nature of these optima makes comparison with real phenomena difficult. Despite such drawbacks, the model proves itself to be a powerful technique for structural analysis, and it has been necesary to limit its application and interpretation mostly to the basic solutions.

It should be said that this enquiry did not begin with the setting of the particular questions above followed by a process of casting around for a suitable technique with which to answer them. Rather, there were some broad areas of interest relating to structural change and capital accumulation, and it appeared that the technique chosen would be an excellent exploratory device. Some of the questions would undoubtedly be better answered by alternative techniques, so there is a strong element in the empirical part of this study of a desire to explore the possibilities of the model purely for its own sake. No apology is made for this; if nothing else, the study exposes the usefulness and limitations of this method of empirical analysis.

In Chapter 5 an attempt is made to draw together the conclusions of both the historical analysis of class formation and the empirical analysis of accumulation and structural change. One of the overriding themes to emerge from both sides of the study is the fundamental importance of the state in South Korean industrialization. Chapter 5 discusses the relationship between the class structure and the state, the means whereby the South Korean government regulated the industrialization process especially through manipulation of the price mechanism, and the economic and political effects of foreign influences. Some serious criticisms of both dependency and orthodox theories of Third World development emerge.

CHAPTER 2
The Class Basis of Korean Industrialization

2.1 Introduction

The specific question that this chapter seeks to answer is how industrial capital became the dominant economic force in South Korea. The fact that it did become dominant follows tautologically from the nature of industrialization which occurred in the sixties and seventies. 'Industrial capital' refers to the capital tied up in accumulation processes in those private manufacturing and service businesses which rely on wage-labour, and its spread is the spread of industrial capitalism. Industrial development in South Korea was carried out mostly by private capital[1] although a large part of the argument of this and subsequent chapters concerns the ways in which the state has influenced the form of accumulation. The dominance of industrial capital over other forms of capital and over the working class and the peasantry is the product of a historical process of class formation and in itself is not quantifiable, although aspects of it are. This chapter seeks to convince the reader that it is the answer to *this* question, that of how industrial capital becomes the driving force of society, that is at the core of the explanation of Third World industrialization. It has been almost wholly ignored by development economics.

The term 'industrialization' can be used misleadingly if it is meant to refer simply to the expansion of the share of industrial production in national product. A much deeper conception of the process lies in the phrase 'the accumulation of private capital in industrial form', and this can be understood as raising two related and fundamental questions about an economy. Firstly, how is the social surplus product generated, under what social relations (feudal, capitalist, petty proprietorship) and using what productive forces (resources of land and labour, fixed captial, a certain technology)? Secondly, how is the social surplus product, once produced, used? Is it consumed luxuriously, remitted overseas, reinvested in industry or trade or agriculture, or taxed by the state? In other words, the essential explanation of Third World development lies in determining who gets the surplus, under what circumstances, and what they do with it. These questions can only be answered historically and involve such issues as modes of production, foreign intervention, political power, wars, and the nature of government. It is in these issues that an understanding of how Korean industrialization came about is to be found. The issues which usually exercise the minds of development economists -

---

[1]In 1963 private enterprises produced 87 percent of non-agricultural GDP; the same figure applied in 1972. In the latter year it accounted for 85 percent of value-added in manufacturing and was outweighed by public enterprise only in electricity, water and sanitation, and finance. However, public enterprise absorbed about 30 percent of total investment over the period 1962-73. All figures are from Jones & Sakong (1980, pp148-50).

import liberalization, exchange rates and interest rates, scarce resources, comparative advantage and so on - must be interpreted in terms of the processes of class formation and development. The seeds of industrial development are sown in the soil of class structure, and it is this that we seek to expose in this chapter.

The class structure as it had evolved to the eve of the period of rapid industrial development in Korea was, inevitably, the product of the whole of Korean history. But to understand its form and interrelations it is necessary to examine in some detail the period of Japanese colonial occupation (1910-1945) since this had a profound impact on all aspects of Korean society. The society which emerged at the end of the Second World War was a product of Japanese colonialism imposed on a traditional foundation, and the political economy of the post-war period is obscure without some explanation of it. As for the forties and fifties, the political and economic (and military) developments of the time were the spawning ground for the future classes of Korean industrial capitalism. We therefore devote the next two sections to the colonial period, and the post-war political economy.

Most accounts of South Korean industrialization attribute enormous impact to the policies of the state, almost as if industrialization occurred by fiat. But the inadequacy of focussing on the policies of the state in isolation is becoming increasingly plain - the formulas of the World Bank are not marked by practical success - because it is empty to do so without an understanding of the social foundations on which the state rests. Only the latter can reveal whether or not particular policies have a chance of achieving their putative ends. Moreover, such policies, in the orthodox stories, appear like *deus ex machina* from the scientific theorizing of economists and their advocates do not stop to ask what the social basis of a feasible policy is. Adoption of a more materialist position may, for instance, make us question the effectiveness of the import liberalization of the early sixties in Korea since there were no indigenous social forces clamouring for such a profound change of economic tack. These suspicions would have been borne out by recent detailed work which has shown the alleged liberalization to be a chimera (Luedde-Neurath, 1983).

Nevertheless, in the following study there will be a great deal of discussion of the state for it appears as a primum mobile at every stage of class formation. There is no attempt, however, to develop a theory of the state, not only because it is an extremely difficult subject, but also because this writer is not convinced that it is valid to do so. Instead the state is interpreted in terms of the mode of reproduction of society or the process of accumulation. The policies of the state, their means of implementation, and their effectiveness are examined in the light of their impact on the class structure and insofar as they reflect the class structure. If nothing else, the history of modern Korea tells us that the state is not necessarily the instrument of a particular class (although at times it has been), but it remains true that the nature of the state at any time develops in the process of class struggle. It represents not a particular class but the articulated structure of class relations under the dominance of a particular class. This structure of class relations contains contradictions, and these contradictions find expression in the state. One thing is clear: no state can survive in the long term if it does not conform to the broad interests of the dominant social class. In the case of Korea this means indigenous industrial capital in alliance with US and Japanese capitalism. The issue of the interpretation of the state will be taken up again in the final chapter.

2.2 The Effects of Japanese Rule on the Korean Economy and Class Structure

Japan's colonization of Korea quickly put to death the declining Yi dynasty, the last two hundred years of which had seen the slow decay of traditional Korean society. Rural destitution and exploitation were coupled with corruption and nepotism in the cities. Peasant revolts, the customary manifestation of social decay, occurred frequently throughout the nineteenth century culminating in the bloody Tonghak rebellion of 1894. Japan imposed its will on this weakened society with growing insistence after its victory in the war with Russia in 1905 and finally annexed it as a colony in 1910.

Japanese colonial policy in Korea - as in Formosa and Manchuria - grew out of the needs of an economy in the early phase of industrial development. Primarily, Japan needed to supplement its food supplies for the burgeoning Japanese proletariat, and its colonies were carefully organized so as to provide an agricultural surplus for export. Korea became, like the other colonies, and integral segment of the Japanese empire for it provided not only food grains (mainly the high-quality Korean rice) but also, in the twenties and thirties, large numbers of immigrant workers, important industrial minerals and a site for the location of Japanese industry.

In the early part of Japanese rule a large portion of the land in Korea was, by one means or another, tranferred into the colonizers' hands. The main instrument for this was the cadastral survey of 1911-18 which set out to regularize the system of land entitlement and to improve the tax base, and had the not-accidental effect of dispossessing the many owner-cultivators and landlords who failed to register their holdings or did so incorrectly. This was of historical importance because in the process of rural reorganization the Japanese introduced the concept of private ownership in land and turned land into a saleable commodity, something that was alien to previous dynasties. The Japanese Government-General also nationalized all village common land and most royal lands as well as arrogating to itself all unclaimed land. More land fell into the hands of the colonial government when Korean occupants failed to pay their taxes. Most of the land acquired in these ways was sold off cheaply to Japanese land companies, settlers and absentee landlords. The biggest buyer was the Oriental Development Company (which Korean sources invariably prefix with the word 'notorious') which had been established in 1908 for the express purpose of expanding Japanese influence in agriculture by replacing Korean peasants with Japanese immigrants.[2] In time there were reportedly 300,000 tenant farmers on this company's land (Sohn, 1970, p256). Prior to 1918 the Government-General also used the company to help bring from the homeland some 98,000 farming families (380,000 people) plus 590 absentee landlord families for resettlement in Chosen (the imperial name for Korea)(Sohn, 1970, p258).[3] The resettlement programme, however, was considered to have failed; the Japanese had underestimated the population density (Moscowitz, 1974, p85) and emigration to a backward, overcrowded and hostile land was unalluring to Japanese farmers.

At the time of Japanese occupation, Korea was overwhelmingly an agricultural country - in 1910, 84 percent of all households were reported to be engaged in agriculture or forestry (Kuznets, 1977, p13) - and the land system was

---

[2]On the history of the Oriental Development Company see Moscowitz (1974).

[3]Keim (1979, p8) says that only 10,000 families from Japan had settled up to 1922.

such that ownership was concentrated heavily and retained by absentee landlords who took rents of around 50 percent of the tenant-cultivators' annual product. Some writers use the term 'feudalism' to describe the precolonial agrarian social structure, but in fact it bore only superficial resemblance to the European model. Firstly, the concept of private land ownership was not well established[4] since ownership of all lands was legally vested in the royal household which allocated it as favours to nobles and officials. Various noble and official families were entitled to collect revenues from estates, and their agents did. The tillers generally had no claim to the land and at the turn of the century around 75 percent of Korean peasants were full or part tenants (Cumings, 1981, p39). However, at certain times over the dynastic period the idea of hereditary entitlement took root and certain *yangban* families grew wealthy and powerful enough to challenge central authority ('...the Yi state danced to landlord tunes' [Cumings, 1981, p40]), in much the same way as independent feudal lords forced a decentralized power structure on European societies. The *yangban* were the traditional aristocracy who wielded local political power and although they usually controlled and collected rents from landed estates, their position was not defined by their landlord status. Secondly, the lord-peasant relationship in dynastic Korea, especially in the later Yi dynasty, was far less rigid and authoritarian than on the European demesnes. In the former, the peasant was 'free' and not a serf legally bound to the lord; landlords could not control peasants' mobility nor did they have the right to interfere in their personal lives (approving marriages and the like); nor could they forbid a peasant from acquiring land. These legal powers, which were enjoyed by European serflords, were absent in Korea.[5] Nor did the landlord demand corvée labour - manorial estates would have been an encumbrance to absentee landlords. Not only was extra-economic compulsion absent but by 'the force of public opinion tenant farmers were given virtual rights to control the land they rented and to renew their leases every year' (Shannon McCune quoted in Brun & Hersh, 1976, p44). Thirdly, although village self-sufficiency was more or less the rule for centuries - until foreign penetration in the latter part of the nineteenth century spread commercial relations - there was not the cohesiveness of the village community centred on the lord's manor which marked European feudalism (see Henderson, 1968, p50).

There does not appear to have been a significant growth of capitalist social relations in agriculture with the coming of the Japanese but as we will see the effects were nevertheless profound. Historically, the hiring of wage-labour to till the fields had been rare since it was more advantageous for the land-owner to lease it out to a tenant family at a fixed rent than to pay the daily subsistence of a wage-labourer. Grajdanzev shows that the proportion of Korean farm workers classified as agricultural labourers rose from 2.9 percent in 1932 to 3.8 percent in 1938, but suggests that more accurate reckoning may show it to be considerably larger (Grajdanzev, 1944, p109). The upheaval in the countryside certainly created growing numbers of itinerant rural proletarians, but the land system could not support them as hired labour and they were forced to emigrate to the cities and thence to Japan or Manchuria. Essentially, the overwhelming number of Korean

---

[4]'The concept of land ownership simply had not developed' (Hatada, 1969, p113). See also Brun & Hersh (1976, p43).

[5]'...in the course of the dynasty unfree labourers such as slaves and bond servants were largely replaced by commoner tenants whose relationship to the landowner was more contractual than personal' (Shin, 1975, p50).

farmers spent their lives in a landlord-tenant relationship both under the Yi dynasty and Japanese colonialism (see below); in this respect there was more continuity than change with the advent of colonialism. However, in addition to the confiscation of some cultivators' land, and the greatly increased insecurity of tenancy which was responsible for an enormous level of tenants' rights transfers (Cumings, 1981, p44), colonialism had other effects which historically have shown themselves to be preconditions of the development of capitalism. On a subjective level these were the spread of ideas subversive to the *ancien régime*, of education and a sense of the world beyond. There was the new experience of a centralized and powerful government with direct political control of activities all over the country. More fundamentally perhaps, there was the decline of farm and village self-sufficiency and the spread of exchange relations which inevitably followed from the colonial policy of extracting the maximum agricultural surplus for export.

The reorganization of land ownership under the colonial regime had two immediate effects. Firstly, it caused the transfer to Japanese possession of a large portion of the land. The exact acreage is unclear, but Kuznets concludes that if 'government property is included, the Japanese may have controlled more than half of the land in Korea' (Kuznets, 1977, p17). The figure is probably somewhere between 25 and 50 percent,[6] but it was concentrated in the more productive paddy fields of the south and was the source of much more than a quarter of grain production. The second effect was a marked increase in pure tenancy: of all farm households, pure tenants (those who owned none of the land they worked) accounted for 39 percent in 1913-17 and for 56 percent by 1938.[7] This implied an increase in the concentration of ownership.

All this by no means signalled the demise of the traditional Korean landed aristocracy for the Japanese land acquisitions were made primarily at the expense of the weaker owner-cultivators. The old *yangban* class became more explicitly a landlord class rather than an idle aristocracy concerned with consumption, courts and classics.[8] The class of rich landlords survived in effective alliance with the encroaching Japanese, for continued access to the privilege of land ownership was extended only to those who would submit to and accept the new rulers. However, they were seriously weakened, no longer with access to positions of influence in government. While the majority of landlords in Chosen remained Korean (Brun & Hersh, 1976, p45), the social composition of the indigenous landlord class appears to have changed significantly as a result of Japanese intervention. The traditional landowners, the *yangban* connected to the court, comprised by the thirties comparatively few of those with substantial holdings while enterprising small-owners and the former *ajon* (rural clerks and tax collectors with detailed local knowledge) expanded their holdings greatly (Henderson, 1968, p404 n22).

The proliferation of Japanese landlordism was an efficient means of extracting an export surplus from agricultural production. Rents continued to be set at about 50 percent of the crop but could be up to 90 percent in the fertile paddy fields of the

---

[6]See Grajdanzev (1944, pp106 & 110). Foster-Carter (1977, p74) reports that in 1942 25 percent of cultivable land and 80 percent of forests were Japanese-owned.

[7]Kuznets (1977, p16). If part-tenants are included then around 80 percent of the Korean population in 1930 were tenants (Cumings, 1981, p43).

[8]'The Yi aristocracy lost its official component and its control over the central bureaucracy ... [but] Japanese rule rooted the aristocracy even more firmly in the land, for land was the last bastion of its strength' (Cumings, 1981, p41).

south (Cumings, 1981, p44) (unlike in the pre-colonial system in which half was a legal maximum - a law not always enforced). Most of the rice collected as rent was exported. The government too took a substantial proportion in taxes, for the new land tax of 1918 had the effect of increasing revenue from the land two and a half times between 1910 and 1930.[9] These exactions in themselves are insufficient to establish an increased exploitation of the peasantry to feed the Japanese economy, but when combined with the following three trends the effect of colonialism is more apparent.

In the first place, the output of Chosen agriculture (inefficient in comparision with Japan's) rose by 74 percent between 1910-12 and 1939-41[10] under the impact of the colonial administration's plans to expand rice production through land improvement (irrigation), increased material and capital inputs and more intensive application of labour.[11] Secondly, there was an intensification of agricultural pauperization in the colonial period, and a decline in per capita consumption of rice and other food grains (Kuznets, 1977, p17; Grajdanzev, 1944, pp118-119; Han Woo-Keun, 1970, p480). At the same time real wages of urban workers fell by nearly a third in the thirties (Kuznets, 1977, p23). Grajdanzev (1944, p118) gives an index which shows a secular decline of per capita rice consumption in Korea from 100 in 1915-19 to 56 in 1934-38.[12] A contemporary observer reported that in the mid-twenties most owner-cultivators managed to break even, but of tenants and part-tenants around 96 percent lived below subsistence (Keim, 1977, p10). One effect of this, as we will see, was to drive a large proportion of the rural population off the land. The numbers were extraordinary: at some point during the Japanese occupation around 4 million Koreans worked in Japan and 2 million in Manchuria, and in 1944 11.6 percent of all Koreans were living outside Korea.[13] Thirdly, there was a tremendous growth in rice exports to Japan over the same period, rising six-fold between 1912-16 and 1927-31 so that in the early thirties it accounted for 42

---

[9]Cumings (1981, p41). After all of the payments due, tenants were often left with only 15-25 percent of the crop (Grajdanzev, 1944, p114).

[10]Kuznets (1977, p19). The population increased by about 63 percent between 1911 and 1939 to around 23 million (Grajdanzev, 1944, pp73-74).

[11]Brun & Hersh (1976, p45) dissent from this view arguing that little capital was invested in rice production and that human power, more than ever abundant, gradually replaced animal power. There does not appear to be a detailed study of the means by which the Japanese went about improving agriculture in Korea.

[12]Consumption of other cereals and beans also declined per capita, except for a slight rise for millet (Grajdanzev, 1944, p119). The Government-General itself reported that in 1930 6 million people were hunger-stricken. In 1936, 87 percent of farm households consumed less than the Government's subsistence level (Sohn, 1970, p288). The decline in rice in the diet was partially compensated for by imports of inferior food grains (especially millet) from Manchuria. These imports were subject to customs duties while exported rice was purchased cheaply from farmers.

[13]Cumings (1981, pp56 & 54). Concerned about the revolt that may have been caused by falling rural consumption and neglect, the Government-General launched in 1934 the Movement of Rural Revival which stressed 'self help, self-reliance and spiritual mobilization' (Grajdanzev, 1944, p120). This apppears very similar to President Park's Saemaul Undong or New Community Movement of the early seventies which aimed at self-help, community mobilization and 'raising village consciousness'.

percent by volume of the total annual crop.[14]

While Korea remained primarily a source of agricultural produce and crude materials throughout the Japanese interregnum, there was a degree of development of industry in the thirties which was remarkable for any colony. Industrial development in nearby colonies and at home was encouraged after the decision to pursue an import substitution policy aimed at diminishing reliance on imports from outside the Yen Bloc. The manufacturing growth which occurred in Korea (and in Formosa and Manchuria) was determined by the requirements of Japanese industrialization and was in no sense autonomous. The contemporary observer George McCune commented (well before dependency theory had appeared):

> The Korean economy was Japanese-owned and Japanese-directed and in no sense an entity in and of itself, but rather the geographical location of a portion of the wider configuration of the economy of Japan (McCune, 1950, p37).

Prior to Japanese occupation, industry and commerce in Korea were minimal.[15] There was some metropolitan merchant activity and handicraft industry, but most requirements were hand-produced on the farm. In the late nineteenth century a market economy had barely developed in Korea and the commercial class, such as it was, was weak and poor and not well-connected. Even before Japanese occupation, business was foreign-dominated (Cumings, 1981, p18). A few industries had been developed by foreign interests - notably electric power, lumber and rice milling - but the number of manufacturing concerns did not begin to multiply rapidly until the twenties, after the repeal of the Corporation Law (see below). New business began producing mainly light manufactures (processed food, textiles, ceramics, lumber and printing)[16] often at the expense of handicraft production. In the thirties, however, there was a new wave of industrial expansion including the development of heavy industry. Between 1929-31 and 1939-41 the net commodity product of manufacturing grew two and a half times with the most rapid growth occurring in the early years of the decade, so that on the outbreak of the world war 29 percent of total net commodity product originated in manufacturing (Kuznets, 1977, p19). This figure was high even for an advanced country. There was greater stress on chemicals (especially fertilizers) and on industrial raw materials[17] as the demands of heavy industry and military expansion increased. The bulk of this new industrial growth took place in the northern part of

---

[14]Sohn (1970, p287) also Kuznets (1977, p14). Candidly, the Japanese referred to this as 'hunger export'.

[15]Manufacturing made up 6.7 percent of net commodity product in 1910-12 and fewer than 1 percent of all households were engaged in manufacturing in 1910 (Kuznets, 1977, p19). Much of the information on the development of trade and industry in this period is from Kuznets (1977, pp9-23).

[16]In 1930, three quarters of factory output originated in these sectors, especially food and textiles (Kuznets, 1977, p20).

[17]By the time of the war, Korea supplied nearly all of Japan's requirements for magnesite, graphite, cobalt and molybdenum, and significant portions of its supplies of bauxite, coke, steel and fertilizers (Foster-Carter, 1977, p74).

the country.[18]

This industrial development was very much contingent upon industrial expansion in Japan. The volume of Korean trade rose to a very high level by the outbreak of the world war - increasing more than ten-fold between 1910-12 and 1939-41 - to the point where the trade ratio (roughly calculated) stood at over 50 percent.[19] The growth in trade was almost exclusively within the Yen Bloc with 99 percent of Korean exports going there (and around 90 percent to Japan) in the twenties and thirties while well over 90 percent of imports came from within the Yen Bloc (with around 80 percent coming from Japan in the thirties) (Kuznets, 1977, p10). Until the late thirties, Korean exports were dominated by unprocessed food (around 60 percent) although in the years before the Second World War minerals and processed goods became more important.[20] Imports were primarily of finished manufactures for consumption (except for some food grains - mainly millet from Manchuria - in the twenties) and increasingly industrial materials and equipment with the import substitution of the thirties (Kuznets, 1977, pp10-11).

Throughout the occupation of Chosen the colonial administration was careful to restrict the development of indigenous capital, even though in some industries to compete against companies such as Mitsui and Mitsubishi was extremely difficult for most Korean manufacturers. In fact the Government-General from 1910 enforced the Corporation Law which empowered it to approve the establishment of new firms. It was designed to circumscribe the development of businesses in Korea - other than those connected with agriculture - which could compete with Japanese industrial imports. It made it difficult for new Japanese enterprises to be established, and virtually impossible for new Korean firms. The law was used to dissolve two prosperous Korean-owned firms in 1911.[21] It was repealed in 1920 as part of the 'liberalization' which followed the independence demonstrations of 1919, although according to Hatada (1969, p118) the prosperity of Japan after the First World War made apparent the desirability of industrial investment in Korea and the abolition of the Corporation Law was at 'the request of Japanese capitalists'. Administrative measures continued to discriminate against indigenous businesses. Local domestic industry continued to survive if not to prosper despite being excluded from the subsidies, exemptions and administrative favours which benefitted Japanese enterprises in the twenties and thirties. But competition with

---

[18]Concentrated in the south were light industry (including textiles), grain production, machine industry and two-thirds of the population; in the north were concentrated heavy industry, fertilizer production, bean crops, electric power and gas (Joungwon Kim, 1975, p33).

[19]Kuznets (1977, p10). This pattern of 'export-led growth' coupled with substantial import substitution in the twenties and thirties displays a remarkable similarity to that of the sixties and seventies.

[20]While rice exports had been the *raison d'être* of Japanese colonial policy in the first decades of occupation and were motivated by food shortages at home (there were serious rice riots in 1918), the world-wide food glut of the early thirties saw Japanese landlords demanding restrictions on food imports, especially from Formosa and Chosen. The Government-General's 30-year rice production plan for Korea was cancelled in 1933, and new plans emphasized the potential of Korea as a source of industrial raw materials, especially cotton (Grajdanzev, 1944, pp92-93).

[21]The 'Regulation for Fisheries Associations' of 1912 advanced the penetration by Japanese fishermen of the fishing industry.

the modern industrial businesses became increasingly formidable, particularly for textile and related industries which drew on limited supplies of raw materials. Grajdanzev observed that in this 'struggle for raw materials the Japanese administration applied unusual methods' including compulsory sales to Japanese agents, forbidding the use of and destroying looms in villages, and punitive taxation; this resulted in 'the forcible destruction of domestic spinning and weaving in Korean villages' (Grajdanzev, 1944, pp152 & 105). The development of light manufacturing in the twenties and heavy industry in the thirties did not provide many opportunities for Korean capital - most investment was financed by Japanese banks, which quickly asserted control over investment and the monetary system (now based on the yen).[22]

Throughout the period, industrial production was overwhelmingly dominated by Japanese business. Although the data are very uncertain, the following figures give an indication of the hegemony of Japanese capital: in 1938 Japanese-owned enterprises produced three-quarters of the gross value of industrial output, comprised 60 percent of all firms, and accounted for 90 percent of paid-up capital.[23] Moreover, industrial production was highly concentrated - a tendency toward oligopoly favoured by the administration - with a mere 1.2 percent of all firms producing 80 percent of all factory product in 1939.[24] According to Joungwon Kim (1975, p23) the Japanese held a 'virtual monopoly in every area of the economy', with significant Korean interests (i.e. over 20 percent of sectoral paid-up capital) only in trade, agriculture-forestry, real estate and non-bank financial institutions.

After the repeal of the Corporation Law many new businesses were established. Those in Korean hands tended to be much smaller than those owned by Japanese. In commerce for instance, a sector containing a large portion of Korean capital, Korean firms in 1938 had an average paid-up capital value of 125 thousand yen while Japanese firms averaged 1,250 thousand yen (Grajdanzev, 1944, p175). (The average size of Korean firms had declined over the period.) This was indicative of the size difference. Another conservative estimate put Japanese firms at 6 times bigger than Korean ones and probably much more (Grajdanzev, 1944, p175). The latter also reports (p282) that in 1938 there were 2,504 Korean factories, 2,308 of which employed fewer than 50 workers. In manufacturing as a whole in 1938 Korean firms accounted for 12.3 percent of paid-up capital investment. These indigenous businesses were largely restricted to small-scale operations in brewing, medicines, rice processing and textiles. We should not dismiss entirely the development of indigenous firms; after all, those 2,504 Korean-owned companies were mostly there because of the Japanese presence and, despite the limitations imposed by the colonial government, factory production by Korean firms expanded under the Japanese.

The contemporary observer Grajdanzev suggests that the Japanese could easily have chosen to squeeze Korean businessmen out of industry completely but

---

[22]The number of Korean banks fell from 12 in 1923 to 3 in 1938 with a corresponding halving of paid-up capital (Grajdanzev, 1944, p173).

[23]Kuznets (1977, p22). Sohn (1970, p240) reports that between 1910 and 1929 the share of paid-up capital of wholly Korean firms fell from 17 to 6 percent, while that of wholly Japanese firms rose from 32 to 62 percent. These figures, however, exaggerate the real situation since Korean firms were relatively under-capitalized.

[24]Capital export to Korea was very profitable for Japanese business. Grajdanzev (1944, p156n) reports that textile corporations earned net profits of 50 percent in 1939-40.

may have refrained from doing so because, as one Japanese economist then argued, this would directly set Korean workers against Japanese capitalists with unwelcome political and industrial consequences (Grajdanzev, 1944, p177). There did develop, then, a significant, if noncohesive and feeble, class of indigenous commercial and industrial capitalists in the twenties and especially the thirties. They were mainly engaged in the grain trade at all stages, money-lending and the more traditional industries which required little capital outlay. Cumings suggests (1981, p21) that there were two types - those who branched into industry and commerce from a base in landed assets, and those with commoner or despised origins who fought their way up 'through sheer enterprising talent'. The latter in particular cleaved to the Japanese and were branded as traitors in years to come. The former, the landlord-entrepreneurs, were more inclined towards the gradualist camp of nationalists. Both groups were to be of great significance after liberation but the upshot of the industrial expansion of the twenties and thirties was to confine the incipient classes of Korean capitalists and merchants largely to the interstices of the colonial economy.

The growth of industry in the twenties and thirties required increasing numbers of wage-labourers. Hatada (1969, p127) argues that the colonial agricultural exactions, by creating a vast pool of impoverished peasants, when coupled with the greater freedom to control labour in Korea were decisive factors in the attraction of Japanese capital to Korea in this phase of industrialization. The supply of workers greatly outstripped the demand. On the land, the exactions of landlords, the loss of land tenure through debt or trickery, and the simple inability to scratch a living from tiny plots drove thousands of families from the farms every year. The pace of urbanization was rapid; by 1946, 11.6 percent of the population lived in cities of over 50,000 inhabitants, compared with 2.6 percent in 1910 (Joungwon Kim, 1975, p32). But the cities could not have coped with the huge numbers of newly marginalized Koreans, and the pressure was relieved only by mass emigration. Without this exodus Japanese colonial rule would have been seriously threatened by social instability. Over the forty year period nearly 15 percent of the entire population emigrated; by 1944 Japan and Manchuria each accommodated 1.5 million Koreans.[25] (Most of these emigrants returned to Korea after the liberation from Japan.) By and large the emigrants earned a living as labourers in the lowest paid and meanest jobs in and around Japanese industry.

Within Korea there developed a substantial industrial proletariat. In 1938, according to Grajdanzev's calculations, there were something over one million wage-workers in Korea, which meant that about one in four households included a wage-earner (1944, p178). About two thirds of these workers were employed in mining,

---

[25]Figures from Joungwon Kim (1975, pp18,29). Nearly one million of these 3 million left Korea after 1940; big waves of emigration occurred in the late twenties and late thirties. Kuznets puts the total of emigrants to Japan and Manchuria in 1940 at 2.7 million (Kuznets, 1975, p.23), compared to Kim's 2.1 million. The population of Korea, according to Kuznets (1975, p23) increased by 95 percent to 26 million between 1910 and 1944, including 780,000 foreigners. The population growth swelled the number of potential tenants thereby driving rents up and hastening the rural diaspora.

industry and construction, mostly in Japanese concerns.[26] The growth of the industrial workforce in Korea quickened considerably in the early forties as the Japanese conscripted and otherwise coerced Koreans into the industries of war. Many more were sent to Japan. In 1938, 30 percent of industrial workers were women (children made up a further 9 percent) and they were concentrated most heavily in textiles (81 percent of that sector's workforce) but also in ceramics, chemicals and food processing. Their proportion of the workforce had in fact declined from 35 percent in 1931 as heavy industry expanded more quickly. Women workers worked longer hours than men.[27]

The occupations of Korean wage-workers were almost invariably those of least skill and responsibility.[28] Where Japanese workers were not available there was some technical education to train skilled Korean workers, but in Kim's words 'virtually all managerial and technical personnel were Japanese'.[29] This extended to senior levels of the bureaucracy (Grajdanzev, 1944, p243) although from the early thirties Koreans began to fill middle-level positions in the bureaucracy so that (by design) it was often the case that Japanese rule had a Korean face. While colonial policy formally included the extension of literacy and primary education, the predominance of Japanese in places of higher learning effectively excluded Koreans from pursuing higher administrative, technical and managerial positions.

The conditions for workers in industry, Japanese and Korean-owned, were execrable, and worsened through the thirties. The Government-General had no interest in intervening; Japanese industrial policy in the thirties sought to promote industrial development in its colonies to exploit the low cost of labour. Grajdanzev comments sardonically that contemporary Japanese economists looked favourably on 'the absence of labor legislation hampering the bold imagination and initiative of the Japanese entrepreneurs' (1944, p179). Wage levels were generally less than half those of Japanese workers in Korea, and showed a steady decline throughout the thirties. Grajdanzev has calculated that from a base of 100 in 1910 real wages had declined to 67 in 1940 (1944, pp179 & 181) and having studied consumption needs comments that the 'only logical conclusion possible in these circumstances is that

---

[26]Grajdanzev (1944, p178) gives the following breakdown of the numbers of wage-labourers: mining 224,000, industry 273,000, construction 193,000, fishing 60,000, transport and communication 150,000, and commerce 30,000. Within manufacturing the great bulk of workers were concentrated (in 1937) in the three sectors textiles, chemicals (mainly oils, rubber products and fertilizers, but also gunpowder and explosives), and food processing (Grajdanzev, 1944, p300).

[27]These figures are from Grajdanzev (1944, pp183-84) who observed that the idea persists that 'the Oriental woman in general and the Korean woman in particular does not work outside her home or her family's fields'. In 1931, the 35 percent of industrial workers who were women compared with 13 percent for the USA in 1930, and this 'clearly shows that in the Orient women play a much larger part in industry than they do in the United States'.

[28]This was consistent with the imperialists' conception of the qualities of the Korean worker. Japanese economists saw them as naturally submissive with low expectations and willing to withstand long hours of monotonous work. These were their 'good points'. Their bad points were that they were lazy, irresponsible, unambitious, uninventive, undisciplined and intellectually incapable (Grajdanzev, 1944, p151).

[29]Joungwon Kim (1975, p33). In 1933, 81 percent of technicians and engineers in Korean manufacturing industry were Japanese (Jones & Sakong, 1980, p26).

these wages are not sufficient to support a family'.[30] Farmers continued to leave the land for these appalling conditions because there was no alternative; without land that could produce a surplus above rent, taxes, input costs and debt repayments there was no means of livelihood.

It barely needs mentioning that Korean workers were not permitted to organize into trade unions (but that did not prevent numerous labour disputes including general strikes in Wonsan and Seoul at the end of the twenties [Hatada, 1969, p128]). This was part of the general system of repression instituted by the Government-General aimed primarily at quashing any expression of nationalist sentiment. The efficiency and severity of the police force were responsible for the absence of any effective nationalist organization within Korea at the time of liberation. In fact there were very few organizations of Koreans of any kind other than religious ones.[31] However, communist groups were sporadically active throughout and appear to have gained widespread popular recognition for their anti-Japanese activities. The Japanese elaborated and enforced a 'cultural policy' which permitted but carefully controlled newspapers, books and the like, regulated school curricula (in the early years teachers had been required to wear military-type uniforms), banned the teaching of the Korean language and rewrote the country's history. A contemporary missionary called Korea 'a well-regulated penal colony' (quoted in Sohn, 1970, p253). The aim of the policy of cultural genocide was to integrate Korea into the Japanese empire body and soul, but it contained the contradiction of all more 'enlightened' forms of imperialism that the colony should form a fully integrated part of the ruling country yet still be subordinate to it. The explanation lies in the subordination of the Japanese working class.

Growing out of these conditions there developed in Chosen deep-rooted, anti-colonial feeling, which achieved its most dramatic expression in the 'March 1st Independance Struggle' of 1919, a broadly-based series of demonstrations and actions across the country in which Japanese property and police stations were attacked. Several thousand deaths resulted. It marked the Declaration of Independence calling for a free Korea and replacing the old despotic regime with a democratic constitution guaranteeing civil liberties. Although the movement was crushed and the masses sank back into the despair of the everyday struggle for existence, the movement stirred a deep nationalist sentiment. The Korean Provisional Government (including Syngman Rhee) was established in Shanghai exile and, despite factional squabbles, became a centre of nationalist opposition outside Korea. Shortly after this, the Korean Communist Party was founded but its attempts to organize and agitate within Korea appear to have been speedily quelled each time and its participants arrested. The independence movement shook the Japanese, and their colonial policy moved away from one of arrogant military might towards a cultural policy designed to assimilate potentially sympathetic

---

[30]The same author makes the remarkably prescient observation that Japanese (and Korean) firms could pay less-than-subsistence wages because the expenses of rearing a family had been borne by farm income, and the surplus of potential workers leaving the farms meant that wages did not need to be high enough to reproduce the worker's family in the city (Grajdanzev, 1944, p182).

[31]Repression became more intense as total war loomed. In the last decade of colonial rule the Japanese decreed the 'Ordinance on Constant Surveillance and Domiciliary Confinement of Korean Thought Offenders', and the equally Orwellian 'Thought Criminals Preventive Custody Law'.

elements of Korean society with the ultimate end of an independent Korea within the Japanese empire. It was a classical policy of divide-and-rule. It was effective in coopting many 'gradualist nationalists' who were thereby compromised by association with colonialist organizations and ideas, and the struggle for independence was left largely to leftist forces drawn from the ranks of workers, farmers, students and intellectuals.

Japanese colonialism, then, had a profound effect on the class structure of Korea, shaking it out of the stagnation of the Yi dynasty. The first act of the new master was to abolish the monarchy - the emperor was forced to abdicate in 1907 - and along with it the old bureaucracy and nobility were swept away.[32] The purchase and seizure of lands by the Japanese weakened the traditional landed aristocracy. Not only was part of its control over agriculture's (and thus the nation's) primary resource diminished but its political power, locally and centrally, was abrogated. The only course open to the rural gentry was to form a *de facto* alliance with the occupying forces and to bide their time. Though enfeebled under the Japanese, their continued possession of such essential resources put them in a position to assume political power on the Japanese departure, though under changed circumstances to be sure.

On the other hand, there had been a great increase in tenancy; by the end of the thirties pure tenants made up over half of farm households with part-tenants making up another quarter, with a concomitant decline in petty owner-cultivators. The tenants were reliant on contracts with landlords, were subject to extortionate rents and frequent turnovers, and the stability of village life was disturbed forever. Capitalist social relations in the primal form of wage-labour did not penetrate agriculture to any marked degree, although by the time of liberation perhaps one in twenty of the rural workforce was an agricultural wage-labourer. But the imperatives of export production had introduced exchange relations on a wide scale and had destroyed the self-sufficiency of the traditional economy. In addition, Japanese occupation exposed the peasant masses to a degree of centralized government intervention in daily life which was previously unknown. More than that, the poverty and hunger of the peasantry under the Japanese forced millions of the rural-born to discover new modes of existence beyond the village, in Korean cities and foreign lands where they were reproduced as proletarians.

Off the land, a radical transformation of Korean society had been wrought by the growth of industry in the twenties and thirties. Although it was an industrialization built largely by Japanese capital and conditioned by the economic structure of Japan proper its impact on Korea was profound. Korean capital was limited in most industrial sectors and was largely confined to trade and small-scale industry,[33] but the Korean-owned enterprises which did emerge generated a group of perhaps a few thousand businessmen who assumed a position of influence after liberation and formed an important component of the new class of commercial and industrial capitalists which grew up in the fifties.

---

[32]Henderson (1968, p77) writes that 'the Imperial Household pensioned off 3,645 Korean officials, selected with a detailed Japanese knowledge of the Korean upper class and its fractions. The infiltration and undermining of the leadership class had been ... an old and long process. Its final elimination was now extraordinarily thoroughly accomplished ... . At least from 1919 on, Korea may be said to have become a country without a leadership class'.

[33]'... it was the Japanese who constituted almost the entire middle and upper classes of Chosen' (Henderson, 1968, p97).

Population growth, transformed agrarian conditions and rural pauperization forced droves of poor families from the land but the social pressure of these marginalized masses was dissipated by large-scale emigration. Around six million people left for Japan and Manchuria, most of whom returned after liberation. A further one million or so, a third of whom were women, joined the ranks of the swelling proletariat in mining, manufacturing, construction, transport and commerce. They were largely untrained, unskilled and illiterate. A mere trickle achieved managerial or technical status, although some did acquire factory skills.

That trickle, however, was to be important, for those in business and the bureaucracy, as well as Korean technicians and landlords and policemen, who had become integrated into the system of colonial control would be those who could apply their worldly knowledge and ownership of productive resources to bid for political power after liberation. There was no possibility, however, of a return to pre-colonial Korea. Japanese colonialism had introduced capitalist social relations on a wide scale, it had sapped the traditional legitimacy of the landlord-tenant relationship in the popular consciousness and had destroyed the authority of the old ruling class. Korea had irreversibly entered a period of profound change.

2.3 Formation of the Post-War Nation-State

A revolutionary wind swept Asia after the war. Nationalism which had stirred under the repressive forces of various colonialisms was unleashed in the turmoil of the Japanese defeat. Those nationalists in former Japanese colonies were quick to take advantage of the surrender and, for a time at least, were leaders of independent nations. In Korea, the nationalist emotion had penetrated almost every corner of society for even in the remotest villages the harshness of Japanese rule had been felt. The nationalist movement had formed and developed and split in exile but elements of it had provided persistent and worrying armed resistance to the Japanese in Manchuria, especially Kim Il Sung's Northeast Anti-Japanese United Army. Such was the efficiency of Japanese repression within Korea that all expressions of indigenous dissent were quickly quashed and their leaders gaoled or forced to flee. Factions within independence movements united in the face of common enemy; peasants and workers, and elements from the professional, *yangban* and bureaucratic classes who felt deprived and frustrated under colonial rule were driven towards policies of radical social reform; national liberation became associated increasingly with a new social order to replace the discredited and effete *anciens régimes*. The form of this new social order was vague, to be determined upon liberation, but as that day approached it precipitated irresolvable divisions within the nationalist movements. The imminent seizure of power undermined the surface cohesion provided by a common goal.

The political history of South Korea from the time of liberation (and the division of the country into administrative districts under US and Soviet occupation) to the consolidation of the Park regime is far too convoluted to present in detail here. Yet aspects of it are essential to an understanding of the emergence of the class structure which existed on the eve of the period of rapid industrial growth.

At the time of Japanese surrender, there was no indigenous political structure or organization capable of assuming immediate control, and because those who had remained were almost imvariably collaborators, potential leaders with a claim to legitimacy were in exile near or far. Emphatically in Korea,[34] Japanese occupation had destroyed the legitimacy of the traditional governing class. Immediately, there was a great upsurge of popular political activity, uncoordinated, spontaneous and decentralized. All over the peninsular local People's Committees sprang up, sometimes with the cooperation of local communist cells and everywhere fired by national spirit. These committees took control of their areas, disarmed the Japanese, released political prisoners, and punished collaborators. They seized factories, took over administration, controlled transport and communications and in rural areas drew up plans to redistribute land. When US officials arrived in South Cholla province two months after the Japanese surrender they found 42 of the province's 50 factories in operation. Now the enterprises were being run either by the Korean workers on a profit-sharing basis or by the local People's Committee (Jones & Sakong, 1980, p32). Henderson has written:

> Rarely has a nation been so suddenly, so radically stimulated toward revolutionary political and economic development and almost all possible manner of accompanying property and social change (Henderson, 1968, p118).

The People's Committees, it is agreed even by hostile sources, were generally representative and embraced conservatives and radicals of many hues. But in a time of great popular unshackling their inclination was towards radical social change. In the north where the Soviet army had occupied, they were looked on with favour as an expression of popular will. In Seoul a 'central government' was formed by a committee of moderate nationalists and communists and took the title of the Korean People's Republic.[35] According to Henderson 'the People's Republic had made genuine progress in setting down local roots and achieving a degree of legitimacy'.[36] For a few weeks a popular Korean government, represented in the provinces by the People's Committees, achieved de facto sovereignty throughout the country and proved the Korean capacity for self-government. The combined activities of the People's Committees and the People's Republic sent a shiver of fear through the propertied classes and those others who had swum with the Japanese imperial tide. Many thousands of political prisoners were released and many became immediately involved in the local Committees. Collaborators were hounded out of their districts, but lesser landlords often participated in these experiments in local democracy which expressed the demands and aspirations of the long-suffering peasantry. In the factories the formation of unions had been rapid and collectively they formed the National Council of Korean Labor Unions which was to lead the general strike of 1946.

The arrival of US forces a few weeks after the Japanese surrender brought a

---

[34]Henceforth 'Korea' refers to South Korea, the Republic of Korea, unless it is otherwise obvious.

[35]Although communists in the south supported the People's Republic it was criticized by communists in the north as a 'bourgeois republic' (see Brun & Hersh, 1976, pp77-78, and Halliday, 1977, p23 nl).

[36]Henderson (1968, p120). Western reporters confirmed that the People's Republic had popular backing including strength in the countryside - see McCune (1950, p50).

new government to South Korea. The United States Army Military Government in Korea (USAMGIK or, more simply, AMG) refused to recognize the People's Republic and established an administration served by Koreans who had worked in the Japanese bureauracy and police. These forces immediately began to spread out into the countryside and into towns and cities and to wrest control from the local People's Committees. The latter were soon declared illegal, and all property of the Japanese - factories and farms which had been seized and operated by local communities - was appropriated by the AMG. The People's Committees had in many areas set down firm local roots and it was some months before the AMG could, with force, suppress them and reinstate the Korean officials who had worked for the Japanese, including the police who had gone into hiding. The AMG lent its support to reactionary forces, small but wealthy, behind the newly-founded Korean Democratic Party (KDP) which gave allegiance to the Korean Provisional Government.

Thousands of nationalist activists returned to Korea in the months following liberation. Among them was Syngman Rhee who had been in US exile for some 40 years and who was regarded by some in the State Department as a danger to stability because of his burning hostility to the USSR with whom the US sought to negotiate in the months after the war. The dilemma for the AMG was that it was required to prepare a government of nationals to assume control in due course (this at a time when unification was still being negotiated), yet apart from the powerful communists, the only leaders with a claim to legitimacy were the intensely nationalist founders of the Korean Provisional Government in exile. The AMG had been instructed in 1946 to give no encouragement to Syngman Rhee, Kim Koo and their organization but to seek out a group of 'younger, more liberal' leaders (Joungwon Kim, 1975, p65). At this time, however, moderation was in short supply in Korea. Meanwhile the US forces had earned the hostility of the people: firstly by taking local control from the People's Committees and in the process rearming the Japanese-trained police who had been disarmed by the people; secondly by announcing that the Japanese administration would be temporarily retained (a decision quickly reversed in the face of popular wrath); and thirdly by reaching an agreement with Moscow to put Korea under a five-year trusteeship rather than grant immediate independence.

In 1946 the AMG set up an interim legislature, half elected, half appointed, and wholly resented, as a prelude to the 1948 elections for the Korean National Assembly, which was to form an independent government in the South. There was universal suffrage and elections were supervised by the United Nations Temporary Commission on Korea (UNTCOK). There was widespread opposition to the holding of these elections since they were to give some permanence to the partition of the country. Indeed, a month before the election a unification conference was held in Pyongyang involving the government of the north and representative of every significant political organization in the south with the exception of the Syngman Rhee clique. Syngman Rhee had been always dependent on US support, political and military, and came to the early conclusion that unification under prevailing conditions was undesirable. His fanatical anti-communism drove him to this at a time when only the left articulated mass demands. Throughout this period there were popular uprisings against local administrations set up by the AMG and a general strike which led to many deaths. In particular there was a bloody revolt in October 1946 in the Taegu area during which the police were attacked; many policemen were killed and mutilated. The Military Government needed troops to suppress the rebellion.

Although supervised by UNTCOK the elections have been called by others a 'complete farce' conducted under conditions of police terror and a general strike (Brun & Hersh, 1976, p84). When the Assembly convened, around two-thirds of the members were affiliated either with the landlord-backed Korean Democratic Party (KDP) or Rhee's National Society which was dominated by the nationalists of the Provisional Government in exile. Rhee was overwhelmingly elected chairman and, on independence, president of the Republic. Once in power Rhee continued the policy of the AMG of eliminating radical and communist influence wherever it could be found. The State Department discarded its commitment to liberalism and backed the anti-communist purges vigorously. Rhee claimed legitimacy because of his unsullied record of opposition to the Japanese (and his claimed *hyangban* - lesser, local nobility - origins). In the months that following there was a wholesale purge of 'disloyal' elements in the army, police, press and educational establishments. Some ninety thousand people were arrested in an eight month period in 1948-49 (Henderson, 1968, p163). By this process, Rhee and his US backers carried through a process of rooting out and destroying the left opposition and cowing popular protest, although it was several years before the parliamentary liberal-left was wholly exorcised from the South Korean body-politic. When elements of the parliamentary opposition challenged Rhee's power in 1949 the police responded with arrests, torture and imprisonment (see Henderson, 1968, pp165-67).

The first basis of Rhee's support was undoubtedly the USA. Although the relationship was often uneasy, no government could have long survived without US support, as the near future was to reveal. Rhee's initial rise to the presidency was supported by landed property interests in the KDP,[37] but Rhee chose his cabinets mainly from the independence activists. Undoubtedly, the domestic foundation of his power lay in the two most powerful domestic organizations in Korea at the time, the bureaucracy and the police.[38] Although a fervent nationalist in his opposition to the Japanese occupation Rhee was an anti-communist first, and that allowed him to ally with these discredited and despised groups. Both bureaucrats and police were trained by the Japanese and served them in the colonial task. The AMG had restored them to power after the People's Committees had spurned them. The bureaucracy was perhaps more powerful than ever since it did not exist to serve private capital but controlled most of the economy directly itself. It was intimately tied to the US forces in Korea. It chose to support Rhee because he was the best guarantee against the reprisals of popular nationalism.

Similarly, members of the police force had once sworn loyalty to the Japanese imperial government; many had fled the north from charges of collaboration to join the force in the south. They were a tightly-knit and largely uncontrollable force - disciplined, authoritarian, often brutal, loyal to themselves. (Says Henderson, 'ordinary Koreans hated and despised them more than they did many Japanese' [1968, p80].) Above all they had a terror of the people - from the time of liberation

---

[37] The KDP, writes Cumings (1974, pp57-58), 'was not simply a party of landlords and collaborators. Also present were highly educated Koreans (some educated in the West), some Christians, business entrepreneurs, and various conservatives'.

[38] The army's loyalty remained uncertain. Although built into a significant military force under the tutelage of the AMG, and under the direct command of the openly fascist 'General' Yi Pom-sok, it was not wholly loyal to the new government and was capable of mutiny when sent to quell popular revolt (Henderson, 1968, pp141 & 162). Most of its senior officers had served in the Japanese army (Cumings, 1974, pp72-73).

the police had been periodically attacked by incensed mobs and often killed with ferocity. In the 1960 'student revolution', the target of demonstrations was the police. They carried out a campaign of ruthless suppression of the left opposition on behalf of Rhee. Not only the left suffered. Opposition assemblymen in an unwise attempt to undermine Rhee's power base passed in late 1948 the National Traitors' Law designed to expose and punish collaborators in the bureaucracy and police. When this was put into practice the police responded by arresting and persecuting the assemblymen involved.

As the left was weakened by police terror and popular uprisings were put down, the parliamentary opposition became a focus of dissent. This effectively meant the Korean Democratic Party (from 1949 the Democratic Nationalist Party) which had initially supported Rhee's presidency. The KDP was composed of and represented absentee landlords and businessmen connected with the landlords, and was supported by the important *Dong-A Ilbo* newspaper. In no sense did it represent a more liberal, democratic set of principles as an alternative to Rhee's government. Indeed it is reported that Rhee would not appoint KDP 'capitalists' to his cabinet because the UN might deny recognition to the new Republic since many countries would see it as too 'right wing' (Joungwon Kim, 1975, p119).

The post-war balance of class forces found some expression in the National Assembly. From the perspective of later industrial development, the key issue was land reform. The landlord-dominated Interim Assembly had rejected it in 1948. The AMG had initally been suspicious of such a radical measure but could soon see the political danger of maintaining the old system, particularly in the light of the popular favour in which the land reforms of the north were held, and followed McArthur's lead in Japan. It began distributing to tenants the substantial government holdings that had been confiscated from the Japanese. More than 90 percent of formerly-Japanese land was passed to Korean cultivators immediately prior to the National Assembly elections of late 1948. The effect of this redistribution on landlords was not material but it gave them a good whiff of the winds of change. Popular feeling on the issue was intense. It had fermented under the pressures of rural pauperization and growing land concentration during the Japanese period; nationalism and land reform for many went together and the northern example beamed bright. Indeed there had been, from the day of the Japanese surrender, killings of landlords and seizure of land. The landlord class was too enfeebled to mount a sustained resistance; they had been weakened in possessions, legitimacy and political power by the Japanese. The land reform bill introduced in 1949 aimed at abolishing tenancy and landlords. Although they dominated the National Assembly, the landlords were to pass the bill and effectively to destroy their own traditional material base. Many, however, had already diversified into industry and commerce; many had already sold their land in anticipation of reform. Ban, et al. (1980, pp285-86) provide figures which show that, compared to the 330,000 hectares redistributed by the government, around 570,000 hectares were sold directly by landlords to tenants between the end of the war and the implementation of the reforms. Moreover, the profitability of land ownership had fallen precipitously in the post-war years. In some areas, landlords could not command the authority to collect rents; elsewhere, because of the AMG's grain collecion programme landlords ended up with only about 7 percent of the output on tenanted land, a very low rate of return compared with over 50 percent before the war (Ban et al., 1980, pp288 & 439n6). The provisions of the reform bill appeared to be financially attractive - owners of estates of over 3 hectares were, it seemed, to receive a good price under the circumstances, to be paid in government bonds exchangeable for ownership shares in former Japanese industries. However, Ban et al. (1980, p287) conclude that ultimately land reform 'involved much more expropriation than compensation'. It ought to be noted that the Assembly enacted the bill in February 1950 over Rhee's presidental veto, although the reason behind Rhee's opposition remains unclear.[39]

The US-Rhee alliance was an unstable one throughout. Prior to the Korean War the US and Korean governments were in constant conflict over economic policy. The nationalistic Rhee wanted autonomy in decision-making; the US had an investment to protect and the lever it resorted to time and again to impose its will was the threat of withdrawal of the aid which formed the greater part of the government's budget.[40] Only US aid after the Korean war made possible the economic growth which sustained Rhee. The price of this support was pervasive US influence over Korean affairs, economic and otherwise. This influence was first felt in the US attempts to ensure that elections would produce a goverment sympathetic to its wishes.[41] Although the AMG threw its weight behind Rhee, and participated in the crushing of popular opposition, it could not rely on Rhee to be compliant. The influence of the AMG spread, however, to the police and the bureaucracy, which were beholden to the US for restoring them to power, and above all to the military which, during and after the Korean War, was built by the US, supplied by the US, and trained in its techniques and methods of organization. Large numbers of officers were trained in the US, for South Korea had become the front-line of the US empire in Asia. As we will see, the effect of US hegemony was not only to sustain conservative political forces but to influence the economic structure of Korean society so as to foster the growth of a native bourgeoisie.

The outbreak of hostilites in 1950 saved Rhee from an apparently inevitable fall from power after the defeat in the National Assembly elections of that year.[42] After the war the regime remained, always beseiged, for several years with the grudging support of the US. There developed no solid social foundation for Rhee's dictatorship. In the fifties South Korea was a society being transformed - capitalism was emerging as the dominant form of social relation economically and the political power of capital was on the ascendant. Rhee's bedrock of support in the police and bureaucracy could not continue to prevail in the face of the countervailing power. Nor was Rhee, always the dogmatist, willing to bend with the wind. Capitalism brings with it a preoccupation with economics, but Rhee ignored the pressures from domestic sources and US aid officials to attend to the economy. Although there was fast growth in some years with the support of economic aid and military spending, the foundations were shaky, and growth was liable to decline at the hint of adverse conditions. Moreover, it became clear that the economic development which was taking place was an edifice built on the quicksand of aid - it was not self-sustaining,

---

[39]Joungwon Kim (1975, p125) argues that Rhee in fact gave the bill his blessing since he calculated that it would undermine the economic and thus political power of the DNP opposition.

[40]Indeed the US Congress, tired of the US's factious protégé, reduced economic aid from $180m in 1948 to $59 in 1950. The war changed this trend.

[41]The State Department issued a directive this way to the AMG in 1946 (Henderson, 1968, p133).

[42]Some writers who have gone beyond Cold War propaganda about the causes of the war (ideas still abroad today) argue that Rhee's oft-claimed intent to reunify by force was put into action in the sure knowledge that the US would enter the war.

and it was increasingly apparent that the aid could not last for many more years. Indeed as if to prove the case, economic growth fell rapidly in 1959 and 1960 in response to sharp cuts in US aid.[43] Business was squeezed and the recession was compounded by a poor harvest in 1959-60. Not only were the economists ignored, but the regime persistently sought more aid by maintaining an exchange rate which discouraged exports and neglected agriculture so that food aid would continue to flow.[44] For his part, Rhee estranged the remnants of his conservative support with his obsession with the North and fanatical anti-communism. His autocratic leadership was even more intolerable as he increasingly cut himself off from the realities of Korean society and refused to recognize opposition opinion. The new entrepreneurs who were largely created and sustained by the regime's control of aid funds (see below) and who formed the financial backbone of Rhee's Liberal Party, began secretly to channel funds into the opposition Democratic Party as they lost confidence in the government (Joungwon Kim, 1975, p160).

The US was increasingly worried by these developments. Concern over Rhee's neglect of economic issues and over his obsessive nationalism were closely related. The US had begun to evolve a new East Asian strategic plan which foresaw a strengthened Japan assuming some of the USA's commitments, economic and military, in the region. This would require rapprochement between Korea and Japan, something that was anathema to Rhee.

The end was quick. When police fired on and killed students protesting at election-rigging in April 1960, US officials made it clear that the US would no longer support the regime and that Rhee must resign. The 'student revolution' saw a brief period without effective government (an interim government was formed with US sanction) before the elections of July 1960 caused the old Democratic Party to be swept into office on the slogan 'Economic Development First'. The new government pledged to

> ... utilise the industrious and intelligent labour of Korea to produce commodities for export, as successfully demonstrated by Japan in the early stages of industrialization and by Hong Kong more recently ... and to make an all-out effort in normalizing relations with Japan with a view to promoting mutually beneficial economic arrangements (quoted in Payer, 1975, p155).

Acutely aware of the power the US could exert by withdrawing aid funds, the new government assiduously sought the approval of the US government and its officials. The government readily agreed to the two key US demands, resisted by Rhee, of direct US supervision of aid funds (which had been a source of corruption) and a big devaluation. The latter had disastrous consequences in deepening the recession, and was very unpopular. The Democratic Party was not in any way representative of the forces which carried out the revolt. Its members and backers were not easily distinguishable, in social background and material interests, from Rhee's Liberal Party. It was a faction-ridden, conservative coalition largely

---

[43] Between 1958 and 1959 aid was cut from $321m to $222m, almost by a third, and the growth rate of GNP fell from 7 percent to 5.2 percent (Joungwon Kim, 1975, p160) and fell further in 1960.

[44] Agricultural production figures were falsified to further the impression of dependence on US aid (Cole & Lyman, 1971, p79).

representing propertied interests, mainly the old landlord class, but also elements of the ascendant bourgeoisie and disaffected bureaucrats. Of the Democratic Party assembly members 40 percent were the sons of former landlords and a quarter of them had served in the Japanese civil service (Joungwon Kim, 1975, p209). They were less committed to nationalism than the stalwarts of the old Provisional Government who had surrounded Rhee.

The new government was ill-fated. Although it purged the police, the law could not regain control of the streets and the villages. Moreover, it alienated the military by ignoring it, by its factional disputes and by its sycophancy towards the US. The military became alarmed at demands by students for reunification with the north and plans to meet North Korean students to discuss the issue. Senior officers who had access to information about developments in North Korea had become concerned about the rapid economic growth there which made the South's record look very poor (Joungwon Kim, 1975, p219). In addition there were signs of the left in South Korea reorganizing, and popular disturbances, especially in the south-eastern region, were gaining a threatening character. Disunity in goverment and unrest on the streets precipitated a military coup in May 1961.

Perhaps unusually in recent history the US appears to have had no foreknowledge of the coup and would not have supported the overthrow of such a compliant government. The coup was carried out by a coterie of young colonels with Park Chung-Hee, a major-general, playing a leading role.[45] The source of all of the original plotters was the eighth military class of 1948-49, men who, having borne the brunt of the fighting during the civil war, felt overshadowed by more senior officers most of whom were immersed in the corruption of the Rhee regime. Promises by the new government that the senior ranks would be purged of the corrupt were reneged on (under intense US pressure), causing widespread bitterness. The conspirators assumed a high moral posture, denouncing the conspicuous consumption of the rich, attacking degenerate western influences (they had trained with and fought alongside GIs), purging the army and the bureaucracy of the corrupt and dishonest and announcing measures to confiscate 'illicit fortunes' accumulated by wealthy businessmen under Rhee. They were, however, by no means anti-business.

The first sympathies of the colonels lay with the increasingly impoverished peasantry - starvation on a large scale appeared possible - and two of their first acts were to rewrite the terms of usurious rural debts and to extend agricultural credit. A military career was not one of high social standing and officers were generally of rural, and often peasant, origin. Of the coup's authors and subsequent military rulers, 71 percent came from rural areas (Joungwon Kim, 1975, p221).[46] More generally their economic orientation was aimed at less reliance on the US by encouraging import-substituting heavy industry and improved agriculture to achieve self-sufficiency and export growth. Much of this was not in accord with US

---

[45]Park was trained at the Japanese military academy in Manchuria in 1940-42 and then served in the Japanese Kwantung army as Lieutenant Okamoto Minoru. In 1948 he was arrested for participating in the Yosu rebellion and sentenced to death. His sentence was commuted and in 1950 he was reinstated in the army (Joungwon Kim, 1975, p230).

[46]Another study found that of officers who graduated from the Military Academy between 1955 and 1962, 60 percent were sons of farmers or small bussinessmen, 20 percent were sons of white collar workers and 6 percent had fathers with professional occupations (Cole & Lyman, 1971, p274n2).

planning for South Korea although there was some relief in the fact that the colonels were more concerned with the material benefits which could ensue from cooperation with Japan than with excoriating that nation for past crimes. Still contributing half of the national budget and three quarters of the defence budget, the price the US extracted for its indispensable support was the release of gaoled Liberal Party leaders and a commitment to return to civilian rule 'at the earliest possible date'.[47]

The transition to formally civilian rule and the election of Park to the presidency in 1963[48] also witnessed the emergence of a new leadership group within the political party formed by the colonels and their supporters, the Democratic Republican Party (DRP). The 'Young Turks' of the eighth class had envisaged a radical change in the whole political structure; they talked of reshaping society so that it could be modern, democratic and egalitarian. Park and the more senior officers wanted to eliminate corruption and instability, but had no plans for shaking up the immanent forces within Korean society. The latter group attracted the support of the US and business leaders and the bureaucracy, and over the next couple of years managed to assume clear dominance of the DRP and the government. The economic and political orientation of the Park government will become clearer in a subsequent section but essentially it sought to cooperate with domestic capital to advance industrial growth. Its economic strategy was consistent with, but not uniformly subservient to, US designs. An important test came with the issue of normalization with Japan, and presented the government with a serious crisis. Normalization, which involved substantial reparations and loans to Korea as well as the opening up of trade relations, was strongly favoured by business groups, the bureaucracy, Japan and the US. There were still strong ties between Japan and powerful interests in Korea, among them senior DRP politicians such as Park and Kim Jong Pil who had served in the Japanese army, senior officers in the army and bureaucracy and businessmen who had established themselves in the colonial period. Through these links the Japanese could apply pressure to draw South Korea into its sphere of influence. In opposition stood virtually the rest of Korean society who feared creeping subservience to the former colonial master.[49] The pressure applied by the US, eager to release some of the financial burden, was intense (see Joungwon Kim, 1975, p258), and aid had been steadily declining from 1962. When the treaty was signed in 1965 it was done so under conditions of martial law and sparked rioting thoughout the land.

---

[47]Joungwon Kim (1975, p234). This was, after all, Kennedy's new era.

[48]Park beat his main (right-wing) opponent narrowly. Political activity had been banned for the larger part of military rule, most political leaders had been gaoled, and the newly-created and powerful Korean CIA directed its well-funded efforts at ensuring Park's victory.

[49]Joungwon Kim (1975, p257) whose book is generally very valuable, attempts an implausible alternative explanation to prove that Korean opposition to normalization was *not* 'a reflection of an irrational or emotional Korean reaction to the Japanese because of the bitter experience of Japanese rule'.

2.4 Formation of the Classes of Korean Capitalism

Although capitalist social relations had thoroughly penetrated Korean society during the Japanese period, the economy remained predominantly agricultural and based on landlord-tenant relations. Precapitalist forms continued to dominate immediately after the war. The fifties, however, saw a further radical transformation of Korean society, one which laid the very foundation of the industrial growth of the sixties. This was the deepening of primitive accumulation in which capitalist social relations became the dominant social form politically and economically. Although it was not until well into the sixties that the output of capitalist manufacturing and service industries began to outweigh that of agricultural peasant-proprietors, it was clear by the end of the fifties that capitalism was the moving force in South Korean society and had taken hold irreversibly. The alienation of the US, of Korean capital and of the urban working and professional classes from Rhee stemmed largely from his failure to recognize this.

The process of primitive accumulation in South Korea, which began under the Japanese, was one of separating labour from the land and reconstituting it as an industrial working class. It was at the same time one of transforming the physical and social basis of money-making from agriculture to industry, of transforming rentier assets into capital which multiplies and accumulates through productive investment.[50] The importance of the process lay not in the amassing of fortunes by individuals or firms - although there was plenty of that - but in the creation of conditions in which capital could be accumulated through industrial production using wage-labour. No matter how large fortunes grow, capital will continue to be invested in land or merchant trade as long as it is more profitable to do so. This was the case in immediate post-war Korea where the bulk of capital was rooted in the soil - the figurative soil of exploitative agrarian social relations. The transition to capitalist industrialization came about in two broad phases; the transformation of rentier assets into commercial capital in the fifties and the transformation of commercial into industrial capital in the sixties (see Hamilton, 1984). This, of course, is a generalization - in the fifties, significant industrial growth took place - but we will show it to be a reasonable one reflecting the broad trends of accumulation in South Korea. The genesis of industrial capital is, *pari passu*, the formation of an industrial proletariat, and the whole process of the formation of the classes of Korean capitalism is intimately and inseparably bound up with the tranfiguration of agrarian social relations. We will look at all of these together.

The transformation of landed wealth into merchant capital in the fifties came about in response to forces both of repulsion from the land and attraction to commerce. Rentier capital was repelled from the land as a result of the land reform, reflecting the diminished political and economic power of the landlord class, and attracted to commercial pursuits in response to economic circumstances characterized by a flood of US aid and a shortage of foreign exchange which made possible windfall profits through trade. These will be explained in more detail.

The land reform, promulgated in its final form in March 1950, was based on the principle of land-to-the-tiller and it attacked the problem directly by outlawing

---

[50]Since post-war Korean agriculture was not based on capitalist production relations it is not strictly accurate to talk of 'agricultural capital' and 'rentier capital' and thus the 'transformation of capital'. The essential transformation was of the mode of production.

tenancy.[51] Along with land distributed by the AMG and land sold to tenants in anticipation of land reform, the law within a couple of years saw the redistribution of the largest part of tenanted land in South Korea. The new law set an upper limit of 3 *chongbo* (about 3 hectares) per household and although there were some exemptions and a degree of cheating[52] there is no doubt that the reform successfully tranferred the vast bulk of agricultural land to the ownership of the cultivator. Consequently there was a profound change in agrarian social relations, with the rural power of the landlord class effectively eliminated.[53] Between 1945 and 1965 the proportion of farm households wholly owning their land rose from 14 percent to 70 percent, and the proportion of pure tenants fell from 49 percent to 7 percent (see table below).

Table 2-1: Owner-tenant distribution of farm households, 1945-65

	1945	1964	1965
Full owner	13.8	71.6	69.5
Owner-tenant	34.6	23.2	23.5
Tenant	48.9	5.2	7.0
Farm labourers and burnt-field farmers	2.7	-	-
Total	100.0	100.0	100.0

Source: Ban et al., 1980, p286

Effectively, then, tenancy was eliminated.[54] The revolution in agrarian relations did not, however, have any large impact on plot size or farming technique (apart from some initial decline in investments with the withdrawal of landlord capital), and the serious problem of land fragmentation persisted.

What effect did the land reform have on landlords? First of all the reform confirmed the decline of the political and economic power of landlords. Already, as we have previously commented, land ownership had become a less attractive proposition because rents, traditionally very high, were more difficult to collect from an increasingly truculent peasantry and had been diminished as a result of the state's grain collection policy. The Land Reform Act decreed that former tenants were to pay for their land 1.5 times the normal annual output of the main crop, payable over five years to the government. Landlords were to receive the equivalent in government bonds (whose value was to be expressed in terms of rice). However, since the government often did not redeem the bonds on time and since most

---

[51]The new constitution of 1962 again prohibited tenancy outright.

[52]A 1965 survey suggested that exempted land and land illegally rented out amounted to about 16 percent of total cultivated acreage (8 percent each) (Ban et al., 1980, p287).

[53]Keynes's 'euthanasia of the rentier', this time on the land.

[54]Tenancy and absentee landlordism have more recently reemerged on a minor and illegal scale, but these new 'landlords' are generally small farmers who have moved to the cities and wish to maintan their stake in the land (Pak in Park et al., 1980, p69). The extent is difficult to estimate but one report (*Dong-A Ilbo*, August 12, 1976) put the proportion of partial or full tenants at 25.5 percent of all farm households, a very high level.

landlords could not use them as collateral on business loans, the market price of the bonds fell sharply. Ban et al. conclude that landlords received compensation equivalent to around 15-25 percent of their former land assets (1980, p290). The difference accrued partly to the former tenants and partly to the government which took 30 percent of the main crop to finance the war effort. According to one expert on the period, most landlords went bankrupt in the early fifties (Pak & Gamble, 1975, p33), but these were the smaller owners who had not dissociated themselves from the land in advance. As we have seen in the last section, more land was sold privately by landlords to tenants in the 1945-51 period than was appropriated under the land reforms (Ban et al., 1980, p286, also Pak & Gamble, 1975, p32) and was disposed of on terms much more favourable to the landlord. Moreover the bonds of the dispossessed landlords were exchangeable for industrial facilities formerly owned by the Japanese, and several of today's large industrial concerns emerged in this way.[55] However, it was not always the landlords who acquired the vested property this way, for many bonds were sold on the market (for prices between 30 and 70 percent of their face value[56]) to thrusting entrepreneurs. These latter were often technical or managerial employees of the same companies under the Japanese. The factories were often sold at prices well below their actual worth and financed by low-interest government loans, frequently in return for political favours. Jones and Sakong observe that the attempt at 'converting landlords into capitalists is generally held to have been a failure' (Jones & Sakong, 1980, p35-36).

The evidence on the direct conversion of landlords into merchants and industrialists is scarce. If we accept the comment of Jones and Sakong, which applies specifically to the scheme of exchanging assets in land for assets in Japanese-built factories through the issue of bonds, this does not mean that landlords did not find a path into the business world by some other means. Indeed, if it is true that despite the confiscatory element of the land reform many rich landlords were left still wealthy after disposal of their land through private sale or government acquisition, they must have found some other place to put their capital. In the fifties, after the cessation of hostilities, opportunities for profitable investment arose both in commerce, particularly importing, and in import-substituting industrial production. From the viewpoint of the accumulation of capital the important point, however, is not whether landlords were converted into capitalists but that asset-holding and investment in land declined while commercial accumulation accelerated. Even so, it is worth noting that the wealthier landlords formed a disproportionate number of the capitalists who financed the industrial growth of the sixties and seventies. A survey of manufacturing firms in 1976 found no less than 47 percent of entrepreneurs' fathers had been 'large-to-medium landowners'.[57]

The South Korean economy suffered extensive damage as the world war drew

---

[55]Including the OB Company, the Sunkyung Group and Korea Explosives (Jones & Sakong, 1980, p39).

[56]Quoted in Jones & Sakong (1980, p35); another commentator suggests that it was closer to 12 percent (Ban et al., 1980, p289).

[57]Jones & Sakong (1980, p228). The rest had fathers who were merchants (19 percent), factory owners (16 percent), civil servant (6 percent), teachers (4 percent) or professionals (7 percent). See also the study referred to by Cole & Lyman (1971, p17): 'Many of Korea's modern entrepreneurs are thus descended from the former landlord class'. In the Jones & Sakong study, large-to-medium landowners would have been, given the agricultural techniques, also landlords.

to a close and the Japanese withdrew, and again during the civil war of 1950-53. The withdrawal of the Japanese left many factories without key technical workers and it took time before the facilities returned to full capacity operation. The AMG was also very slow to return factories to operation. Moreover, the structure of the economy in the south was even more distorted than under the Japanese because the north, now cut off, had produced most of the peninsular's metallic and chemical products and electric power. All this led to severe shortages of manufactured goods throughout the late forties and fifties, particularly of consumer goods while the 'easy phase' of import substitution was going on. This made for lucrative opportunities, which subsequently led to widespread charges of profiteering. The basis for the accumulation through trade lay in foreign exchange allocation and US aid. No systematic study has been made of this period and evidence is almost wholly anecdotal. Jones and Sakong give some examples of what they call 'zero-sum' activities, i.e. those which did not involve adding value or productive activity (1980, pp272-73). Kyong-Dong Kim has analyzed the development of the chaebŏl (family-based industrial conglomerates) in the fifties as a process of political favouritism allowing windfall profits on commercial deals:

> With some private capital at hand, they sought the best opportunities for economic ventures in the existing political economy - i.e. in foreign aid. The best access to this source was the use of political connections (Kyong-Dong Kim, 1976, p468).

For instance, in 1952 the Rhee administration illegally allocated 3 million dollars of foreign exchange earned through tungsten exports to forty private firms. The funds were used to import grains and fertilizers which, when sold at monopoly prices and taking advantage of the discrepancy in foreign exchange rates, earned enormous profits some of which flowed to Rhee's Liberal Party. Similar gains were made by cement-producing firms which also imported quantities of cement which were sold at vastly inflated prices responding to high demand. Kim's conclusion is thus:

> In this period of rising costs and a predominantly consumer-oriented economy, these entrepreneurs accumulated capital mainly through such 'non-rational' processes as speculation, price fixing, tax evasion, and taking advantage of cumulative inflation (Kyong-Dong Kim, 1976, p469).

In markets where imported goods fetched very high premiums, foreign exchange was a precious commodity. Since exports were relatively small the source of most foreign exchange was aid. According to Byun and Kim (1978, p10), 'it was a privilege to get a foreign exchange allocation since import itself guaranteed profitable opportunities because of the general shortage in every kind of consumer good'. If access could be had to a foreign exchange loan, imports could generate massive profits. Preference in allocation was given to exporters (mainly of agricultural and mineral products) and domestic producers dependent of imports of capital goods. Loans for these industries accounted for 45 percent of total imports in the 1945-61 period (Byun & Kim, 1978, p10). In the words of the last-mentioned authors, 'this access to loan rather than production itself must have been the backbone of profitable capital accumulation at that time'. Often, it was reported, loans were granted on the understanding that the recipient firm would make a donation to the Liberal Party.[58] In addition, many traders were able to take advantage of the multiple exchange rate system which, when combined with an official exchange rate that fell well below the market rate, acted to subsidize the cost of imports from government coffers (Byun & Kim, 1978, p11).[59]

US aid was essential to this process. Dollars and imported materials flowed to selected businesses, and whether or not these resources were used to add value domestically or were simply resold at a premium the mark-up attracted by these scarce commodities could be prodigious. Access to productive inputs which were limited by the shortage of foreign exchange guaranteed some sort of monopoly over the sale of goods produced with them. Not only could big profits be made through access to dollars or imports directly, but the flood of army supplies which accompanied the US forces after each war permitted individuals with a little capital and political influence or well-placed contacts to build fortunes. This was augmented later by 'the hundreds of millions of dollars' worth of surplus Army material disposed of in Korea [which] permitted some practitioners of "buy-and-sell" to become established merchants and even importers' (Sung-Jae Koh in Sung-Jo Park et al., 1980, p373). Later, when aid was allocated for specific projects, collusion and political favouritism in the bidding for government and US military contracts was a further source of easy accumulation. This method is said to have led to the emergence of the 'Five Men' of the construction industry.[60]

As for the argument above that the dominant trend during the period was the emergence of capital in merchant form, this should be tempered by recognition of the considerable import-substituting manufacturing growth which also occured in the fifties. The real gross fixed capital stock grew at an average annual rate of 5.1 percent between 1953 and 1962.[61] Moreover, although superprofits could be had through access to foreign exchange and import licences, the goods so obtained were often used in processes of production which represented industrial accumulation. As we have seen at least 45 percent of imports in the 1945-61 period went to domestic industrial concerns. Even so, one solid piece of evidence for the dynamism of commerce in this period is supplied by Byun and Kim in their study of the 'Fifty Groups', South Korea's fifty most powerful industrial groups consisting of over 500 firms nearly 60 percent of which are in manufacturing (Byun & Kim, 1978). Of the fifty groups, 31 were established in the period under consideration, 1945-1961 (13 in

---

[58]See eg. Kyong-Dong Kim (1976, p468) and Jones & Sakong (1980, pp106 & 272). Much evidence on these practices became public after the Student Revolution of 1960.

[59]'Because the dollar was undervalued, those firms which could secure the precious licences permitting them to deal in matters involving foreign exchange could make a large profit by purchasing foreign goods at far below true market costs and selling them at a tremendous profit' (Joungwon Kim, 1975, p153).

[60]Kyong-Dong Kim (1976, p469). The close relationship between the state and segments of private capital was one of the most important sources of accumulation:

....a major characteristic of Korean entrepreneurship in the fifties was that it was far easier to make money from government-derived favours than from productive competitive activity, and entrepreneurs naturally followed their pocket books (Jones & Sakong, 1980, p37).

[61]Hong (1979, Table 2.6, pp20-21). In the next 9 year period, 1962-1971, it grew at 16.5 percent per annum.

1945-1952, 18 in 1953-1961). Of these 31, no fewer than 11 began business in foreign trade.[62] It might be objected that the official figures, so far as they are accurate, show for example that wholesale and retail trade in fact grew a little less fast than manufacturing in 1953-60 (see ESY, 1967, pp10-11), but a very large part of the trading activity that was taking place in South Korea at this time was illegal and immeasurable and not likely to be accounted for in the official statistics.

There is no question, however, that a great deal of import-substituting production began in the fifties and that this represented the growth of industrial capital.[63] The conditions for this were excellent. First of all, there were a great number of factories built by the Japanese which by one means or another passed into Korean hands. Nor should we ignore the significant development of Korean-owned industry in colonial times, most of which continued to operate and expand after the war. Jones and Sakong (1980, p28) give the details: there were 2,400 Korean-owned manufacturing factories (in 1937) 160 of which employed more than 50 workers; there were 7,000 Korean managers, 28,000 professional and technical workers, 58,000 engineers and technicians and several hundred thousand industrial workers (not to mention the millions who returned from Japan and Manchuria, perhaps more to the North though). Thirteen of the future fifty groups predate the world war (Byun & Kim, 1978, p8). Through the stimulus of shortages and abetted by government policy, import substitution in the fifties emphasized basic consumer industries such as textile manufacturing, flour milling and sugar refining. In the 1953-61 period mining and manufacturing grew at an average annual rate of 12.2 percent (ESY, 1970, p50). Although this new production did replace potential imports, the fact is that there was an *increase* in import dependence in many manufacturing sectors during the fifties, including processed food, clothing, printing, and almost all heavy, chemical and machinery sectors (but not textiles, wood products and paper).[64] Nevertheless the government had taken certain measures to encourage the development of domestic manufacturing.[65] The multiple exchange rate helped and so did high tariffs on both aid and non-aid financed imports. The overvalued exchange rate was offset by a system of tariffs whose rates rose in accordance with the degree of competitiveness of the imports with domestic production (but with very heavy rates levied on luxury goods) and were low on necessary imports of raw materials and capital goods. A system of tariff exemptions helped channel imports at reduced cost to selected domestic indutries.[66] Undesired competition from imports was further discouraged by quotas and tax exemptions, and domestic industrial firms had access to bank loans at cheap rates for expansion.

---

[62]Byun & Kim (1978, pp11-23). Another 5 of the 31 began in textiles, with others in transport (2), food (4), liquor (2), printing (1), chemicals (2), briquets (1), glass (1), iron and steel (1) and electricity (1).

[63]Youngil Lim (1981, p49) argues that figures on rates of establishment of new enterprises suggest that 'vigorous entrepreneurial activities started during the latter half of the fifties, long before the policy changes came into effect in the mid-sixties... the potential, long-run force of industrialization and the willingness of entrepreneurs to enter the manufacturing sector and to take risks seems to have begun operating long before [the accession of the military government]'.

[64]The details of these and more are in Suh (1975, Tables 5-1 & 5-2).

[65]The UN-sponsored Nathan Report of 1954 recommended, shades of the IMF, that Korea revert to the colonial pattern of exporting rice and minerals while importing manufactures.

[66]On all this see Hong (1979, pp45-49), and Suh (1975, pp198-199).

These measures, which aimed at expanding profits and hastening accumulation in domestic enterprise, were the more effective in that their impact was largely concentrated on the bigger companies, the emerging chaeból (Jones & Sakong, 1980, p271).

By the end of the fifties it was becoming clear that the economic system that had overseen the decline of the landed rentier and the rise of the capitalist could not sustain itself. The economy was a derivative one; Korean industry and agriculture were dependent on imports for survival. The value of imports was at least ten times that of exports, and only US aid kept the economy afloat.[67] The significance of this had been brought home through the cuts in aid in 1958-60 which were accompanied by falling growth rates. The problem of the foreign exchange gap began to exercise the minds of economists and politicians as it became evident that US aid would not last for many more years. Social stability rested on imports and aid. But although this suggests why a change in the economic structure became necessary for future development, it does not explain how that change came about.

The transitional period, auguring the passage of economic and political supremacy from commercial to industrial capital, was launched by the Student Revolution of 1960 which toppled the corrupt Rhee regime that had so transformed society from its agricultural base. The revolt might be seen as a product of the political strains brought about by the inability of merchant capital to provide for the needs of the people. As if to confirm our argument about the dominance of commercial capital in the fifties and the methods by which it was created, the anger of the populace was directed foremost against the profiteers, the parasites, the corrupt and the abusers of authority. The military government which succeeded the civilian one took up the same theme and was willing to act on popular demands for retribution. The Special Law for Dealing with Illicit Wealth Accumulation was designed to punish those who 'accumulated wealth illicitly by taking advantage of their positions of power' (quoted in Jones & Sakong, 1980, p280), the latter defined to cover those who had made illicit profits from foreign exchange allocation, contracts for public works and commodity supply, cheap bank loans, tax avoidance and overseas transfer of wealth. The Park Military Government immediately arrested most of Korea's leading businessmen, and stood poised to confiscate their assets. A deal was subsequently struck, reflecting the changed economic emphasis of the new administration, whereby criminal charges would be dropped if the businessmen agreed to build factories and donate them to the state. Jones and Sakong (1980, p278) have summed up the transition this way:

> ...under Rhee much, if not the bulk, of chaeból accumulation took place as a result of government-controlled transfers that produced relatively few compensatory benefits for society as a whole.

Under Park, the 'zero-sum activity' of the fifties was largely replaced by 'positive-sum activity' and the illicit wealth accumulation episode inaugurated a pattern 'whereby substantial assistance was given to established businessmen who proved

---

[67]Hong (1979, Table 3.2, p46). In 1957-58 grant-aid paid for five sixths of imports (Cole & Lyman, 1971, p132).

themselves capable of initiating new manufacturing and export activity'.[68]

Just as the transition from land rent to commercial business came about under forces of repulsion and attraction, so it was in the transformation of merchant into industrial capital. The repulsion of capital from its old commercial circuit was due to the elimination of the opportunities to make big profits simply through trade and access to foreign exchange. In large measure this was due to the fact that the military government, unlike its predecessor, was not initially dependent on donations from the wealthy, and by the time civilian rule and elections came around industrial capital was sufficiently well-organized to deliver strong support to the Park government. More than that, the mood of the country had changed.

As the sixties progressed it became increasingly more difficult to multiply capital simply though access to foreign exchange, aid funds and government favour. These things continued to exist but the profits which attached to them were increasingly tied to productive activity, the adding of value. The ability to import through access to foreign exchange which had been so lucrative in the fifties was made more and more dependent on matching productive activity. The export-import link system, introduced in 1962, (discontinued in 1964 but reintroduced in 1966) gave domestic manufacturers who could achieve export success access to import licenses for the most restricted, and most rewarding, imported commodities.[69] The impact was to encourage the growth through exports of industries whose profit margins would not otherwise have led to such expansion. While the plethora of export promotion policies introduced in the sixties can be seen in this light, the value of the export-import link system was that it encouraged productive activity by making available funds which would otherwise have fattened merchants. It was not the only scheme to use the scarcity of foreign exchange to provide incentives for productive activity. The wastage allowance, which permitted exporting firms to import intermediate inputs over and above the technical requirements of production, provided another source of profit tied to expansion of value-added. Indeed the problem was attacked directly in 1961 when in order to register as a foreign trader it was necessary to export over $5,000 of goods. This was raised to $30,000 in 1962 and $50,000 in 1966.[70] With the import substitution of the fifties it became easier in the sixties to limit severely imports of the consumer goods which had been such bountiful profit-makers for traders. The political climate made it feasible to clamp down hard on the import of luxury goods. This was achieved not only by simple prohibition but also by the series of big devaluations of the won which followed the ousting of Rhee. By making imports much more expensive they removed much of the excess demand for imports which had dominated the fifties.

---

[68]Jones & Sakong (1980, p282). One of the comments to emerge consistently in the interviews by Jones & Sakong (1980, Appendix A) with small and medium businessmen was the belief that the fifties were more corrupt, and that in the sixties government became 'more efficient and more impartial', less subject to favouritism and more supportive of business.

[69]The export-import link system had also operated between 1951 and 1955, but since exports were so small in that period, and such exports as there were tended to be primary products, it was not an effective inducement to industrial expansion.

[70]Up to 1961 the requirements for registration as a foreign trader were considerably easier - see Hong (1979, pp50-51).

In keeping with the military-turned-civilian government's productionist bias, everywhere bureaucratic discretion, which has been a pillar of Korean industrial development, has favoured manufacturing expansion over commercial activity. Industrial promotion policies were the mark of a government that measured its success by the growth statistics. In the taxonomy of Jones and Sakong, only one of the main zero-sum activities of the fifties was not eliminated in the transitional period. 'The remaining element, domestic and foreign credit, is the dominant target of zero-sum accumulation under Park' (1980, p273), but even here excess profits could be obtained by access to cheap bank credit only on the condition that the loan be used for industrial expansion.[71] The government had assumed control of the commercial banks in the 'illicit fortunes' confiscations of 1961, and this control over finance was used to promote industrial growth by lengthening the time-spans of loans so that industrial projects with long gestation periods could secure finance. The importance of bank lending in the economy was enhanced by the interest rate reform of September 1965 which attracted a great flow of deposits into banks and out of the short-term curb market.

As we have come to expect, the US hand in all of this was crucial. From the mid-fifties, US aid officials and US government policy had been pressing hard for the more efficient and productive allocation of aid funds. After reconstruction the US demanded of Korea that it pursue an economic policy to build up the economic viability and strength of the country so that it would be less reliant on US aid and able to develop on its own resources. A large part of the explanation of the withdrawal of US support for Rhee lay in the latter's unwillingness to embrace their view of Korea's economic future. As for the flows of aid which were so instrumental in the accretion of merchant wealth in the fifties, certain changes occurred in the early sixties which all but cut off this source of commercial accumulation. First of all there was the sheer decline in the volume of aid, both in absolute value and relative to national income. Total aid (undeflated) averaged US$325 million per annum in 1956-58, $222 million in 1959-61 and $199 million in 1962-64, and these represented respectively around 14 percent, 8 percent and 6 percent of Korean GNP.[72] Secondly, in the fifties the aid dollars had been sold to selected importers at the official exchange rate which was about half of the estimated parity rate during 1953-61, and this was the source of windfall profits (Hong, 1979, p138). The exchange rate reforms of the early sixties largely eliminated this gap. Thirdly a growing proportion of US aid took the form of PL 480 surplus agricultural commodities; the share of PL 480 in total US aid rose from an average of 11 percent in 1959-61 to 38 percent in 1962-64. Consisting almost wholly of wheat and cotton (especially after 1959), these flowed directly into the flour-milling and textile industries (Hong, 1979, Table 6.8, p137). Finally, as the diminishing volume of aid was replaced by foreign loans and investment, the government could itself carefully regulate the inflow of finance. The 1966 Foreign Capital Inducement Law, empowered the planning minister to approve foreign capital inflows if they contributed to export production or the development of key industries (Hong, 1979, p142).

There was one further factor which, although not confined to the sixties, was

---

[71]Jones & Sakong (1980, p277). However, some industrial credit was used for speculation in land.

[72]Hong (1979, Table 6.6, p135). In 1965-67, total US aid averaged $111 million and stood at around 2 percent of GNP.

fundamental in the accumulation of industrial capital - the growth of the proletariat. The availability of an abundant source of labour is, of course, essential to the development of industrial capital. The period of Japanese colonialism had created huge numbers of wage-labourers and in the sixties, as we will see, government policy ensured that the supply of workers did not dry up. By the end of 1948, an estimated 2.5 million Koreans arrived in the southern zone either repatriated from Japan and Manchuria or having returned home from the north. On the other hand, several hundred thousand Japanese in Korea were sent home. After the civil war 646,000 refugees are said to have arrived from the north. (Set against this was the ghastly toll of the war, which claimed approximately 1.9 million dead in South Korea.)[73] Most of these displaced persons swelled urban populations, and the marginalized masses managed through the fifties somehow to eke out a living until the industrial expansion of the sixties began to soak up appreciable numbers of surplus industrial workers. The data on population are scarce and unreliable for the years 1945-60, and figures on industrial employment are more or less nonexistent before 1960.[74] It is clear though that there was a great labour surplus until the late sixties at least; for instance, until that time it was extremely difficult for rural workers on the overcrowded farms to find work in the cities (Ban et al., 1980, p340). This was the case up to 1967 when the situation changed dramatically. The annual net out-migration from farm households rose from 243,000 in 1960-66 to 568,000 in 1966-70, which represented a rise in the rate of net out-migration from 1.8 percent to 4.2 percent. Whereas in the earlier period more of these migrants had been men than women, in the later period the women substantially outnumbered the men as demand for young female labour in the labour-intensive manufacturing industries mushroomed (Ban et al., 1980, p377). After 1967 the farm population began to decline absolutely, its numbers falling from 16.1 million in that year to 13.2 million in 1975. It was in these 8 years that agriculture contributed the largest part of the 9 million farmers who entered the non-agricultural workforce between 1953 and 1975 (Ban et al., 1980, pp24 & 321). Joungwon Kim (1975, p283) quotes government figures which show that in the two-year period 1968-70, ten percent of the total farming population, one and a half million people, left their farms. The cause of this rural diaspora, as we will see, lay in the government's grain pricing policy and neglect of agricultural development which reduced millions of rural families to penury.

The study of the development of the classes of Korean capitalism has a recurring theme: primitive accumulation and the rise of industrial capital has been as much a political process as an economic one. In the reordering of agrarian social relations and the ruin of the landlord, in the promotion and expansion of commercial capital and then its transformation into industrial form, and in the provision of a vast supply of wage workers, the state has played a fundamental role; land reform, distribution of aid, allocation of import licences and loans, then confiscation of illicit fortunes, curbing corruption, tying profitability to productive activity through a range of policies, cracking down on speculative and short-term capital, and sponsoring massive rural-urban migration, each has been instrumental in generating industrial capitalism. This is not to claim, however, that these

---

[73]Figures from Joungwon Kim (1975, p30), Ban et al., (1980, p320), Henderson (1968, p137).

[74]See Ban et al., (1980, pp320-21), Hong (1979, Table 2.6, p20). The latter records a population of 21.05 million in 1953 and 24.95 milion in 1960.

measures were, necessarily, deliberately taken to achieve the actual outcome, nor to claim that the state was a neutral decision-maker immune to the influence of the forces it was helping to create. We can only claim that, whatever the motivation, the results followed.

2.5 Aspects of the Class Stucture During Early Industrialization

The foregoing has analysed the development of the class structure up to the threshold of the period of rapid industrial growth in the middle to late sixties. But it would be wrong to imagine that the pattern of class forces that had developed in the fifties and which was the social foundation of industrialization was somehow fixed and fully adequate to the task. Class relations are constantly changing. In the process of Korean industrial development there were certain evolving aspects of the class structure that were essential to the form of industrialization which should be discussed, if only briefly, in this final section. We can identify four aspects of the evolution of class relations in the sixties that were of central importance. Firstly, there was the squeeze on agricultural incomes which yielded a surplus that helped to finance industrial investment. The second aspect, closely connected to the first, was the suppression of the general level of wages and control over the working class through political repression. Thirdly, there was the emergence of the specific form of industrial capital particularly as it was influenced by the trade regime, and what this revealed about the relationship between industrial capital and the state. Fourthly, there was the subordination of financial capital to industrial capital. It would be inappropriate here to attempt to review all of the economic developments of the sixties and seventies, and we take only a partial view by dealing with the aspects suggested above.

Although the colonels who seized power in 1961 were sympathetic to the plight of the farmer, the emergence of the Park group and the assertion of US influence over economic policy placed primary emphasis on the growth of industry. In a country where natural resources are scarce it was felt that economic progress could best be achieved through that sector which could most effectively enhance the productivity of the most abundant resource, labour. Given the historical experience of most countries, capitalist and socialist, it would be surprising if the South Korean agricultural sector had not been squeezed to support the growth of manufacturing. Ban et al., (1950, Chapter 2) have the peculiar argument that agriculture contributed very little to economic development because in the sixties rural savings and taxes were negligible. The obvious error of this, exposed by Lee (1979, p511), is that it ignores the foremost mode of transferring surplus out of agriculture and into industry in Korea, viz. 'unequal exchange' between the two sectors.

The statistics show that the agriculture-industry nominal terms of trade moved against agriculture in the 1963-69 period and did not return to their 1963 level until 1972. In Table 2.2 1974 has been chosen as the base year because, although it gives the strongest impression of rural exploitation, it is in that year that per capita rural real incomes, while still remaining below them, most closely approached urban real incomes (see Column 2). These terms of trade can be misleading in that it does not follow from them that the farmers were worse off in the sixties as a result of the decline in the terms of trade. That farmers *were* worse off is revealed in Column 3. Indeed the movement of the terms of trade is even more remarkable because the growth rate of agricultural value-added during the 1961-71 period was 3.7 percent (Lee, 1980, p497) compared with an overall GNP growth rate of over 10 percent with manufacturing growing still faster.

Table 2-2: Agricultural terms of trade, income and product prices

	(1) Agricultural terms of trade 1974=100[a]	(2) Rural/urban per capita real income (per cent)	(3) Index of real income per rural household 1963= 100[b] (percent)	(4) Ratio of govt purchase price to market price for rice[c] (percent)
1961	71			87.7
1962	70			58.9
1963	93		100	59.4
1964	92		105	89.3
1965	83		84	92.1
1966	78		87	88.2
1967	79		88	83.7
1968	78		92	81.7
1969	81		103	89.0
1970	90	67.4	106	97.9
1971	92	79.9	131	88.9
1972	98	84.5	142	101.6
1973	101	83.6	149	93.4
1974	100	95.0	147	88.4
1975	100	92.9	152	
1976	99	84.5		
1977	99	76.4		
1978	99	65.4		

a. Index of prices received by farmers divided by index of prices paid by farmers.
b. Nominal income per household deflated by the rural price index, rounded up.
c. Clearly, the market price would be lower if the government share were sold privately.

Sources: (1) ESY (1981, p266), ESY (1970, p352); (2) Kim & Joo (1982, Table A-7, p30); (3) Lee (1980, Table 3, p497); (4) Ban et al., (1980, Table 105, p240)

The cause of the declining terms of trade after 1963 lay in large measure in the government's farm price policy.[75] The government, from before the civil war,

---

[75]Wideman, who worked in the villages and carefully studied South Korean agricultural statistics, comments as follows:

Analyzing the grain purchase price paid to farmers, we note that for most of the harvests between 1965 and 1971, farmers did not even obtain adequate cost-of-living increases for their grain. This was directly due to the low government purchase price (Wideman, 1974, p279).

had acquired grain from farmers at government-fixed prices by means of direct purchase (sometimes compulsory), by the rice-fertilizer barter scheme and by collection of farm taxes in kind. While in the fifties the government's share of total marketed rice was less than 10 percent it had grown to over 50 percent by 1975 (and 90 percent for barley).[76] Up to 1960, the government's purchase prices for rice were much lower than the estimated costs of production, but as the share of government in the harvest rose in the sixties it was necessary to raise the prices above production costs (Ban et al., 1980, p240). However, throughout the sixties the government's purchase price was consistently below the market price and usually well below it (see Column 4 of the table above).[77] This policy was undoubtedly the prime cause of the decline in rural living standards up to 1967 and led to a substantial transfer of 'surplus' to the industrial sector. Essential to the government's agricultural policy were supplies of imported grain through PL 480 aid. Rice imports became increasingly necessary. The proportion of imports in total rice supply rose from none in 1964/65 to 6 percent in 1967/68 to 25 percent in 1970/71 (Brown, 1973, Table 12, p119). By augmenting the domestic supply of grains without draining foreign exchange reserves, the government could afford to neglect agricultural development and to ignore the disincentive to production of its pricing policy. Experience in the seventies has shown that farmers will respond to higher prices by raising marketed output.[78] After being neglected in the first two five-year plans, greater agricultural self-sufficiency became an important item in the third plan beginning in 1972. Ban et al. (1980, p12) observe that 'when the terms of trade did shift in favor of agriculture in the seventies, it was a result of a deliberate change in government policy...'. Farm incomes rose partly in response to the increased government purchase price (which was up by around a real 15 percent in the seventies), but more so as a result of the increased agricultural production stimulated by higher prices and by greater application of chemicals. In fact the government's attention had been attracted to agriculture in the late sixties when it became evident that US food aid to South Korea would soon expire with the very unwelcome consequence that grain imports would become a substantial drain on foreign exchange reserves.

Having acquired a large proportion of marketed rice at a low price the government sold it in the cities or distributed it to government workers and disabled war veterans. It did so without making a profit, the purpose of the whole rice collection programme being to keep food prices stable and low so that the hiring of industrial workers could be kept cheap. Up to 1969 the government resold rice for purchase price plus handling costs, but since then rice has typically been sold at a loss.[79] The grain procurement scheme has been only one aspect of the

---

[76]Ban et al. (1980, p238). This however, represented only 6.1 percent of the total rice crop in 1959 and 17.2 percent in 1975 (ibid., Table 52, p131).

[77]The ultra-neoclassical Brown (1973, p120) has the extraordinary argument that government procurement policy had the principal effect of bringing rice prices closer to their 'equilibrium' levels. As will be seen in Chapter 5, the orthodox accounts of Korean development consistently try to portray government intervention of all sorts as rectifying market distortions rather than itself being the cause of distortions.

[78]It was also proven with the 1965 sweet potato crop - see Wideman (1974, pp283-84), also Brown (1973, Chapter 5).

[79]See Ban et al., (1980, pp246-47). The losses on barley have been even greater. The financing of these losses on the grain account has had inflationary consequences (ibid., p250).

attempt to keep industrial wages low. It might also be argued that the neglect of agricultural development, by keeping farm productivity and incomes lower than they would otherwise have been, had the effect, intentionally or not, of keeping industrial wages low in the manner of Lewis.[80] Low wages were recognized as being essential to the expansion of export industries. The data on wage levels are conflicting and official figures are unreliable[81] especially on issues like wages and unemployment. According to official figures real wages fell slightly in each of the years 1960 to 1965, although manufacturing wages rose a little (BOK, *Review of the Korean Economy in 1965*, p115). While manufacturing real wages rose by an average of 2 percent per annum in 1962-66, from 1967 they have appeared to rise much faster, averaging 12 percent in 1967-71 and 5 percent in 1972-76 (Hong, 1979, Table 8.3, p210). However, we can still find an official publication declaring in 1969: 'Needless to say, the wage level of this country still does not exceed the minimum living expenses to a substantial extent'.[82]

Undoubtedly, a large part of the movement in wages can be explained by the level of unemployment. Officially, the unemployment rate has declined from around 7 percent in the mid-sixties to around 4 percent in the mid-seventies (ROK, EPB, *Social Indicators*, p68), but this counts as employed everyone who has worked at least one hour per week. If we count all who worked less than 18 hours a week as unemployed then the rate, for farm and nonfarm households, stood at 16.3 percent in 1964, 12.8 percent in 1967, 9.2 percent in 1970 and 7.7 percent in 1973 (Byun & Kim, 1978, p95). Hong has further accounted for disguised unemployment in agriculture and shows that the rate of unemployment in the early seventies was something over 15 percent (Hong, 1979, p215n6).[83] At the end of the sixties, official organs were talking about 'the chronic, deep-rooted unemployment in this country' (ROK, EPB, *Economic Survey* (for 1968), 1969, p121); a government minister said in 1976 that the first priority of the government was to increase

---

[80]According to Lewis (1954), in a dual economy the wage level in the capitalist sector depends on earnings in the subsistence sector, since labour migration provides a (nearly) equalizing force. Ideally, industrial capital would like high agricultural productivity with low prices, but the prices must be low enough so that increased productivity does not raise farm incomes. This also assumes that the product is marketed. As a rule, however, increased farm productivity is a response to higher prices.

[81]See eg. FEER (June 30, 1966) and Lee (1979, p497).

[82]ROK, EPB, *Economic Survey* (for 1968) (1969, p124). This publication argues that continued restraint of working class consumption through suppression of wages is justified by 'taking into consideration the philosophy that sufficient contentment in the future is more valuable than insufficient contentment at the present', although the working class may not adhere to this philosophy. As late as 1976, the Office of Labour Affairs reported an average male worker's salary of $93 per month while the Economic Planning Board held that the minimum requirement of the average family was $142 (McCormack, 1977, p63). See also FEER (June 23, 1966) where living standards are said to be 'barely above subsistence', repeated in FEER (April 27, 1967).

[83]See also ROK, EPB, *Economic Survey* (for 1968) (1969, p121). Sedjo (1972), in a piece of work extraordinary for its ineptness, came to the conclusion that Korea stopped being a labour-surplus economy in 1964. According to the FEER correspondent (June 30, 1966) 'knowledgeable observers' estimated that of a labour force of 10 million in 1966 3.3 million were jobless. For those who could obtain full-time employment, these jobs were very insecure. In 1967, 51.2 percent of employees were either temporary or daily workers; by 1976 this had fallen to 42.9 percent (Byun & Kim, 1978, p96).

employment (Long, 1977, p33) (hardly consistent with an official unemployment rate of 3.9 percent). Since the late sixties, however, there have been shortages of skilled workers[84] which have enabled these privileged workers to push their wages up considerably (especially in sectors such as construction, electric power and business services[85]). This has put a gloss on the wages figures, disguising the fact that the bulk of workers received not much above a subsistence minimum.[86] There is little doubt that the government's agricultural policies, by design or otherwise, assisted in this by encouraging, especially from 1967, massive migration from the farms to the industrial centres. The weakness of the working class in resisting this, and its inability to maintain its share in the national wealth has been fundamental to the growth process in Korea in the sixties and seventies. In the words of Wontack Hong: 'the trend of wage movements in Korea seems to have been conducive to enhancing the share of entrepreneurial profits' (1979, p211). The maintenance of low wages has been greatly assisted by the policy of the state in unhesitatingly suppressing any form of organized or spontaneous working-class activity and the preference of industry to employ women workers.[87] The history of repression has been so well chronicled as not to require documentation here.[88]

The relationship between business and the state in the sixties is greatly clarified by looking at the trade regime and its means of implementation. This will be discussed in more depth in the final chapter, but for the present we observe that the period of rapid industrialization was marked as much by continued import-substitution as by export-expansion. A detailed study of this has been made by Suk Tai Suh and the conclusion is worth quoting at length:

> The remarkable export performance under liberalized trade policies [in the sixties] has often been cited as the prime-mover of Korean economic growth. The general impression has been that import substitution contributed a negligible amount. However, we find that there has been continuous ISI [import substituting industrialization] in the light as well as heavy manufacturing industries during the period 1960-74, a finding contrary to the general notion. In fact, we find that the extent of import substitution during the period 1960-74 was far greater than that during

---

[84]See eg. FEER (April 27, 1967); ROK, EPB, *Economic Survey* (for 1969) (1970, p194).

[85]In 1975, workers in these industries received average monthly earnings of, respectively, 62, 104 and 96 thousand won, compared with 38 thousand in manufacturing (ROK, KSY, 1979, Table 34).

[86]The ratio of food expenditure to private consumption expenditure (and this covers the increasingly wealthy business and professional classes) was 59.4 in 1965 and had fallen only as far as 50.6 in 1978 (ROK, EPB, *Social Indicators in Korea*, 1981, p57).

[87]The importance of low wages in manufacturing production is revealed in the following figures. In 1977 there were 803,000 male and 821,000 female 'production related' workers. The average monthly wage for males was 76,000 won and for females 40,000 won, 52 percent of the male wage (ROK, Office of labour Affairs, *Yearbook of Labour Statistics* 1978). The average age of males was 30 and of women 21.

[88]See eg. Long (1977), FEER Yearbook (1981), Gittings and McCormack (1977, Chapter 3), almost any issue of AMPO and especially the harrowing account of the supression of the strike by women workers at the Wuonpoong textile factory prepared by the Japan Emergency Christian Conference on Korean Problems (*Korea Communique* No. 46, February 15, 1983).

the ISI period of 1953-62. Therefore, we conclude that [the] economic growth pattern is characterized by simultaneous export promotion and import substitution.[89]

It is worth pointing out, too, that the 'export-oriented' strategy was stumbled upon quite accidentally by the Korean economists of the early sixties. The First Five-Year Plan did not envisage export-led industrialization but concentrated on bridging the chronic foreign exchange gap through import-substitution including achievement of food self-sufficiency. Export promotion was part of the plan but it stressed the expansion of traditional exports of primary products such as fish, rice, dried laver, raw silk, tungsten, anthracite and other mineral ores. By 1966 manufactures were projected to occupy about one third of exports (Hong, 1979, p63). However, when 1966 arrived the major foreign exchange earners were not those primary products but manufactures such as textiles, clothing, footwear, wigs and plywood, which alone comprised nearly 50 percent of actual exports (*ibid.*). The rapid growth of exports of these products was a surprise to the planners and they began to adjust their plans to it by 1965. Even so, while the Second Five-Year Plan (1967-1971) put more emphasis on exports it also planned a major programme of import-substituting industrial investment. Throughout the period, the foreign exchange deficit dominated development planning, from the time of the early sixties when foreign correspondents were sending despatches full of black prophecies of impending 'catastrophe', of industry collapsing for want of essential inputs, of famine averted only by imports of grain (FEER, July 18 & August 8, 1963), to the induction of massive foreign loans in the seventies.

The second point to be made is that although there was a spurt of export expansion in the early sixties (from an extremely low base), this was not a trend that could sustain itself and bring sufficient foreign exchange earnings to finance widespread industrial expansion. It required government intervention at all levels to redouble the momentum. The government had to twist arms to compel businesses to export, because there is little doubt that it was, as a rule, much more profitable to supply the domestic market than foreign ones, particularly if one were supplying the domestic market with scarce imports. Several studies have shown that export production has been less profitable than production for the domestic market. Seung Hee Kim (1970, p99) reports that in 1967, 'except for a few items, such as tungsten, laver, and raw silk, the profit rate was below the average rate in manufacturing ... . Generally speaking, it is reasonable to say that many exporters would be operating at a loss without government subsidies'. Youngil Lim (1981, pp44-45) found similar results for the 1973-78 period: 'The rate of profit, either on total assets or on net worth, is smaller for export enterprises than for domestic enterprises', and he quotes a further study by L. Westphal and Y.W. Rhee to this effect: 'One might wonder why these producers export at all, but exporting is the price paid to do business in Korea'.[90] This will receive support in our own study in a subsequent chapter.

These studies point to the coercive power of the state over business. Hong (1979, pp58-59) gives an indication of the extraordinary efforts taken by the

---

[89]Suk Tai Suh (1975, p4). It remained true that the import coefficient of the economy as a whole increased throughout 1953-74, while that of many sub-sectors declined.

[90]That exporting achievement did not carry its own financial rewards receives circumstantial support from the habit of President Park of bestowing 'merit medals' on successful exporters.

government to achieve export targets and the willingness of businessmen to concede, and although the carrots in the form of subsidies, tax concessions, and import rights were liberally distributed, the stick in the form of tax penalties, loss of import licences and so on could make a mark. The 'natural' development of the form of capital was moulded by the state to conform to its ideas of economic development. The trade regime which emerged in the sixties aimed not only at encouraging export production but also, emphatically, at protecting domestic capital from the potential ravages of international competition.[91] The barriers to imports, perhaps the least of which were high tariff rates, were formidable indeed and the alleged liberalization of the 1963-64 period, which constitutes a central pillar of the orthodox explanation of the Korean 'miracle', has recently been shown to be a myth (Luedde-Neurath, 1983). Through the sixties there evolved an intricate system of import controls which had the sole purpose of protecting domestic industry and later export industries.

The exclusion of competitive imports was not the only way of protecting domestic capital. Control of investment has overwhelmingly been in national hands, for direct foreign investment has never accounted for a large part of productive capital in Korea. Across the whole period 1962-79, direct foreign investment accounted for a mere 1.2 percent of gross domestic capital formation. While foreign loans made up 18.9 percent, and while there was a surge of direct investment in the early seventies (especially from Japan), the contribution of direct foreign investment to gross capital formation fell from 2.2 percent in 1972-76 to 0.6 percent in 1979.[92] The government has thus been assiduous in shielding domestic capital from foreign competition from within and has as a rule insisted, not only that joint ventures should prevail,[93] but that foreign companies in Korea be export-oriented so as not to compete on domestic markets.[94] The amount, industrial type and market orientation of foreign firms in Korea has been very carefully regulated throughout.

---

[91]Frank et al. (1975, Chapter 10) show that the effective rate of protection on import-competing industries in 1968 was 92 percent.

[92]All figures are from Korea Exchange Bank (1980, p8). The share of net foreign capital inflow in total gross domestic investment had declined but was still high: 1962-66 47.9 percent, 1967-71 39.2 percent, 1972-76 24.8 percent (BOK, *National Income in Korea*, 1982, pp286-289). The Exchange Bank asserts that the changes in guidelines of September 1980 represent 'a radical change in the official philosophy toward incoming business, and the government has clearly recognized the imperative need for much greater foreign involvement in the task of upgrading Korea's technological capabilities in the coming decade' (Korea Exchange Bank, 1980, p1). This says more about the restrictions on foreign investment before 1980 than after.

[93]At end 1978, 57.4 percent of cumulative direct foreign investment was in joint ventures at least 50 percent Korean-owned, and only 31.5 percent was in wholly foreign-owned companies (Westphal et al., 1979, p368).

[94]The pursuit of domestic markets by foreign producers has, according to the Exchange Bank, 'resulted in occasional conflicts of interest between foreign invested enterprises and local firms because of excessive competition' (Korea Exchange Bank, 1980, p13). The share of exports by foreign invested enterprises in total Korean exports rose from 16.9 percent in 1974 to 18.7 percent in 1978 (*ibid.*, p6). We also discover this extraordinary fact: the share of raw materials imports by foreign firms in total raw materials imports stood at 43.0 percent in 1974 rising to 50.1 percent in 1978 (*ibid.*, p13).

Clearly, the Korean state cannot be thought of as the instrument of big business - it has maintained a large degree of autonomy from the power of capital. The 'illicit wealth accumulation' measures were a fiery baptism for big business into the new world of the Park regime, but while this incident showed that the state would act against capital 'in the national interest', the compromises which closed the affair demonstrated the reliance of the state on the performance and support of industrial capital.[95] The independence of the state was maintained, however, so that for instance the May 1974 Presidential Special Directives could impose a set of measures on the chaeból to force and encourage them to sell shares in themselves on the stock market. Strong firms were ordered to go public while those that were financially weak were compelled to take certain measures to improve their debt-equity ratios and general financial soundness (see Jones & Sakong, 1980, pp282-284). The independance of the state from business has enabled the former to establish an elaborate system of business regulation which is in practice highly effective and not subject to the corrosive influence of cosy business-government relationships. This autonomy has been essential for the authority of government interventions - interventions the like of which have been rendered impotent in other Third World countries simply by being ignored by businessmen and bureaucrats alike.[96]

Consistent with its policy of promoting industrial accumulation, the state has taken various strict measures to ensure that industrial capital has not fallen under the control of financial capital. The two forms of capital, which may coexist under the one business roof, earn profits in different ways, ways that may be inimical to each other, and the suppression of finance capital has been to a large extent a continuation of the process of converting commercial capital into industrial capital. The aim of the government has been to ensure that the resources of finance capital have been subordinated to the needs of industrial growth. Several decisive steps have been taken in furtherance of this, although as we will see the unofficial money market has proven remarkably resilient.[97] The grip of rural money-lenders was seriously weakened by the annulling of farmers' debts in 1961 and the establishment of schemes to supply cheaper loans to farmers. In the organized money market, the government achieved overwhelming dominance when it took control of the commercial banks in the illicit wealth accumulation episode, and it has consistently used this dominance to promote industrial growth in general and export industries in particular.[98] Through its control of the commercial banks, special banks and development institutions the government has been able to control a good 90 percent

---

[95]We may agree with Jones and Sakong (1980, p67) when they write that 'the very survival of Park Chung Hee rests on economic performance and thus on the achievement of private business ... [but] the dominant partner is unequivocally the government... ', unlike in Japan.

[96]One survey of businessmen in Korea asked them how effective government policy implementation was under Park and Rhee; 'always implemented, impossible to avoid compliance' was recorded for 78 percent for Park and 3 percent for Rhee (Jones & Sakong, 1980, p137).

[97]In the words of Cole and Park (1979, p42): 'the unorganized financial sector has expanded despite all types of suppression and financial institutional reforms and policies to integrate this sector with the OFS [official financial system] over the years'.

[98]Thus, '... organized finance in Korea provides a textbook case of rationing' (Kuznets, 1977, p194).

of the assets of organized finance (Rhee, 1981, Table 1-1, p7). The government's policy of low interest rates on industrial loans in the sixties - the cost of loans has been far below the average return on investment capital (Rhee, 1981, p18) - resulted in a great demand for them and a short supply of deposits which in turn favoured the growth of the unorganized money market. The curb market (covering moneylenders, money brokers, urban landlords and shopkeepers) has been a growing source of concern for the government because of its very high interest rates and the short-term nature of its loans both of which hinder industrial expansion and impair international competitiveness. Borrowers from the curb have often been large incorporated firms (Cole & Park, 1979, p132). The curb market in Korea has been intensively understudied, but according to one estimate, at the end of 1964 the unorganized money market (which as well as the curb market included local credit cooperatives [Kye], trader's money-lending organizations [Kaekjus], finance companies and 'others') held some 43 billion won of outstanding transactions (Baker & Choi, 1973, pp13-14) compared to total bank loans of 53 billion won and a money supply of 49 billion won (ESY, 1970, pp111 & 84).

Two major attempts have been made by the government to check the growth of the curb market and to weaken its control over industrial enterprises. The first was the interest rate reform in 1965 which saw maximum interest rates raised and the deposit rate set higher than the loan rate. By raising the deposit rates to levels more commensurate with those on the curb market, the government successfully attracted large quantities of savings away from the unofficial lenders and into the banks. The four years after the reform saw a dramatic rise in domestic savings in Korea (a country unusual among the underdeveloped for its low level of domestic savings), so that by 1970 domestic savings as a proportion of GNP had more than doubled (Cole & Park, 1979, p261 also p267). Time and savings deposits doubled in the first year, not only drawn out of the curb market but also affecting holdings of real assets. The inverted interest rate structure could work because only a small fraction of deposits in banks attracted the maximum interest rate (30 percent) while over 60 percent of loans by banks yielded the highest authorized loan interest rate (24-26 percent) (FEER, April 27, 1967). The system and the high rates were substantially modified over subsequent years; the curb market continued to flourish and, according to Baker and Choi (1973, pp13-14), there must have been substantial growth between 1964 and 1972 despite the interest rate reforms. This was due partly to the great inflow of foreign capital after the reforms. The government decided to attack the inflationary pressures brought about by the monetary growth by squeezing domestic credit (export and import-competing manufacturers persuaded the government respectively that neither exchange rate appreciation nor import liberalization were appropriate responses) so that only favoured firms (exporters and those in key industries) would have access to bank credit. The rest turned back to the curb market (see Cole & Park, 1979, pp267-70). Nevertheless, the size of the unofficial money market appears to have declined relative to organized finance during the high interest rate period (Cole & Park, 1979, p155).

By the early seventies the government was seriously concerned about its inability to control the growth of the unorganized market particularly as it appeared to be weakening the competitive ability of manufacturing firms. Alarm was expressed at the mushrooming debt-equity ratios of large manufacturing firms and the extent of debts to private money-lenders. Collectively, the money-lenders and brokers had shown themselves to be capable of imposing their demands on debtors even when these were large industrial concerns, and reportedly had bankrupted several such companies over previous years by discontinuing credit (Cole & Park, 1979, p130n19). Their loans were often very substantial and were secured by notarized property deeds (*ibid.*, p132). The curb market generally lent for periods of no more than one month and charged an interest rate of between 40 and 70 percent per annum, (inflation in the period was about 10-15 percent).[99] According to Cole and Park (1979, pp273-4) the financial insecurity of many big companies had been worsened by the 18 percent devaluation of 1971 which, although stimulating exports, caused a sudden increase in the won cost of foreign debt-servicing. Companies with foreign debts were forced to turn to the curb market to bail themselves out. Moreover, the government was aware that the prevailing financial structure - with insufficient savings in official institutions and the burden of short-term, high-interest curb borrowing in corporate debt - was incompatible with its new industrial development strategy which emphasized a shift into heavy and chemical industries. That could succeed only if there was a large volume of long-term, low-interest investible funds. In the words of the Bank of Korea, the constellation of difficulties covered 'the worsening of the financial structure of some business firms, the vicious circle of prices and exchange rates, the weakening of Korea's international competitiveness and the cancerous enlargement of the curb market' (BOK, *Annual Report*, 1972, pp25-26).

The government attempted to break the tightening grip of finance capital on industrial enterprises with the August Economic Emergency Measures in 1972.[100] The terms of borrowings by enterprises from the curb market were 'adjusted', as they delicately put it, and new cheap loans from the official lending agencies would try to obviate new borrowings from the curb. All curb market creditors and debtors were required to report their lending and borrowing to the tax office or local bank within seven days. The total amount of loans reported by creditors was 356 billion won, and by debtors 345 billion won (BOK, *Annual Report 1972*, p27) compared with total 1972 bank loans of 1198 billion won and a money supply of 519 billion won (BOK, ESY, 1981, pp47 & 10). The new terms to which these loans were compulsorily subjected required the principal and interest to be repaid in equal instalments every 6 months over 5 years after an initial 3 year grace period and the interest rate applied was uniformly reduced to 16.2 percent per annum.[101] However, all loans to firms by their major shareholders (in fact, one third of total reported loans) had to be converted into shares in the enterprises. In addition the government reduced the interest ceiling for which curb market loan interest payments were tax deductible from 33.6 percent to 18 percent for big firms (and 24 percent for small- and medium-sized enterprises), in a further effort to make curb market money unattractive. This was indeed a severe and painful blow to lenders. In order to fill the credit gap created by this attack on finance capital, the government authorized the banks to issue up to 200 billion won of special financial debentures so that firms could replace short-term, high-interest loans with long-term, low-interest ones. At the same time, interest rates on bank loans and deposits

---

[99]Baker & Choi (1973, p14). Since the anti-usury laws specified a maximum interest rate on private loans of 15 percent, the curb's transactions have been (and are) cloaked in secrecy (Cole & Park, 1979, p256). It was reported in 1982 that the going rate on the curb was 26-33 percent per annum, maturing in 2-4 months (FEER, May 21, 1982).

[100]Cole and Park (1979, p271) complain that the Decree 'was a drastic measure, inconceivable in a free enterprise economy'.

[101]The details are in BOK, *Annual Report 1972*, pp25-36.

were lowered (so that for the first time they fell below those prior to the 1965 reform) in an attempt to ease the burden of loans which had been pushing up costs, in the knowledge that the curb market, under threat of further expropriation, would be a less effective competitor.

The real forces which constantly reproduce the curb market could only be suppressed temporarily. Since 1972 real interest rates have tended to be around zero in official markets and it has proven extremely difficult to stamp out unofficial money-lending under such circumstances, particularly when coupled with shortages of credit for those industrial sectors not favoured by cheap official loans. The August Decree was undoubtedly a profound shock for unorganized finance and went some way towards further securing the hegemony of government-controlled organized institutions.[102] While the curb market disappeared for a year or so after August 1972, it reappeared and continued to prosper (Cole & Park, 1979, p132). However, it appears that the relative importance of the curb market had declined substantially by 1980.[103]

Contemporaneous with the August Economic Emergency Measures of 1972, the government attempted to absorb another part of the unofficial money market - the informal bill market - into the official financial system by establishing investment and finance companies to discount short-term bills held by important enterprises. These companies - mostly controlled by the chaeból - have grown fairly quickly since 1972 mainly at the expense of the informal bill and curb markets (Cole & Park, 1979, pp126-29). The enforced expansion of the stock exchange has aided the process of eliminating the influence of private money-lenders. The fact of continuing resistance to the government's attempts to coerce companies into going public is a good indication of the constraints which apply to a state whose economic plans rely on the responsiveness of private capital.

2.6 Summary

This chapter has attempted to explain the emergence of a class structure in which capitalist social relations in general and industrial capital in particular became dominant in South Korea. The underlying argument is that the answer to the question of why South Korea industrialized lies essentially in the evolution of the class structure. The process of evolution in the modern period has its roots well

---

[102]Time and savings deposits with banks rose by 34 percent between 1972 and 1973; this nowhere matched the 130 percent increase in the year after the 1965 reforms (BOK, ESY, 1970 & 1981) but in the later measures the interest rate on two year time deposits had been cut from 17.4 percent to 12.6 percent, with the CPI rising at 3.2 percent in 1972 and 24.3 percent in 1973 (*ibid.*).

[103]One rough estimate put curb market transaction in 1980 at 800-1000 billion won (Rhee, 1981, p15, but see also FEER, May 21, 1983, p52), compared with total bank loans of 12,204 billion won (ESY, 1981, p47). If these figures are accurate then the ratio of curb market loans to bank loans fell from .29 in 1972 to about .07 in 1980. We cannot agree with the conclusion of Cole and Park (who do not appear to like government interference in free markets) that the 'Decree succeeded in achieving none of the objectives for which it was designed' (Cole & Park, 1979, p281).

back in Korean history, at least to the beginning of Japanese colonial domination. Japanese rule not only realigned the economy to provide export crops and, later, industrial goods to support Japanese growth, but destroyed the legitimacy of the traditional ruling class, transformed agrarian social relations and introduced capitalist forms of production.

The social structure which developed in South Korea after the Second World War did so on these foundations. Amid the political turmoil, the fifties and sixties witnessed a double transformation of the basis of social reproduction. Firstly, landed wealth was transformed into merchant capital. It was both repelled from the land by land reform and government exactions and attracted to commerce by the lure of windfall profits to be had through importing, access to foreign aid and government contracts. New, import-competing industries could also provide a profitable haven. Secondly, there was a broad process of transforming merchant capital into industrial capital through both repulsion from pure commerce as a result of government measures to close off unproductive investment, the decline in aid, and legal sanctions, and attraction to industry in response to government measures which tied profit-making to manufacturing.

These changes in the economic mode of reproduction were parallelled by the political and social ascendency of industrial capital and the corresponding growth of the working class. The peasantry, who continued to form the majority, were politicallly weak and while free of the bonds of tenancy remained poverty-stricken.

While these developments laid the social foundations of industrialization, there were several further developments in the balance of class forces which were essential to the progress of industrial expansion in the sixties and seventies. Consistent with experience in other parts of the industrial world, agriculture was forced to provide surpluses to support industrial growth. Closely tied to this was the suppression of the working class so as to ensure that the surplus provided by agriculture was not eaten up by real wage rises. This was of the utmost importance in an industrialization process dependent on exports, exports which provided the foreign exchange to buy the imported inputs on which home industry depended. The government was uninhibited in taking measures to protect domestic capital from foreign competition. It was equally determined that the gains of industrial capital would not be undermined by the pernicious influence of finance capital and thus a return to the days of 'zero-sum' economic activity.

The modern history of South Korea demonstrates that primitive accumulation and the rise of industrial capital is as much a political as an economic process. The influence of the state at every major conjuncture has been apparent, although its actions have not always been progressive from the viewpoint of industrial capital. The USA, looking at South Korea strategically, played a vital role in inducing social and economic changes that would bring about growth and stability.

While this chapter has exposed the class foundations of the industrial development of the sixties and seventies, examination of the process of social transformation cannot itself reveal the details of the industrialization process. We also want answers to questions about structural change, the pattern of integration into the world economy, the details of industrial policy, the sectoral flows of surpluses, technical change and the rate of growth itself. These can be tackled only through a close study of the empirical details of the evolving economy. Moreover, to comprehend this mass of figures requires a means of organization, a model of the economy. The model which attempts to do this is developed in the next chapter, and the empirical results which help us to answer the questions above are presented and discussed in Chapter 4.

CHAPTER 3
A Model of Structural Change and Accumulation

While in the last chapter the aim was to understand the conditions which brought about the transformation of the relations of production into those of industrial capitalism, that is, *how* accumulation occurred, here we want to determine the conditions that allowed *rapid* accumulation of industrial capital so far as these conditions are reflected in the structure of industry, the techniques of production and the 'behavioural' variables of the economy.[1] The model developed here and applied to South Korea is in the broad class of computable general equilibrium (CGE) models. It shares with other CGE models[2] the general equilibrium framework and a set of strong assumptions. It stands apart in its high degree of closedness and its largely static nature. Solved at two points in time, the present model is restricted to structural analysis, comparison of shadow prices and comparison of optimal growth rates under different conditions. This might be considered a strength rather than a weakness since more dynamic models rely on investment functions to link periods. Investment, because of its stochastic nature in unplanned economies, is inherently difficult to tie down to an equation. Since it does not track an equilibrium (or disequilibrium) path, the present model avoids many of the pitfalls of projection and prediction.[3] It is not suggested in the construction of the present model that there is an equilibrium path which the Korean economy has or should have approached, except in a planning context.

The institutional context of the model is one which rejects notions of individual rational choice, although the assumption of profit maximization is made in the solution process. Since consumption is endogenized in terms of the 'technologically-determined' inputs necessary to produce labourers and other consumers there is no obvious maximand. As we assume (in the assumption of fixed coefficients) that in the base years the set of production processes in operation is the most efficient one available, that the choice of techniques has already been made, substitution of techniques and between productive inputs within a technique is not the context in which the solution emerges. This will be much clearer by the end of the chapter.

---

[1]These behavioural variables, it should be made explicit, do not spring from the opaque psyche of some rational economic man but emerge from the objective conditions of the social formation.

[2]See especially that of Adelman & Robinson (1978); also Lysy & Taylor (1980) and the overview of CGE models in Dervis, de Melo & Robinson (1982).

[3]Adelman & Robinson (1978) use an investment function to dynamize their model but simulate a past growth path rather than project a future one.

3.1 Economic Integration and Constraints on Accumulation

Before proceeding to the model it may be useful to say a few words about how the degree of structural integration of the Korean economy makes the present type of model appropriate and how this integration imposes instability on the accumulation process.

The legacy of colonialism has very often been a disarticulated or unconnected economy since peripheral economies were so organized that production was focused on export trade which sustained the links with the centre. The peripheral economy was highly integrated externally but disintegrated internally. In the first place, then, the process of Third World industrialization is one of increasing interindustry integration, of overcoming the internal structural disarticulation and external dependency left over from colonialism.

This structural integration is more often than not merely one aspect of the transformation of the mode of production from a precapitalist one to a capitalist one. The spread of capitalist production is at the same time the spread of the integrative forces of commodity production, generalized exchange and the social division of labour.

In post-war South Korea this process was very clear. As we have seen in the previous chapter the departing Japanese left a disconnected economy oriented towards the production of crops and minerals and manufactures destined for Japanese markets. The economy was, however, quite unusual among former colonial economies in its degree of industrial development and the extent of interindustry linkages. Briefly, the process was as follows. As traditional Korean social relations withered under the weight of political and economic forces, there arose first the economic primacy of petty peasant-proprietorship. This was superseded quickly as commercial and subsequently industrial capital (accompanied by generalized commodity exchange and division of labour) gained the upper hand. Agriculture became subordinate to industry, but did so some time after the class of peasant proprietors became subordinate to industrial capital. As this proceeded the different sectors of the Korean economy became increasingly interlinked (in the fifties the sheer number of significant sectors expanded considerably), both through providing the products desired for consumption by the workers in other sectors and through providing intermediate goods to each other, so much so that by the early sixties the Korean economic planners were building input-output tables.

The type of model developed here makes sense only for an economy with a considerable degree of internal economic integration. The deepening social division of labour associated with the increasing variety of economic activities and later the technical division of labour, the concomitant spread of exchange relations and the development of structural integration have, historically, liberated the productive forces and laid the groundwork for a massive expansion of production under the spur of the accumulation motive. But as well as freeing the productive forces the development of structural integration imposes certain constraints on the accumulation process; certain relations and proportionalities are necessary for accumulation to continue its progress without serious disruption.[4]

The first constraint is that each sector must produce enough to supply the

---

[4]Marx had this idea in mind when he built his schema of simple and extended reproduction (Marx, 1956, Chapters XX & XXI). The price 'dual' of these necessary conditions are discussed by Marx as the credit relations in periods of crisis.

demands for inputs required by itself, by other sectors and by consumers including the requirements for growth. In a discussion of the Hawkins-Simon condition, Harris has written:

> In general, in order for a non-trivial solution to exist, a special condition must be met by the matrix of coefficients. Specifically, the condition is that any industry or sub-group of industries must be capable of producing, in terms of its own output, just enough to meet its own requirements for production and the requirements of all other industries in the economy ... This seemingly simple algebraic condition is one that may be seen to have great economic significance. (Harris, 1982, p29)

Hawkins, like Marx in his schema of reproduction, showed how rigid the conditions are for an expanding economy to remain in a steady state. In fact there is only one valid solution which is consistent with balanced growth, and the economy is inherently unstable. Writes Harris (1982, p30):

> This potential instability is shown to result from lack of a sufficient degree of linkage or 'coupling' between the different branches of the economy in terms of the input requirements of all other branches.[5]

While the degree of sectoral interdependence certainly has implications for the stability of a system (and helps to explain why the disarticulated economic structures of Third World countries makes them very prone to international, and internal, fluctuations) we cannot make any *a priori* connection between the level of interdependence and the growth rate. Indeed, on the face of it, a greater degree of interdependence is associated with a lower rate of growth because it means that more of total inputs are taken up as intermediate inputs leaving less for value added. Growing intermediate input dependence does not (of itself) account for the central roles of fixed capital and labour productivity in the growth process and this is the difficulty which renders irrelevant those theories which seek to explain growth and development by reference to interindustry linkages. Kari Levitt develops a measure of generalized interdependence which would lead one to conclude that greater interdependence is associated with slower growth, contrary to the historical fact that the advanced countries have much higher levels of interindustry linkages

---

[5]Harris goes on to make the extremely percipient comment that 'one might interpret the analytic content of the subsequent proliferation of neoclassical growth models as a (largely unsuccessful) attempt to show how it is possible to eliminate this [instability] property by assuming 'enough' technical substitution and price flexibility in the economic system'.

than Third World countries.[6]

The second constraint on accumulation is that each output must be produced at a price which covers payments for commodity inputs and value added including profits distributed in accord with the tendency to equalize the rate of profits.

If either of these conditions is not satisfied there will be a 'distortion' in the economic system. Such a distortion may or may not be desirable from the point of view of continued smooth reproduction. If it is a result of changes in techniques of production or of consumer preferences or of trading patterns then it is a 'natural' adjustment as opposed to deviations which are due to growth-inhibiting structural disproportionalities in the sense of the Hawkins-Simon condition. Recognition of these constraints will help in the interpretation of the model's solutions.

3.2 Antecedents of the Model

The method to be used draws on the work of Eastern European economists on the application of Leontief-based methods to planning. It may appear peculiar to apply a method developed for a centrally planned economy to a capitalist development process such as that of South Korea, where the foundation of growth and development has indisputably been the accumulation of private capital operating in the comparatively anarchic environment of the free market, albeit with state involvement in many areas.

The truth is, however, that while the structure of the model is on the face of it the same for both capitalism and centrally planned socialism, the categories which are used to construct it are fundamentally different in each case and the relationships between them represent entirely different mechanisms of movement and causation. In the one system resources are allocated by the pressures of markets, in the other largely by centralized decision-making; in the one system prices are formed under the spur of profit, in the other by decisions based on allocative efficiency and social distribution; in the one system the surplus forms a profit which tends towards an equal rate in each industry, in the other the surplus is a social surplus under no endogenous pressure to be equalized across sectors; on the one hand investment is governed essentially by considerations of private profit, on the other by planning strategies; and so on. Moreover, the results that are generated by the method have different interpretations under socialism and

---

[6]See the development of the linkage hypothesis in the explanation of Third World growth from its genesis in Hirschman (1958) to empirical tests such as those of Yotopoulos & Nugent (1973), and many others, all of whom ignore fixed capital (but see Hamilton, 1985). Although she does not connect interdependence with growth and is not in the 'linkages school', the problem with Levitt's analysis (Levitt, 1965) can be stated as follows. If A is the matrix of domestic intermediate input coefficients and X is the vector of domestic outputs then we can form the eigenequation $AX = \lambda X$ in the case of no fixed capital where $\lambda = 1/(1+g)$ and g is the growth rate. Using a difficult mathematical argument, Levitt shows that $k = 1/(1-\lambda^*)$, where λ^* is the largest eigenvalue, can be considered to be a 'general measure of interdependence' (λ^* can be thought of as a kind of average measure of the input coefficients). However, in this working capital model, we also have $k = 1 + 1/g^*$ where g^* is the maximal growth rate, so that high interdependence is associated with a low growth rate.

capitalism. For instance, deviations of actual prices from production prices will produce quite distinct responses under the two modes of production. The concepts of equilibrium under planned and unplanned systems of allocation are also different.

Thus although words such as price, investment, profit, wages, labour, and so on are used to describe aspects of the two systems, the concepts behind the words are, in their essences, different in the two systems. The uniformity which allows the same method of analysis to be applied to the two systems lies in the technological fact that in both systems the production of commodities requires commodities and labour.

3.3 The Model and its Solution Procedure

The essential idea is that with a given technology, trade structure and consumption propensities there is a particular set of physical output proportions and a particular set of relative prices which respectively generate a potential growth rate and a potential profit rate which is maximal in the long run. Just as the prices of production assume an equalized profit rate, so the optimal output proportions are generated on the assumption of a uniform growth rate across sectors.

The details of the model appear in Appendix E and here we present only a schematic representation of it. Starting with the open Leontief system, in matrix notation:

(1) $\quad X = AX + E + C + G + I$

where X is the vector of outputs, A is the matrix of technical coefficients, and E, C, G and I are final demand vectors representing exports, private consumption, government consumption and investment. The system is now closed by successively augmenting the A matrix with columns of coefficients representing exports, private consumption and government consumption and with corresponding coefficient rows representing imports M, labour inputs L, and 'services' provided by the government T (i.e. taxes on production and expenditure). For illustrative purposes we assume that capitalists do not consume, workers do not save and there are no foreign savings.

Define X_j to be the total output of sector j and x_{ij} to be the output of sector i used as inputs into sector j, then

$$a_{ij} = x_{ij}/X_j \quad\quad \text{intermediate input coefficients}$$

$$m_j = M_j/X_j \quad\quad \text{import coefficients}$$

$$a_{Lj} = L_j/X_j \quad\quad \text{labour coefficients}$$

$$t_j = T_j/X_j \quad\quad \text{government services coefficients.}$$

If we also write total exports E, total number of workers L and total government expenditure G,[7] then

---

[7] The last is in reality a value expression but, as we will discuss presently, it is interpreted as a physical index of the output of government services.

$$e_i \;\; = E_i/E \qquad \text{export coefficients (proportion of}$$
$$\text{total exports due to each sector)}$$
$$\phi_{wi} = C_i/L \qquad \text{workers' consumption coefficients}$$

$$\phi_{gi} = G_i/G \qquad \text{government consumption coefficients.}$$

The augmented coefficient matrix is:

$$
\begin{array}{lllll}
a_{11}\cdots\cdots & a_{1n} & e_1 & \phi_{w1} & \phi_{g1} \\
a_{21}\cdots\cdots & a_{2n} & e_2 & \phi_{w2} & \phi_{g2} \\
\cdot & \cdot & \cdot & \cdot & \\
\cdot & \cdot & \cdot & \cdot & \\
\cdot & \cdot & \cdot & \cdot & \\
a_{n1}\cdots\cdots & a_{nn} & e_n & \phi_{wn} & \phi_{gn} \\
m_1 \cdots\cdots & m_n & 0 & 0 & 0 \\
a_{L1}\cdots\cdots & a_{Ln} & 0 & 0 & 0 \\
t_1 \cdots\cdots & t_n & 0 & 0 & 0
\end{array}
$$

We now have a sector, among others, which 'produces' labourers using consumption goods as inputs. Labour is treated as homogeneous in order to keep the work manageable, although in the full treatment we introduce a sector of self-employed workers.

In order to account for the last element of final demand, investment, we need to introduce stocks of fixed capital and thereby to move into a state of expanded reproduction. Net investment then becomes an addition to fixed capital stocks, where a capital good is in effect an intermediate input with a turnover time of more than one year. In a similar way we can augment the matrix of capital stock coefficients to account in particular for the fixed capital necessary in the production of labour, notably educational investment and housing. We can then write investment in commodities produced by industry i as an increment g_i to the stocks of capital provided by that industry in the past. In fact $I_i = g_i \Sigma b_{ij} X_j$ where b_{ij} is the marginal capital coefficient of good i in industry j, and the output of each industry X_i can be written in the following way:

$$X_i = \Sigma a_{ij} X_j + g_i \Sigma b_{ij} X_j.$$

Here, the vector X_i is fully augmented except for investment, and g_i is the rate of growth of output of industry i. In order to make the analysis of growth and structural change tractable we make the fundamental assumption that growth is balanced with each sector growing at the rate g. This assumption, it will become clear, affects the whole nature of the model and the interpretation of the results which emerge. In particular the model becomes one designed for studying structural change at certain points in time rather than for tracking growth paths. We can now write I = gBX where B is the augmented matrix of marginal capital coefficients and X is the augmented vector of outputs, and

(2)   X = AX + gBX.

This immediately throws up a fundamental question, viz: with given technology, defined broadly as the elements of the augmented A and B matrices, what vector of outputs X would ensure maximal (balanced) growth in the system? This balanced growth output vector is found by forming the eigenequation from (2):

(3) $[(I - A)^{-1}B]X = (1/g)X = \lambda X.$

In the form of (3) the system can be solved for the set of eigenvalues λ and the associated eigenvectors X.

It can be seen from this that the assumption of balanced growth imposes a strict proportionality between the structure of the economy represented by $[(I - A)^{-1}B]X$ and the structure of outputs X. Associated with the set of eigenvalues will be a set of eigenvectors, each one representing a vector of possible output proportions. By the Perron-Frobenius theorem, since $(I - A)^{-1}B$ is a square, non-negative and irreducible matrix, it has a maximal eigenvalue, λ(max), which is real and positive. Associated with this maximal eigenvalue is an eigenvector which is strictly positive and unique (it is the only non-negative eigenvector).[8] However, since λ(max) = 1/g, the balanced growth rate g corresponds to $1/\lambda$(max).[9] There may be lower eigenvalues which correspond to higher growth rates in which case the associated eigenvectors will have some negative elements. Such a solution would be economically meaningless except as an indicator of the short-run direction of output changes. Fortunately, Bródy (1970, pp113-117) has shown that the growth rate associated with the maximal eigenvalue is the maximal one in the long run, on the 'turnpike' or von Neumann path. Thus the model presented here is a (non-optimizing) model of optimal growth.

It makes some sense, therefore, for us to talk about and calculate the potential maximal growth rate implicit in the system and the output proportions at which that rate would prevail. It also makes sense to calculate the dual price vector appropriate to the potential growth rate. As is well known, the output 'primal' of equation (2) has a price 'dual' which reflects the symmetrical nature of the economy as on the one hand a flow of commodities and on the other a flow of money, a system of production and a system of exchange.

From our augmented table of inputs and outputs we can write the unit price of production, p_j, of the product of industry j as

$$p_j = \Sigma p_i a_{ij} + r\Sigma p_i b_{ij}$$

where r is the uniform rate of profit. If P is the augmented vector of relative sectoral prices then, in matrix form,

(4)   P = PA + rPB

---

[8]See Bródy (1970, Appendix 1) or Pasinetti (1977, Mathematical Appendix).

[9]To take an analogy from geometry, if we have a rectangle of variable side but with a fixed perimeter, the area enclosed will be at a maximum when the sides are equal, in a square. Technological change will expand the allowable perimeter.

from which can be formed

(5) $P[B(I - A)^{-1}] = (1/r)P$.

Here we must interpret B as the matrix of *average* capital coefficients so that PB represents the vector of values of sectoral capital stocks per unit of output on which profit is earned i.e. so that r is given by any one of the elements of the vector $P(I-A)/PB$. The equalization of marginal and average capital coefficients means that we have assumed that capital stocks and outputs grow at the same rate, or that growth is due wholly to *extensive* capital accumulation, capital widening rather than capital deepening. In other words, there is no technical progress. This will be further discussed in Section 7.

We have assumed that A and B are matrices of physical coefficients. In practice the coefficients are calculated from commodity volumes evaluated at actual prices. This presents no great difficulty, since we need merely to reinterpret the price solution vector. For if R is the vector of actual prices and P* is the vector of prices computable from the matrices of physical coefficients A and B, then we can define the price indices P (for R > 0)

$$P = P^*\hat{R}^{-1}$$

(where a hat (ˆ) indicates the diagonalization of a vector) i.e. for each sector j, $P_j = P_j^*/R_j$. Let A~ and B~ be the matrices A and B expressed in prices R, then

$$A^{\sim} = \hat{R}A\hat{R}^{-1} \qquad B^{\sim} = \hat{R}B\hat{R}^{-1}.$$

Then our production price equation (4) can be rewritten

$$P^*\hat{R}^{-1} = P^*\hat{R}^{-1}\hat{R}A\hat{R}^{-1} + rP^*\hat{R}^{-1}\hat{R}B\hat{R}^{-1}$$

or

(4′) $P = PA^{\sim} + rPB^{\sim}$.

Since in calculating the A and B matrices we chose our quantities so that the coefficient vector for each sector represents the working and fixed capital costs of producing 'a dollar's worth' of each sector's output, (4) and (4′) are equivalent.

Equations (4) and (5) are almost identical in form to (2) and (3). The solution to (5) will provide a left-hand eigenvector P associated with the maximal eigenvalue $\lambda(max) = 1/r$. This set of prices is the one that ensures maximal long-run profits. When there is no consumption out of profits, the profit and growth rates are equal, $r = g$.

Multiplying (2) through by the price vector we can write in the aggregate

$$g = P(I - A)X/PBX$$

a relation that holds in every sector if either the balanced growth output or price proportions prevail (see Taylor, 1979, pp186-88). In the open Leontief model with savings rates fixed and less than unity we have the Harrod-Domar condition:

$$g = s.P(I - A)X/PBX = s/k$$

where k is the capital-value added ratio. In our construction, the rate of capitalists' consumption and therefore the rate of savings out of profits is set exogenously, as are the savings rates of other classes.

3.4 Noncommodity Sectors of the Model

The complete augmentation of the input-output table can be represented in the categories of a social accounting matrix (SAM) which plots all exchanges of money for commodities in the economy. Unlike the standard SAM, however, there will be no distinction here between 'production accounts' and 'institutional accounts' because we take it that the owners of the 'factors of production' own the corresponding institutional accounts. Most importantly, in our SAM there appears no financial sector other than the value-added sector accounting for the savings of each of the other sectors. Financial intermediation is only implicit in the intersectoral flows, for example in returns to workers' savings, except insofar as the government gives what it takes away. The details of the SAMs for 1966 and 1978, which show how the A matrices have been fully augmented, appear in Appendix A.

A sector is a collection of owners of goods and services which sells these commodities to other sectors in exchange for its income. In the full specification there are 39 sectors producing domestic goods and a foreign sector 'producing' imports. There are in addition three sectors corresponding to the three broad social classes of South Korea, and a government sector.

In the *labour sector* workers sell their labour-power to capitalists and buy consumption goods with wages. The *self-employed sector* is composed in agriculture of farmers who own the farms they work (including working members of family) and in industry and services of proprietors of family businesses which do not employ wage-labour (also including working members of family), primarily in wholesale and retail trade. The self-employed earn income through working with their own means of production and they spend it on consumer goods. However, both labourers and the self-employed save and thus in an indirect way they 'buy' investment goods (by acquiring a share of total capital stocks), although they do not necessarily buy the capital used in reproducing themselves (eg. housing). Both receive a return to the ownership of capital in the form of interest on savings.

The *capitalist sector* does not sell a commodity (and formally is not a sector) but is able to derive an income through the exploitation of labour by virtue of its ownership of the bulk of the means of production (on which for institutional reasons it receives a higher rate of return than workers and the self-employed). We divide the capitalist sector into two parts, one which buys consumption goods and thus sustains the capitalists as consumers, and one which buys investment goods enabling the accumulation of capital.

There is a *government sector* which collects an income by levying taxes on the other sectors (in exchange for undefined services) and spends its revenue among the sectors including the hiring of labour and the making of transfer payments.

Lastly, there is a *foreign sector*, essentially an accounting sector, which turns foreign exchange earnings into foreign exchange outgoings. This sector's inputs include exports, foreign aid and foreign savings which enter into the 'production function' in those proportions which were necessary in the base years to produce one unit (a dollar's worth) of the output of the foreign sector. The output consists of imports (which are used as inputs into other sectors), including imports of capital goods. This sector does not use fixed capital in 'production' since its output is not physically produced but swapped for inputs.

The SAM is used to represent the base year values. The base years are 1966 and 1978, spanning the Korean industrialization period. The figures for the base years have been assembled around the 1966 and 1978 input-output tables and complemented from diverse sources (see Appendix A). The 1966 capital coefficient matrix was constructed for 1965 by the second five-year planners and that for 1978 was purpose-built. The details of the construction of the capital coefficient matrices appear in Appendix B.

3.5 Interpretation of the Solutions

The solution to the model consists of an eigenvalue and two associated eigenvectors. The left-hand or price vector shows the prices of production of the system, i.e. the relative sectoral prices that would prevail if the rate of profit were equal in all sectors.[10] The right-hand or output vector represents the sectoral output proportions that would prevail if the outputs of each sector grew at the same rate, i.e. if the system expanded uniformly. The price and output vectors are dual to each other. Prices of production have a practical existence in the sense that there is a tendency towards the equalization of profit rates, and the means of achieving this is the movement of investment out of low profit and into high profit industries thus inducing a tendency, other things being equal (as they clearly are not in reality), towards equalization of sectoral growth rates. In practice, sectoral growth rates and relative prices vary with continual changes in technology, tastes and trading patterns.

How, then, can we interpret the deviations of prices of production from actual prices (all set equal to one) and of balanced-growth output proportions from actual output proportions?

Prices of production fail to coincide with actual prices because sectoral profit rates diverge. This has a direct impact on prices and indirect effects reflecting the general interdependence of prices. The strength of the tendency towards profit rate equalization depends primarily on two factors: the degree of competition between capitals (including the effects of government intervention of all sorts), and the degree of uniformity of sectoral growth rates. In competitive conditions, we would expect a rapidly-growing industry to attract new investment through a higher-than-average rate of profit, and a relatively high price (overpricing).[11] The imposition of prices of production would lower the price of such a sector's product. Industries whose product is underpriced - i.e. the actual price is lower than its price of

---

[10]We could also use the model to generate Marxian values which prevail when profits on fixed capital are zero (see eg. Sekerka et al., 1970).

[11]By eliminating the influence of divergent sectoral growth rates we could thus use price deviations as a rough measure of the degree of monopoly. However, there is no direct association between the degree of monopoly and high relative prices, as we can see in the case of government utilities which subsidize private industry. Each case would have to be assessed individually.

production - are being drained of profits to support overpriced (high priced) industries.[12]

On the output side, a shortfall of an actual output compared with the optimal level[13] indicates, definitionally, that this sector is producing less than would be required if the economy were running at its maximal growth rate. But what can be said about the state of the real economy on the basis of the computed output deviations? So far as the assumption of no technical change holds, if the actual growth rate is near to the maximal long-run rate then actual output proportions must be close to their optimum levels. The correspondence is necessary to sustain high growth rates since large deviations across the economy will drag the actual growth rate down below the maximal long-run rate (see Bródy, 1970, p114). On the other hand, deviations may be due to changes in technology, tastes or trading patterns. We will show later that in South Korea around our base periods the economy was operating near to its computed maximal growth rate. The argument above implies that sectoral demands will be close to their optimum levels so that an 'underproduction' indicates that there is a shortfall of actual supply - a bottleneck. It may be, however, that an underproduction (relative to the optimal level) indicates a sector which is in structural decline for technological reasons - due to substitution for its product as an input or to declining relative consumption or to import substitution. Overproduction may equally reflect the reverse. In interpreting the solutions these caveats, which arise out of the model's strong assumptions, must be kept in mind. These comments apply only to the product markets and not to the labour markets.

The interpretation above amounts to the proposition that in the base years Korea was probably running close to its turnpike. This is not a vindication of Walras, nor even a proof of the skill of South Korean planners, since it is the turnpike which converges on the actual path rather than the real economy which responds to the lure of the turnpike. This is contrary to the interpretation of Murakami et al., for instance, who claim in their study of the Japanese economy that they can 'detect a tendency toward the turnpike', and that the actual path 'clings to the turnpike'.[14] Bródy, although quoting this study approvingly, is a little more careful in calling the eigenvectors

... not equilibrium, but only stationary solutions, bearing in mind that they belong only to the statistical data. There is no ground for claiming that they reflect true equilibrium proportions of the economy (Bródy, 1970, p113).

In neoclassical spirit, Bródy argues that it is only substitution which can bring

---

[12]Of course, since we are solving a model of general equilibrium, overpricing is indicative only of variations in profit rates and not of 'excessive costs of production'.

[13]The words 'optimal' and 'maximal' are used guardedly. They refer to maximal growth rates and associated optimal output proportions which would potentially prevail only under the model's strict assumptions, in particular the fixed technology and fixed consumption basket assumptions. It is not intended that any normative significance be attached to these.

[14]Murakami et al., 1970, pp45-46. Harris (1982, p26n1) is quite right to debunk the conclusion that Japan's experience confirms the turnpike hypothesis, but not because in practice the real economy is far from the turnpike but because the practical calculation of the equilibrium path will put it close to the real economy.

about 'true equilibrium', i.e. a state which draws the actual economy towards itself and which thereby keeps the capitalist (and perhaps even the socialist) economy on the straight and narrow. Our claim that the Korean economy was operating close to its von Neumann ray in the base years is not surprising when we recognize that the actual proportions and the optimal proportions are both generated from the same coefficient matrices. Even in a crisis year the rigidity of most of the technical coefficients - especially in the A matrix - would produce a 'depression turnpike'. The challenge for the model-builder would be to construct a model whose optimal path deviated sharply from the actual path.

The products of the value-added sectors are labourers, self-employed workers, capitalists-as-consumers and government services, and their prices are the wage of labour, the return to self-employed labour, the unit consumption fund of capitalists and a dummy 'price' of government services. Solutions for the value-added sectors need to be interpreted with caution. They are not productive sectors like those which produce ordinary commodities and their 'production functions' are merely artifices. Essentially, when the model is fully closed using the social accounting matrix we treat these five sectors as accounting sectors whose total output values and input values must be equalized.

This also applies to the foreign sector in which, although it produces commodities, or rather a commodity bundle of imports, the 'production function' is in effect only a monetary accounting system in which a certain value of each foreign exchange earner (export) is necessary to produce one unit (a dollar's worth) of imports. We do not consider imports to be produced with physical inputs and therefore do not ascribe fixed capital to the foreign sector.

In all of these sectors (except capitalists' consumption) there is a surplus element; personal savings (net of profit income) in the case of labour and the self-employed, the government deficit, and foreign savings. In the solution process these are treated in the same way as the profits of each of the productive sectors, as investible surplus, and are redistributed among all of the sectors so that each sector, including the value-added sectors, receives an equal rate of profit on fixed capital. In fact, since none of these five sectors uses any fixed capital (see Appendix B), all of their savings are allocated to the productive sectors. When these five sectors have positive savings, therefore, the optimal solution will show them, *ceteris paribus*, to be overpriced. While this result is a peculiar product of the method of treating the value-added sectors, i.e. as accounting sectors, it has a real analogue in the sense that personal savings (like foreign savings) as a rule find their way into productive investment, and we do account for returns to personal savings elsewhere in the SAMs.

In the case of labour, the balanced growth output vector indicates only the number of labourers necessary for this sort of growth and is not to be interpreted as a labour-supply function. With fixed labour coefficients a 10 percent uniform growth rate will require a 10 percent expansion of the workforce. 'Underproduction' of labourers indicates labour 'substitution' which would come about as a result of the structural shifts between sectors in moving to the balanced-growth output proportions. The wage is composed of the commodities (including a certain level of savings) necessary to reproduce the labourer.[15] We cannot think of the wage as the

---

[15]Excluding, for empirical reasons, resources used up in producing skills. Note that the product of this sector (labourers) is, unlike the productive sectors, not the same as the input which it provides to other sectors (labour-power).

price of production of labour-power because this commodity is not produced capitalistically and the savings of labour are not profits generated in production. We can, however, intepret the money wage as that price of the labour commodity which is necessary to reproduce the system including the level of consumption and savings to which labour has become accustomed. The real wage is fixed in the basket of commodities required to produce one labourer. When this basket is evaluated at a certain price vector, underpricing indicates that the base year value of the basket is less than the value of the new basket. Underpricing of labour-power indicates that the wage is less than that necessary to reproduce the system at its maximum, uniform growth rate under the given assumptions of the model. Does this mean that profits would be higher if wages were higher when we ignore changes in technology, tastes and trade? The answer would be in the affirmative if the labour sector were like other sectors in that the latter commodities are produced capitalistically, in which case 'labour-producing capitalists' would sell labour at a higher price. In fact there is no reason to imagine that labourers will share in the allocation of higher profits (except for the marginal effect on interest paid on their savings).

Similar comments apply to the other three value-added sectors. In the self-employed sector 'underproduction' would indicate declining numbers of self-employed workers if the economy were moving to its equilibrium path. For the purposes of this model, the rate of return to their labour is, in a sense, a concept equivalent to the real wage of labour although clearly it is subject to different determinations and does not stand in the same relation to profit. It is equivalent in the sense that it is composed of a bundle of commodities which is necessary to reproduce the self-employed worker at the customary standard. The imputed return to self-employed capital (i.e. fixed capital used in the businesses and on the farms of self-employed people) cannot be considered conceptually equivalent to profit since the latter is a category peculiar to capitalist production. The equalization of profit rates is not a tendency that applies on self-employed capital because those businesses and farms are not part of the domain of capital. Indeed, as we show in Appendix C, the imputed rate of return to self-employed capital is negative. We must bear this in mind when interpreting the solutions.

The interpretation of the foreign sector solutions must be conducted with equal care since it is little more than a dummy sector. The profits of this sector, foreign savings, will be allocated away completely in the solution process because there is no fixed capital used in the simple exchange of exports for imports. This will give the impression, *ceteris paribus*, of overpricing, the actual price of imports is higher than the optimal price, implying that the exchange rate is undervalued relative to the optimal. Usually one thinks of a big foreign deficit as an inducement to devaluation and not revaluation because of assumed differences in price elasticities of exports and imports. In the present model these elasticities are zero as a result of the fixed coefficients assumption. We can isolate the influence of foreign savings in the solution process by recalculating optimal prices with foreign savings set to zero. We may find that in the new optimal solution the prices of exports are higher than their actual prices so that the imported good is underpriced and the exchange rate overvalued.

An overproduction in the foreign sector (actual imports greater than optimal) would be indicative of the growth of import dependence, and an underproduction would be indicative of either the growth of import substitution or a bottleneck in importing.

3.6 The Wage-Profit Frontier

We can use the model to generate a trade-off relationship between the real wage rate and the maximal long-run rate of profit (hereafter simply the 'wage-profit frontier', profit being understood as the maximal long-run rate).

With an endogenous labour-producing sector the model generates a price dual for this sector, the optimal wage rate, as the 'price of production' of labourers. To construct a wage-profit frontier we need, in effect, to exogenize the wage rate so that we can measure the effect of its variation on the profit rate. In fact the real wage - the consumption bundle required to produce one labourer - is part of the exogenously given technology of the closed system.[16] The only difficulty is that the technical conditions of production of labourers include an element of workers' savings.

The model solves for an augmented price vector P of which one element is the money wage w (the price of production of labourers). Selecting the labour sector price equation from (4) above:

(6) $\quad w = P\Phi_w + rPb_w$

where Φ_w is the vector of components of one consumption bundle for workers (i.e. intermediate inputs into the production of labourers) and b_w is the vector of capital coefficients in the labour sector (i.e. fixed capital used in the production of labourers).

We have said elsewhere (see Appendix B) that the main element of fixed capital used in the production of labourers is housing (at least, this is the main element that can feasibly be accounted for since education costs, in the production of skilled labour, are statistically elusive). However, in the construction of the input-output tables the imputed rent on owner-occupied dwellings is counted in private consumption expenditure as purchases from the real estate sector. This means that the capital costs of producing labour, depreciation on housing which is 'embodied' in labourers, is treated as a current cost item and appears as an element of Φ_w. In other words $b_w = 0$. In the solution process, then, savings of labourers are allocated among sectors which invest productively in order to augment stocks of fixed capital.

Now we have

$$w = P\Phi_w$$

and we can ask what the profit rate would be if the real cost of labour were more or less than one consumption bundle. Writing the number of consumption bundles necessary to produce one worker as c_w (this is now the real wage) we have a variable money wage rate w^* from the solution i.e.

---

[16]The 'price of production' of labourers depends directly on the technical conditions of production in the labour sector and indirectly on the technical conditions in the other sectors since they determine relative prices.

$$w^* = P^*\Phi_w c_w.$$

Normalizing prices so that the value of a consumption bundle remains constant (no inflation of wage goods), i.e. $P^*\Phi_w = 1$. then the wage (real and money) is simply given by the exogenous number of consumption bundles

$$w^* = c_w.$$

When c_w is at a maximum, $r^* = 0$ and the associated left-hand eigenvector gives Ricardo-Marx value prices; when $c_w = 0$ and $r^* = r^*(\max)$ the calculated prices are equivalent to what Sekerka et al. (1970, pp188-91) refer to as 'F-two-channel prices' for the case when $c_w = 0$ and the maximum eigenvalue measures the capital-net income ratio.

By similar reasoning for the foreign sector, and in the knowledge that there is no fixed capital used in 'producing' imports, we could alter the terms of trade by specifying exogenously the number of baskets of export goods necessary to buy one (composite) imported good. More export baskets per imported good implies a devaluation. On the assumption of fixed capital coefficients, we could construct an exchange rate-profit rate frontier.

3.7 Assumptions of the Model

Several of the assumptions of the model are very strong and must be borne in mind when interpreting the solutions. The key assumption, which appears in many guises, is linearity. (This is further analysed in Appendix E where a more general model is linearized). The main assumptions are:

* growth is balanced

* production functions are of the fixed-coefficients type

* utility functions are of the fixed-coefficients (Leontief) type

* prices are uniform across sectors

* there is no joint production.

i) *Constancy of technical coefficients* The production function for each sector j under the assumption of fixed technical coefficients can be written

$$X_j = \min[x_{ij}/a_{ij}] .$$

The output of sector j is constrained by the input whose supply is most limited i.e. there is no substitution between inputs. The assumption of fixed coefficients (in addition to the assumption of no joint production discussed elsewhere) in fact involves two statements about the nature of production; that there are no economies or diseconomies of scale, and that there is no technical progress.

Economies and diseconomies of scale become most relevant when large changes of output are involved. However, around the point of actual production, at which the technical coefficients are calculated, the fixed coefficients assumption is a reasonable approximation - in a limited neighbourhood a linear function can quite closely approximate a nonlinear one if the latter is fairly smooth. Our empirical results will show that most deviations which occur in output proportions are less than 20 percent and we would not normally expect economies to cause major coefficient changes within this range.[17] All this is more true of intermediate input coefficients than of capital coefficients (particularly since in the empirical application the latter have been calculated to include inventories) but we will show that the main results are not affected even by large errors in the estimates of the capital coefficients.[18]

ii) *Absence of technical change* While economies of scale relate to coefficient changes *within* a period of production, technical change relates to coefficient change *between* periods of production. The fixed technology assumption amounts to the proposition that the investments that connect up periods of production are always made in the existing proportions. This assumption is important to the solution process of the model because it is equivalent to the assumption that average and marginal capital coefficients are the same, i.e. that output and capital stocks grow at the same rate. However, we know that in reality investment is not purely extensive and that new investment is often undertaken in response to technological developments. This can change the proportionalities both between inputs and outputs and among inputs. It will prove important to be aware of this in interpreting the solutions.

iii) *Linearity of other inputs* The requirements of the model's solution process impose linearity not only on the production functions involving intermediate, labour and fixed capital inputs. We also assume linear relationships in the 'production' of nonproduced outputs, viz. imports, labourers, the self-employed, capitalists-as-consumers and government services. Since these are essentially accounting processes we need only note the assumption in the interpretation of the solutions for these sectors. The implication is, however, that consumer demands for goods are not price-responsive. In fact the subordination of decisions about consumption is one of the model's most non-neoclassical features. However, one could plausibly argue in the cases of the three private consumption and the government sectors that patterns of consumption are quite slow to change over time especially in the early stages of industrial growth (see footnote 86 on page 43 above) and that equilibrium relative prices do not in practice diverge greatly, for this reason, from actual relative prices.

One linearizing assumption, however, is of particular importance. This is the assumption that the level of the fund for capitalists' consumption is linearly related,

---

[17]Bródy argues that because of the more detailed division of labour, greater standardization and automation, modern manufacturing 'will enforce vigorous proportions' among all of the inputs (Bródy, 1970, p18). This is probably more true in the case of intermediate than capital inputs.

[18]See also Bródy's proof that computed levels of the eigenvalue are much less sensitive to errors of the stock than of the flow matrix; 'we can allow ... 10-25-fold errors in B as compared with A' (Bródy, 1970, pp127-28).

by constant coefficients, to levels of output.[19] In reality the level of capitalists' consumption is determined as a proportion of profits (after taxes) and since the latter depends (multiplicatively) not only on the rate of profit but also on relative prices and outputs, all of which are endogenous to the model, the real relationship is highly nonlinear. In a closed model with our solution technique we cannot account for this and so have tried to approximate the level of capitalists' consumption by a linear relation, viz. by assuming that the 'services' provided by capitalists in the production process and for which they receive an allocation for consumption purposes forms a fixed proportion of (physical) output in the same way that labour services are assumed so to form. One consequence of this procedure is that the net product of the system is necessarily invested. Sensitivity analysis shows (Appendix A) that within the range of feasible variations of capitalists' consumption the linear approximation does not significantly affect the results. Precisely the same procedure has been employed to account for inputs of 'government services' i.e. taxes on production (and incomes) which in practice are levied *ad valorem* and thus depend on the levels both of prices and outputs. These key linearizations are discussed in more detail when the model in its general form is presented in Appendix E.

iv) *Closure of the model* and labour as a produced commodity. The model is completely closed and this requires some explanation. The absence of final demands means that all activities, including consumption and investment, are endogenous activities and are not subject to independent decision-making, eg. in particular, consumers cannot change their consumption patterns in response to price changes. Consumption - the usual maximand of linear programming models - is in no sense the object of economic activity but is simply a means of producing labourers, self-employed workers, capitalists-as-consumers and the government-as-consumer.[20] In addition, exports are not external to the system but are treated as the inputs which produce (the foreign exchange for purchasing) imports, and investment is determined within the system by the capital-output ratios and the growth rate. Only the technology - broadly defined to include all of the elements of the augmented A and B matrices - is exogenous.

The treatment of labour as a produced commodity is closely related to the

---

[19]Von Neumann assumed that no surplus goes to labour and that all is invested. Pasinetti says that these two assumptions are not necessary for a determinate system of relative prices (Pasinetti, 1977, p216). In fact, in order to generate von Neumann prices in a model of maximum growth it is necessary to make either this assumption or the linear one made in the present model. The problem with simply ignoring capitalists' consumption (which is necessary to get relative prices exact since the capitalists' consumption fund is deducted from gross profits after prices have been formed) is that it introduces a further element in the deviation of actual output proportions from their optimal levels, one moreover which is difficult to account for. It could perhaps be skirted around by arguing that in an 'optimal world' of maximum growth the 'wasteful' consumption of capitalists will disappear anyway. We do not see any value in comparing actual Korean capitalism with some hypothetical Korean socialism.

[20]In his exegesis of the von Neumann model Koopmans comments thus: 'The purpose of economic activity is by implication assumed to be fastest growth rather than the enjoyment of life by all generations .... [The model has a bearing on] the forced development of an economy in which the aim is to construct a definite productive capacity for some future date without independent regard for the raising of consumption levels in the meantime' (Koopmans, 1970, pp296-97). This describes the South Korean process admirably.

Classical assumption of a subsistence wage since it amounts to specifying the components of the workers' consumption bundle i.e. the physical wage. For Marx, the wage or price of labour-power was determined, like other commodities, by the labour-time necessary for the production of labour-power and this 'reduces itself to that necessary for the production of... means of subsistence' (Bródy, 1970, p28). The subsistence wage, we ought to note, is not necessarily confined to the physical minimum required to keep body and soul together but can incorporate, after Marx, a historical and moral element. The closure of the model in this way has a peculiar relevance to South Korea in the period of rapid industrialization. It was argued in the previous chapter that circumstantial evidence (if not official figures) suggests that the industrial wage was close to subsistence for the great majority of workers until well into the seventies. This was due to the changing structure of the economy which saw very large numbers of workers stream out of agriculture (itself at a near-subsistence level) and into the industrial factories (especially after 1968).

Despite all this, we do in fact partially open the model by varying the technology in the counterfactual experiments. In particular the consumption bundle can be altered so that the wage is in effect determined from without. Nevertheless it remains true that the closedness of the model makes it generally unsuitable for policy analysis since the latter operates by definition on exogenous variables (see Bródy, 1970, p136).

v) *Uniformity of prices* The price solution of each sector enters into the determination of the prices of other sectors. This price is uniform across sectors into which it enters; in other words the unit sale price is the same for all customers. This is the usual assumption of models based on input-output tables. In practice, the domestic price of a product is not equal to its export price - the first is endogenous, the second determined on world markets (ratios of export to domestic prices appear in Appendix C, Table C.4). Taylor & Lysy (1979) write this into their model explicitly. It has not been possible to modify the present model to account for this difference because the exchange rate solution, which enters into the determination of all other prices, depends on the prices of exports which must be determined exogenously. This is made clear in Appendix E. The result is that the prices which emerge in the solution process are average prices, averages of domestic and export prices (weighted by domestic and export shares of sectoral outputs). In order to have the correct determination of the exchange rate, with exports valued at world prices, we could solve the model iteratively, in which case the model specification adumbrated in this chapter provides only a first approximation. Using the 1966 data, the exchange rate and growth rate solutions converge to four decimal places in four iterations and the first approximations are very close to the final solutions (see Appendix E).

3.8 Relation to Other CGE Models

How does the model outlined above compare with other CGE models and in particular with the neoclassical variants which dominate the field? There are four main areas of difference, and, as will be seen, these cover some fundamental issues.

i) *Nature of prices* In neoclassical models the prices that are determined are market prices established by a *tatonnement* which equalizes the supply of and demand for commodities (although some incorporate fix-price commodities). This price *tatonnement* is usually both a theoretical construct which purports to represent the way in which prices are actually formed (through supply and demand pressures rather than the hypothetical auctioneer), and a means of finding a solution to the model. In the model elaborated in this chapter, on the other hand, the prices which emerge are classical prices of production - long-run prices calculated on the assumption of equal profit rates in each sector.[21] The present model is unsuitable for short-run analysis.

In neoclassical models production and exchange operate as separate systems. The exchange system takes all inputs including nonproduced resources as given, and the *tatonnement* process determines relative prices in response to changes in demand. This, in turn, induces changes in techniques. In the present model, a more classical position of no nonproduced inputs is adopted - even labour is treated as a produced commodity. Resources are not taken as given and prices are not calculated as a response to scarcities. Prices are determined without reference to demand - changes in demand only influence levels of output - but depend on the technology and the profit rate.[22]

ii)*Income distribution* Factor prices in neoclassical models are usually determined by factor demands with the 'wage' of each factor equal to the value of its marginal product. In contrast to this endogenous distribution, the present model treats distribution as being determined outside of the system in a Marx-Sraffa fashion. The actual real wage rate is considered exogenous within the time scale represented by the model solution. This is consistent with the arguments of the last chapter.

iii) *Investment demand* This is the Achilles' heel of all dynamic general equilibrium models due to the absence of convincing theories of investment. This simply reflects the anarchic nature of capitalist production. In a dynamic forecasting model, however, a theory of investment is essential since it is investment that drives the model from one period to the next. In the present model the knot is cut by the simple device of assuming a uniform and constant growth rate in each sector with constant capital-output ratios. The solution of the model tells us what the balanced growth rate actually is and thus the level of total investments required. This device has fundamental implications for the interpretation of the results since it amounts to assuming away the influence of changes in technology, tastes and trading patterns on investment. It recognizes the arbitrary and speculative character of the capitalist economic process and it means that we abandon any idea that we know the actual path of investment. Our balanced growth output solutions are interpreted only as those consistent with maximal growth in the economy. This growth rate applies exclusively to the base years and can be extended to the future only by simple extrapolation. Its purpose, therefore, is for structural analysis rather than path-plotting.

The difficulty with dynamic models is not in solving them for a particular set of parametric values but in specifying the mechanism that drives them from one 'year' to the next. Various devices are used to overcome this. The device of

---

[21]The assumption of no joint production is important here. In the case of the output of the foreign sector, a composite bundle of imported goods, we need only observe that the bundle remains in fixed proportions and the only thing to change is an index of its volume.

[22]This result, the independence of prices from demand, is the well-known nonsubstitution theorem. It depends on the assumptions of constant coefficients and the absence of joint production - see Pasinetti (1977), Chapter 6 & Appendix.

Leontief's dynamic inverse, and that of several other consistency models, is to solve the system backwards so that sectoral growth rates are known after prior specification of terminal capital stocks. Other methods assume that all possible techniques are known and the optimal choice determines investment levels. But CGE models generally embody some *theory* of investment. In his pioneeering work Johansen adopted a Keynesian approach by taking total investment to be fixed exogenously with sectoral investments determined within the system. The interpretation put on this (Johansen, 1960, p30) is that total investment is controlled, directly or indirectly, by government policy. The applicability of this to an economic system where investment decisions are taken by private and numerous profit-seekers is limited. (Keynes would perhaps have argued that 'animal spirits' are so volatile that investment levels are unknowable in the longer run). In the exogenous investment model closure, savings rates become endogenous or these rates are fixed and income distribution adjusts to provide the required savings *à la* Kaldor. The similarity of these methods lies in the specification of the level of investment exogenously, while the present model determines the level of investment through the given technology.

Neoclassical model-builders determine the level of total investment endogenously in the capital account. In the model of Dervis, de Melo and Robinson (Dervis et al., 1982) total investment is determinied by equalizing it with total savings and the latter are determined by exogenous institutional savings rates and endogenous institutional incomes (as in the present model). They comment that this 'model of savings and investment is very classical in spirit' (Dervis et al., 1982, p165). But the method for the sectoral allocation of investment goods is the *differentia specifica* of neoclassical models. Dervis et al. note that the simple approach would be to assume that money markets do not exist and to allocate investible funds in proportion to sectoral profits. 'More realistic', they argue, would be to adjust these proportions as a function of the deviation of a sector's profit rate from the average profit rate (*ibid.*, p176). More accurately, and ambitiously, one could determine sectoral investments by the interaction of demand functions for investment dependent on expectations and the accelerator, and a supply function of loanable funds determined in the money market. An adjustment mechanism, presumably a *tatonnement* on the interest rate, would then bring them into equality and allocation would result. This is the method of Adelman and Robinson (1978, pp32-35).

In the model of this chapter sectoral investment allocation is dealt with by the simple expedient of assuming balanced growth and fixed capital-output ratios. Clearly, this deliberately artificial method greatly diminishes the path-tracking ability of the model, but whether it is much less accurate than the money-market specification outlined above is a moot point.

iv) *Notion of equilibrium* All of the models so far discussed are models of general equilibrium; 'general' in the sense that all major aspects of the economic system which are quantifiable are included, and 'equilibrium' in the sense that the solutions that are generated require all variables to be mutually consistent. In neoclassical models, however, there is another, and stronger, sense in which they are equilibrium models: this lies in the interpretation of equilibrium as an active element of the economy whereby real variables are drawn, by the forces of supply and demand, towards the equilibrium solution. For instance, the determination of factor incomes involves the equalization of supplies and demands in the factor markets. In the labour market of the present model the real price of labour is exogenously given (in the fixed 'technology' of the consumption bundle) and there is no reason to suppose that it settles, in the long or short run, at the full-employment level. If the labour demand of the solution were equal to the actual supply of labour this would merely be the result of an arbitrarily chosen scale factor. Equilibrium in the present scheme is a useful construct to be employed in analysis but is not considered to represent a real process.

3.9 Marx's Extended Reproduction

The present model is an elaboration of Marx's extended reproduction scheme. Bródy's purpose is to show that the analysis of his book conducted in terms of matrix methods and the properties of eigenequations is fundamentally similar to Marx's analysis of extended reproduction.[23] In fact Bródy shows that Marx's examples of extended reproduction are two-sector special cases of the n-sector generalization under the assumptions of i) uniform growth rates in all sectors, ii) no technical change (constant organic composition of capital), and iii) turnover times equal to one year (so that all capital is working capital). The first two are the assumptions of the model of this book. Marx maps out the uniform growth paths of the two departments and labour demand, but, like us, his purpose is not to establish any tendency towards equilibrium, rather to point to the strictness of the conditions necessary for continued, smooth accumulation. The models are therefore useful for structural analysis, for exposing the relation between sectors in the accumulation process. In Marx's reproduction schema (Marx, 1956, Chapter XXI), the fact of extended reproduction and the rate of accumulation itself are taken as given. In the present model the rate of growth is shown to be implicit in the inter-departmental relations themselves in that the level of surplus is embodied in the interrelations of the various processes of production. More precisely, the rate of growth is a potential one contingent upon the investment behaviour of capitalists so that we too in this framework make the supposition that accumulation will take place.

This is the case for the output primal of the present model. The connection with Marx's analysis is much more clear on the price side. Both take prices of production as the relevant prices for analysing the accumulation process. The dual solution of the present model reflects the duality which runs through Marx's work, including the dual form of labour, abstract and concrete, producing exchange and use values (see Bródy, 1970, pp66-67). It ought to be noted that Bródy argues that in his model strictly speaking we are not working with prices of production because in addition to the wage as a cost element of prices we should have, in the augmented B matrix, investment in workers, i.e. the resources tied up in producing skilled labour and the fixed capital necessary to reproduce all types of labour, such as housing.[24] With this fixed capital also entering costs we would in the complete model in fact have what are known in Eastern Europe as 'two-channnel prices'

---

[23]'The purpose of this book is to translate Marx's original approach into mathematical terms and to indicate the path leading from it to modern quantitative economic reasoning' (Bródy, 1970, p9).

[24]For empirical reasons, however, we do not include fixed capital in the production of labour in our augmented B matrix - see Appendix B.

which are found as the left-hand eigenvector of the total system incorporating stocks in the labour column (see Bródy, 1970, pp80-81). Correctly, one should include a mark-up on *wages* as a return to these capital stocks, and the average profit rate no longer exceeds the attainable growth rate.

What is the relation between the model of the economy presented in this chapter and the labour theory of value? The labour theory of value is an explanation of the accumulation process in terms of the capital-labour relation - a social relation rather than a market relation although it finds expression in the latter - and centres on the division of the product between paid and unpaid labour. Its central elements are the wage, the rate of exploitation, the industrial reserve army, the organic composition of capital and the labour process.

... the relation between capital, accumulation and the rate of wages is nothing other than the relation between the unpaid labour which has been transformed into capital and the additional paid labour which is necessary to set in motion this additional capital.[25]

The model used in this study allows precise quantification of the division between paid labour (the amount of labour required to produce the real wage) and unpaid labour and, under certain conditions, the effect on the path of accumulation.

The labour theory of value also draws our attention to the sectors of the economy which are not dominated by the capital-wage labour relation and the effects of these sectors on the accumulation process. These effects can be looked at quantitatively using the present model and indeed the comparison of different base years can give an accurate picture of the change in the relation between the two modes of production. By examining the degree of interindustry dependence between capitalist and non-capitalist sectors (in input-output terms), the 'wage' of self-employed labour, the rate of return on self-employed capital, the capitalist-non-capitalist terms of trade, the overpricing and underpricing of non-capitalist products, the deviation of the output of the self-employed sectors from that necessary to reproduce the system - by examining all of these we can assess the degree to which capital relies on the non-capitalist sectors to bolster its exploitation of labour and the degree to which its rate of accumulation is held back by the self-employed sectors.

---

[25]Marx (1976, p771). 'It is therefore in no way a relation between two magnitudes which are mutually independent, i.e. between the magnitude of the capital and the numbers of the working population'.

CHAPTER 4
Prices, Outputs, Surplus and Accumulation in Korea, 1966-1978

4.1 Structural Change

Price and output solutions, 1966

Prices of production for the year 1966 are presented in Table 4.1. These relative prices have been normalized in such a way that the value of gross domestic output is equal to one; in other words, the optimal output proportions of gross domestic output (GDO) have been chosen as the set of weights (see note 'a' to Table 4.1). Calculated prices of production should be compared with actual prices which are all equal to one. Where the price of production is greater than one we will refer to this as 'underpricing' because the actual price is less than the calculated optimal price, and where the price of production is less than one we will speak of 'overpricing'. The results in Column 1 are referred to as the 'base run' results because the technology from which they are calculated (the A and B matrices) are unaltered while the results in Columns 2 and 3 are the solutions to counterfactual experiments in which some elements of the technology are changed.

One of the striking features of the base run price results for 1966 (Table 4.1 Column 1) is the difference in the way actual prices for agricultural and manufactured goods deviate from their prices of production on the long-run comparative dynamic growth path. The grain, forestry and fishery sectors (as well as coal) show significant degrees of underpricing in comparison with the case where profit rates are equal, indicating that a good part of per unit surplus was being drained from these sectors.[1] However, when the optimal exchange rate is allowed to approach its actual level, i.e. when we eliminate foreign savings as in Column 2 of Table 4.1, the price deviations are flattened out considerably and the agriculture-industry differences, though still apparent, are not so marked. This is indicative of

---

[1]The size of the deviation is due partly to the construction of the augmented matrix in which by definition there is very little profit in agricultural sectors. However, it is shown in Appendix C that the rate of return on fixed capital in the agricultural sectors is negative so that there is no 'unrecorded surplus' being spirited away in the assumption of no capitalist profit in these sectors. In other words, if agriculture were organized along capitalist lines there would still be this much, in fact more, underpricing. The absorption of negative returns into self-employed income thus disguises greater underpricing. See also the substantial *overpricing* in the agricultural sectors in 1978 with a SAM constructed in the same way.

the central importance in a country like Korea of the exchange rate in determining sectoral relative prices and profit rates.

The price difference between industry and agriculture was particularly significant given the weight of agriculture in the economy. These results are consistent with the squeeze on farm income at a time when government policy set low agricultural terms of trade (see Chapter 2). The degree of underpricing would have been higher if not for the fact that grain shortages during the early part of the year, before the bumper autumn crop reached the market, drove prices up. This inflation would have been greater if it had not been suppressed by the government by the release of stores of grain. An exception to the underpricing of primary products was 'other mining', a sector whose output of tungsten and iron ores formed a large proportion of Korea's traditional exports and which apparently had a comparative advantage and a naturally high profit rate.[2]

On the other hand, manufactured goods were almost all overpriced indicating that above average profits were being accumulated there. The sectors which stand out in this regard are the textiles group (9-11), lumber and plywood, pulp and paper, rubber, fabricated metal products, electrical machinery and miscellaneous manufactures. These tend to be industries which were the major export earners. Together with other minerals, these nine sectors accounted for two-thirds of Korea's visible (non-service) exports in 1966.

It will be argued that this does not necessarily mean that big profits were to be earned on exports. Our average prices do not indicate differences between domestic and export prices. Indeed, much qualitative evidence suggests that many export items were sold at a loss (see also the export-domestic price ratios of Appendix C, Table C.4). Losses on exports, however, were usually compensated for by sales on the home market. For instance, a Korean-made car which was sold to overseas buyers for $2,500 could be sold on the domestic market, once export requirements had been met, for over $5,000. The 'wastage allowance' allowed exporters to import more inputs than were strictly required for their own production so that the excess, imported duty-free, could be sold for windfall profits at domestic prices. Most major export industries had a wastage allowance set at a fixed proportion over and above their technically determined requirements for export production. This applied particularly to inputs into the production of plywood (veneer logs), cotton thread (raw cotton) and synthetic fabrics and made-up articles (nylon yarn).[3] A third device which profited exporters was the export-import link system which permitted imports of popular consumer items, which fetched huge premiums, in the same product category as exports, eg. Mercedes-Benz imports for exports of locally-produced vehicles, high-quality radios and televisions for exports of low-quality electrical goods. However, by 1966 this system was operating in a quite limited way.[4]

Other manufacturing sectors which were significantly overpriced were pulp and paper, other chemicals, steel products and transport equipment - all quite new

---

[2]Price solutions for similar models applied to centrally planned economies have consistently shown underpricing in agriculture. On Hungary in the sixties see Brown & Licari (1977, p204) and Walker (1973, p18). Bródy (1970, p157) reports major *overpricing* for Hungarian agriculture in 1962 (and comments that this 'runs counter to our understanding of the economy') and this suggests an error in the calculations.

[3]For the details see Hong (1979, Table B.18).

[4]On all this see the very useful study by Youngil Lim (1981).

Table 4-1: Prices of production, 1966[a]

	(1) Base	(2)[b] $S_f=0$	(3)[c] $S_f=T_f=0$
1 Grain	1.03	1.00	0.97
2 Other agriculture	0.99	0.97	0.95
3 Forestry products	1.09	1.04	1.01
4 Fishery products	1.11	1.05	1.00
5 Coal	1.09	1.04	1.01
6 Other mining	0.89	0.87	0.86
7 Processed food	0.97	0.97	0.96
8 Beverages & tobacco	1.00	0.98	1.04
9 Fibre spinning	0.95	1.05	1.05
10 Textile fabrics	0.94	1.00	1.00
11 Finished textile products	0.93	0.97	0.96
12 Lumber & plywood	0.85	0.98	0.97
13 Wood products & furniture	0.95	0.98	0.97
14 Pulp & paper	0.93	0.96	0.96
15 Printing & publishing	0.97	0.98	0.96
16 Leather & products	0.96	0.95	0.95
17 Rubber products	0.89	0.97	0.97
18 Basic chemicals	0.98	1.01	1.00
19 Other chemicals	0.90	0.94	0.95
20 Chemical fertilizers	1.06	1.04	1.00
21 Petroleum & coal products	0.97	1.01	1.02
22 Nonmetallic mineral products	1.00	0.98	0.96
23 Pig iron & raw steel	0.99	1.07	1.03
24 Iron & steel products	0.95	1.02	1.00
25 Nonferrous metal products	1.00	1.01	0.98
26 Fabricated metal products	0.93	0.99	0.98
27 General machinery	0.97	0.99	0.97
28 Electrical machinery	0.91	0.94	0.94
29 Transport equipment	0.95	0.99	0.98
30 Miscellaneous manufactures	0.92	0.96	0.96
31 Building & public works	0.96	0.97	0.96
32 Wholesale & retail trade	1.01	0.95	0.94
33 Transport & warehousing	1.36	1.23	1.15
34 Finance & real estate	0.88	0.85	0.87
35 Electricity	1.19	1.08	1.05
36 Water & sanitary	1.28	1.16	1.09
37 Communications	1.05	0.97	0.93
38 Social & other services	1.23	1.13	1.07
39 Other	1.02	0.97	0.97
40 Foreign trade	0.73	1.01	0.99
41 Labour	1.08	1.05	1.03
42 Self-employed	0.97	0.94	0.92
43 Capitalists' consumption	1.03	1.01	1.07
44 Government	1.06	1.05	1.34
Average percentage deviation[d]	7.8	4.7	5.0

a. These are normalized by setting P'X' = 1, where P' is the normalized price vector and the weights are X', the (augmented) vector of optimal output proportions itself normalized so that its sum is 1.
b. $S_f=0$ - foreign savings set to zero with exports making up for the deficit.
c. $S_f=T_f=0$ - foreign savings and foreign aid set to zero with the foreign aid gap made up by increased government debt.
d. Average percentage deviation of sectoral prices from the weighted mean (=1).

and heavily capital-intensive industries. Within manufacturing five sectors were underpriced or nearly so, and each of these was government owned or controlled to a greater or lesser extent. In beverages and tobacco, the government had a monopoly on the production of cigarettes. In non-metallic mineral products the biggest item, cement, was government controlled. Fertilizers were also a government monopoly. Under the rice-fertilizer barter programme the government sold fertilizers to farmers at a heavy discount and farmers in fact chose to pay in cash rather than barter with rice.[5]

In the service sectors there was generalized underpricing. There was severe underpricing in transport and storage, electricity, water and sanitary services and social services. Against the trend, however, there were excess profits being accumulated in the finance, insurance and real estate sector (this despite the fact that a large portion of profits in this sector have been recorded as income of the self-employed). Real estate speculation, riding on the back of the building boom was a major feature of Korean commercial life in this period and reflected the preference of Korean moneyed classes to hold their wealth in urban land rather than financial assets (see Chapter 2). It was reported in 1966 that a third of current capital investment went into real estate speculation (FEER, June 30, 1966). This was consistent with the negative real interest rates on bank deposits which prevailed in the inflationary early sixties.[6] The government was to adopt several measures to induce and coerce capital out of land and into productive enterprise, in particular the interest rate reform of September 1965 which saw nominal rates raised very substantially and a successful expansion of bank deposits.

In the case of transport and storage, large profits were being made in some areas but the fixed capital costs were so high (the 1970 capital coefficient for this sector was 5.8) that the actual rate of profit was quite low.[7] Moreover, with railways forming the backbone of Korea's transport system until the seventies (Brown, 1973, p80) the government used rail freight charges to cheapen the costs of key industries and to provide cheap public transport (fares were raised substantially in 1965 and 1967). This sector appears as a major export-earner in 1966 but most of this is no more than an accounting phenomenon since the transport margins on all exports are recorded in this sector. Electricity, water and sanitary services, on the other hand, were underpriced because of their status as government utilities whose output was largely geared to the requirements of industry, especially export industry.[8] The underpricing of electricity is even more startling in the knowledge that 1966 was marked by a 25 percent increase in electricity charges (see BOK, RKE, 1966, pp68-69) at a time when continued expansion of power-generating

---

[5]See Pal Yong Moon (1974, p38) and Brown (1973, pp126-28).

[6]See Hong's figures (1979, Table 7.7). These figures could not pick up the transactions of the substantial curb market in which inflated profits were being made during this period (see Chapter 2).

[7]This underpricing of transportation is not, apparently, confined to capitalist economies. Ganczer (1965, p76) and Walker (1973, p18) report similar low returns for Hungary in 1961 and 1959 when actual prices are compared with prices which allocate surplus on the basis of stocks of fixed capital. Allende discovered from the truck drivers' strike that this can have grave political consequences.

[8]See Hong (1979, pp53-63). Westphal reports that the contribution of price reductions in overheads to export costs has always been quite small and stood at only 0.4 percent of the value of exports in 1968 (Westphal, 1978, p451).

capacity was still a priority. The study by Brown (1973, Chapter 4) of government pricing policy concludes that the major government utilities set prices at 'less than their short-run competitive market equilibrium levels' at least until 1968 (p79). Our results will show that in 1978 this underpricing was much more severe. The explanation of the underpricing of social and other services is explained by noting that the largest part of it was comprised of educational and health services which, when state-run, are not organized on the principle of profit maximization.

The output solutions for 1966 are presented in Table 4.2. The optimal output proportions are those which would be necessary for balanced growth at the maximal long-run rate. They are presented under different assumptions in Columns 2, 3 and 4 as sectoral proportions of gross domestic output (where GDO=100) for simple comparison with the sectoral proportions that actually prevailed in the base year (Column 1). Where the actual output proportion exceeds the computed output proportion it is referred to as 'overproduction' and where less to 'underproduction'.

The fact that there were very large shifts occurring testifies to the rapidity of structural transformation at the time. Bródy reports that a 10 percent deviation of actual outputs from balanced growth proportions is a reasonable expectation for more mature economies, so some of these deviations are very large indeed. Bródy also observes that for more mature economies relative prices deviate much more widely with a 20 percent error not uncommon (Bródy, 1970, p126); our Korean results show much more modest price deviations except for government-influenced industries which subsidize private profits, although the 1978 results will show more radical variation.[9]

Certain straightforward patterns emerge from the output proportions for 1966 (comparing Columns 1 and 2 of Table 4.2 with their differences recorded as percentages in Column 5), and we can see that there are some very substantial deviations from optimal outputs.[10] Significant positive deviations, indicating those sectors growing faster than average, occur in other mining, the textiles group (9-11), wood products and miscellaneous manufacturing. These tend to be export-oriented sectors (these six sectors accounting for more than half of manufactured exports) and their overproduction reflects the very rapid expansion of exports at the time. The reason that fast-growing sectors are not more apparent is probably that imports were expanding so rapidly (the actual share exceeding the balanced-growth share by 19 percent). The overproduction of grain in 1966 was due to the bumper rice crop in that year, the harvest recording a 20 percent rise over 1965 (FEER Yearbook, 1967, p340).

Sectors in apparent decline or facing bottlenecks were nonmetallic mineral products, the four metal sectors (23-26), the three machinery-producing sectors (27-29) especially, and building. The substantial negative deviations of several manufacturing sectors suggests that these were industries which the economy was drawing on more and more but which were having difficulty keeping up with demand. The alternative explanation of underproduction - that these sectors were in structural decline because of substitution by alternative products or by imports - is

---

[9]Computuations for Eastern European economies show large price deviations, for example those for Hungary in 1964 calculated by Brown and Licari (1977, p206) in which the ratio of actual to production price was 1.19 for total industry and 0.72 for agriculture.

[10]The word 'optimal' is used to describe balanced-growth outputs and production prices and only in the sense that these output and price proportions are the ones associated with the maximal rate of growth, other things being equal.

clearly untenable for the capital goods-producing sectors at a time of early industrialization involving capital widening and booming home demand for capital goods. In 1966 serious bottlenecks were reported in the production of coal, cement and iron and steel (see BOK, RKE, 1966, pp9-10) as well as a severe shortage of briquettes for home heating due to the fact that the production of anthracite had reached its limit. The coal shortage does not show up in our figures. The dominant feature of the underproducing sectors is that they are capital goods-producing sectors (building and machinery) or major suppliers of capital goods producers (the metal industries and cement).

The underproducers also tend to be sectors with a large proportion of total supply imported and which depend heavily on imported inputs (the metal and machinery industries in particular - see Appendix C, Table C.5). We will look at this in more detail presently. Note that these large negative deviations are significantly cut into (and reversed in the case of building) when foreign savings and foreign aid are set to zero (Columns 4 and 6 of Table 4.2), suggesting that the underproduction is closely connected to the trade regime. At the time there was stringent rationing of foreign exchange in the continuing attempt to preserve meagre foreign exchange holdings and no industry could freely import all of its requirements. This appears to have hit the machinery sectors very hard. Our figures point to an undervaluation (overpricing) of the exchange rate (one eliminated when foreign savings are set to zero, bearing in mind the limitations of the results in the foreign sector) suggesting that imports were too expensive relative to the exchange rate associated with the maximal growth rate (see below). Whether this was the case or whether it was simply that foreign exchange was very hard to acquire, some import-dependent sectors were not getting the imports they needed and were underproducing as a result.

Water and electricity had been striving to keep up with distended demand and the big investments in power generation and water facilities prior to 1966 appear to have warded off severe bottlenecks. However, serious shortages were still reported since future demand had been underestimated (Brown, 1973, p87) and in 1968 there was a tight squeeze on power use by big companies. A further, much needed, power plant had been begun in 1966 (RKE, 1966, p56) but it was not until the early seventies that excess capacity appeared (Brown, 1973, pp90-91).

Some of the underproducing sectors were heavily influenced by the state of the building and construction sector, itself underproducing to the extent of 13.7 percent in 1966. We refer particularly to nonmetallic mineral products (glass, stone and clay products) and the iron, steel and nonferrous metals group. The large degree of underproduction in nonmetallic mineral products was partly overcome at the end of 1966 with the opening of a big cement factory which was scheduled to increase Korean cement production by 25 percent. A new factory with four times this capacity was started in 1966 and was due for completion in 1968 by which stage the supply constraint should have been fully eased (see RKE, 1966, pp60-61).

The big deviations for the building and machinery sectors may be due to errors in the capital stock matrix. Bródy shows that much larger errors in the B matrix can be tolerated than in the A matrix (1970, p128). Sensitivity analysis with our figures confirms this; very large deviations in the capital coefficients have only slight effects on the output proportions and negligible effects on relative prices. In compiling the 1978 capital stock matrix the danger appeared to be error on the conservative side. The output deviations suggest that stocks may have been overestimated in the case of fixed assets in the shape of buildings (because higher capital-output ratios in the building sector would appear to drive up the optimal

Table 4-2:   Output proportions, 1966[a]

	(1) Actual	(2) Base	(3)[b] $S_f=0$	(4) $S_f=T_f=0$	(5) (1-2)/1	(6) (1-4)/1
1 Grain	8.35	7.99	8.01	8.13	4.4	2.7
2 Otherag	6.14	6.27	6.34	6.48	-2.1	-5.6
3 Forest	0.91	0.94	0.93	0.93	-3.3	-2.3
4 Fishery	0.82	0.80	0.83	0.88	1.8	-6.8
5 Coal	0.51	0.51	0.52	0.54	-0.4	-4.4
6 Othmin	0.51	0.47	0.51	0.57	6.9	-11.8
7 Profood	3.31	3.23	3.31	3.44	2.4	-3.9
8 Bevstob	1.91	1.89	1.95	2.04	1.0	-7.0
9 Fibresp	1.36	1.22	1.33	1.47	9.7	-8.2
10 Textfab	1.43	1.33	1.43	1.55	6.7	-8.7
11 Fintext	2.06	1.98	2.09	2.25	4.0	-9.3
12 Lumply	0.76	0.73	0.76	0.81	3.0	-7.1
13 Woodpro	0.23	0.21	0.21	0.21	6.0	8.2
14 Pulpap	0.63	0.62	0.62	0.62	0.9	1.0
15 Print	0.51	0.51	0.52	0.53	0.6	-3.0
16 Leather	0.29	0.29	0.29	0.30	-1.8	-6.1
17 Rubber	0.49	0.48	0.50	0.54	2.2	-10.1
18 Baschem	0.24	0.23	0.23	0.24	3.7	0.2
19 Othchem	0.83	0.82	0.83	0.84	0.6	-1.5
20 Chfert	0.16	0.16	0.16	0.16	3.2	1.0
21 Petcopr	1.22	1.21	1.23	1.26	0.1	-4.0
22 Nonmet	0.76	0.83	0.76	0.72	-9.5	5.1
23 Irost	0.26	0.28	0.26	0.25	-9.5	3.8
24 Steelpr	0.53	0.61	0.57	0.55	-15.8	-4.2
25 Nonferm	0.18	0.24	0.22	0.22	-31.8	-18.6
26 Fabrmet	0.40	0.43	0.42	0.42	-5.2	-4.6
27 Nonelm	0.38	0.63	0.51	0.43	-67.0	-15.3
28 Elmach	0.51	0.88	0.74	0.64	-73.9	-27.0
29 Transeq	0.83	1.38	1.15	0.99	-65.3	-18.4
30 Miscman	0.70	0.66	0.71	0.77	5.5	-10.5
31 Build	4.35	4.95	4.33	3.83	-13.7	11.9
32 Trade	5.80	6.11	6.00	6.04	-5.3	-4.0
33 Transto	2.60	2.60	2.68	2.80	0.0	-8.1
34 Fininre	2.08	2.00	2.02	2.04	3.5	1.9
35 Electr	0.65	0.66	0.67	0.69	-0.4	-5.0
36 Water	0.11	0.11	0.11	0.12	0.0	-4.9
37 Commun	0.37	0.38	0.38	0.38	-1.2	-3.3
38 Socserv	4.03	4.00	4.11	4.21	0.9	-4.4
39 Other	2.06	2.06	2.21	2.41	-0.1	-17.3
40 Foreign	6.97	5.66	5.53	5.53	18.8	20.6
41 Labour	10.73	10.85	10.87	10.91	-1.1	-1.7
42 Selfem	13.77	13.65	13.66	13.88	0.8	-0.8
43 Capscon	4.21	4.32	4.32	4.40	-2.6	-4.6
44 Govern	5.09	4.83	5.21	3.99	5.2	21.7
Average percentage deviation[c]					9.1	7.5

a. Normalized so that the sum of actual outputs and the sum of optimal outputs (representing different distributions of GDO) are both equal to 100.
b. For explanation of column headings see notes to Table 4.1.
c. If X_i is the actual output and X_i^* is the optimal output of sector i then the average deviation is given by $[\Sigma|X_i-X_i^*|/X_i]/44$.

output proportion) and underestimated in the case of capital imports. This is not so, for a halving of the 1978 capital coefficients reduces the output deviation of the building sector only a little, and raises the deviation of the foreign sector by a small margin. Relative prices are almost wholly unaffected.

It does appear then that the underproduction in the building sector in 1966 was in fact due to a supply constraint. While there was a 31 percent growth in the output of the industry in 1966 (RKE, 1966, p10) - and gross domestic fixed capital formation as a proportion of GNP had leapt to 20 percent in 1966 from an average of 13.4 percent over the previous three years (ESY, 1970, p11) - demand was rampant, to the point where in the second half of the year the government found it necessary to suspend, almost totally, the issue of building permits (RKE, 1966, p11). This rebounded on the nonmetallic mineral products sector (underproducing by 9.5 percent) which sold 71 percent of its total output to the building sector. Moreover, 1966 was a year when South Korea was sending engineers to South Vietnam to fulfil lucrative construction contracts let by the US forces there.

One of the most remarkable features of the 1966 results is the size of the deviations of both outputs and prices in the foreign sector (see Tables 4.1 and 4.2). There is substantial 'overproduction' (18.8 percent) indicating that imports were growing much faster than the rest of the economy (but still not fast enough for the import-dependent sectors) and revealing the growing import-dependence of Korean industrialization. In other words, the marginal propensity to import was considerably greater than the average propensity. The emphasis of production was such as to favour those sectors which were heavily dependent on imported inputs and which on the balanced growth path would have grown considerably more slowly. The gross 'overpricing' in the foreign sector (the actual price exceeded the optimal price by 37 percent) reflects the size of the current account deficit in 1966 and the reliance on foreign borrowing to finance imports. Overpricing here means that the exchange rate was undervalued (by 37 percent) in relation to the long-run comparative dynamic growth path.[11] We might interpret this undervaluation as the effect of intense pressure to export reflected in high foreign savings. In fact there had been a major devaluation in May 1964 (from 130 to 255 won per US dollar) and the exchange rate had been allowed to float thereafter (and stood at 272 in 1966). During the year import prices rose less than domestic prices (RKE, 1960, p14). Wontack Hong (1979, Chapter 7, Section 2) argues that imports of capital goods at the time were underpriced, not as a result of effective tariff rates but due to the government loan allocation policy which provided foreign exchange at low interest rates for imports of necessary capital goods. The evidence is conflicting on this point, but we might interpret actual events as reflecting short-run pressures in the foreign sector with the solution of the model reflecting long-run pressures. However, as we will see in the counterfactual experiment that sets foreign savings equal to zero, the overpricing of exports is more a result of the construction of the model than a reflection of disequilibrium on the foreign exchanges.

We can get a clearer picture of the influence of particular sectoral characteristics on the 1966 price and output deviations by aggregating the sectors

---

[11]Bródy's 1962 Hungary example (1970, pp156-57) shows an 11 percent overvaluation of the exchange rate and this, he argues, reflects 'an enormous drive to import' in a country with a big trade surplus. The 'excessive foreign trade' appears in the results as an overproduction in this sector; we have argued above that overproduction in the foreign sector is not inconsistent with a shortage of imports but reflects the rapid growth of trade.

according to three criteria: 1) export-oriented versus domestic market-oriented industries - here we take export-oriented industries to be those which export more than 10 percent of their output (in fact they averaged 20 percent); 2) users of domestically produced inputs versus those reliant on imported inputs, the latter defined as those sectors which rely on imports for more than 10 percent of their inputs (average 24 percent); 3) sectors in which total supply is domestically produced versus sectors in which a large part of their total supply is imported. Again in the last, the cut-off point is 10 percent of total supply (though in fact import-dependent sectors had an average import content of total supply of 36 percent).[12]   We exclude the agricultural sectors 1-4, and the foreign and value-added sectors 40-44.

Dealing first with outputs, in Table 4.3 entry A is the actual 1966 output proportion, B is the weighted average deviation obtained by summing actual and optimal outputs and C is the unweighted average deviation obtained by averaging all of the sectoral deviations in each category. Both types of deviation are expressed as percentages. We use both methods of averaging (B and C) because in the former a small deviation in a big sector can swamp a big deviation in a small sector. The first part of Table 4.3 puts category 1 against 2 and the second part puts 1 against 3. Quadrant numbers are in roman numerals.

The two methods of averaging give broadly the same picture. Industries which did not import much of their inputs or their total supply did not deviate very far from their balanced-growth output proportions; the only exception was the building sector which we have discussed in some detail already. On the other hand, those sectors which depended heavily on imported inputs or imported supply, whether export or domestically oriented, displayed a very marked degree of underproduction. In fact this applies to those which depended heavily on both imported inputs *and* imported outputs since these show the biggest negative deviations.

What can be said about prices? Here we simply take the unweighted average of the base-run prices for 1966.

The calculations reveal that sectors oriented towards the domestic market were substantially underpriced when compared with export-oriented industries. This was particularly so for those using domestic inputs and importing very little of their total supply, largely because this category includes the government-controlled service sectors and utilities. While export-oriented sectors appear consistently overpriced it does appear that those which relied on imported inputs achieved higher profit rates than those which used domestically-produced inputs. This is consistent with the argument, expressed in Chapter 2, Section 5, that export production was not in itself profitable but was made so by government incentives and, in particular, access to foreign exchange for importing as a reward for exporting. Our figures do not break down each sector's sales between domestic and export sales and so it is difficult to confirm the contention that many manufacturers

---

[12]See Appendix C for the detailed breakdown of sectors.

Table 4-3: Summary output measures, 1966

		Export oriented I	Domestic oriented III
Domestic	A	4.62	A 27.66
inputs	B	+2.5	B -2.7
	C	+3.6	C -0.9

		II	IV
Imported	A	4.99	A 5.73
inputs	B	-7.4	B -11.7
	C	-13.7	C -15.9

		Export oriented	Domestic oriented
		I	III
Domestic	A	4.67	A 28.86
supply	B	+4.9	B -2.2
	C	+4.6	C -0.5

		II	IV
Imported	A	4.49	A 4.54
supply	B	-9.8	B -17.5
	C	-16.7	C -16.7

Note that in the top part of Table 4.3 quadrant I accounts for 32 percent of total exports and quadrant II for 24 percent, and in the bottom part quadrant I accounts for 22 percent and quadrant II for 34 percent of total exports.

Table 4-4: Summary price measures, 1966

	Export oriented	Domestic oriented		Export oriented	Domestic oriented
Domestic inputs	.95	1.06	Domestic supply	.92	1.05
Imported inputs	.92	.96	Imported supply	.94	.97

were recouping their losses on exports through sales to the domestic market.[13]

---

[13]Park & Cole (1979, p268) make this point. See also the studies which support this argument by Seung Hee Kim (1970, p99) and Youngil Lim (1981, pp44-45). Figures compiled by Hong (1979, Table 8.6, p218) show that in 1966 there was a 6 percent rate of subsidy per dollar of exports. This does not account for the 'hidden subsidies' related to access to foreign exchange. Frank, Kim & Westphal calculate that the effective rate of subsidy on export sales by export industries in 1968 was 13.5 percent (Frank et al., 1975, p199).

However, Frank et al. (1975, pp201-206) calculate that several of the major export commodities were sold at a loss on world markets.

Overall the 1966 results suggest that owner-cultivator agriculture and government-operated service industries subsidized the profits and growth of manufacturing industries and export industries especially. However, there were severe bottlenecks in some sectors, particularly the capital goods-producing sectors and their suppliers. Growth was highly unbalanced. The effect was to restrain the growth of those sectors which depended on imported inputs and this reflected the general shortage of foreign exchange. These results point to a crucial element of the Korean economic structure of the mid-sixties: imports were very hard to get but were very profitable once obtained, whether sold directly to final consumers or used as inputs.

Price and output solutions, 1978

Comparing the 1966 with the 1978 figures in Table 4.5 shows in detail the structural pressures and structural changes which prevailed in the period. The first thing to note is that the average deviation of production prices from actual prices increased from 7.8 percent in 1966 to 11.8 percent in 1978. There is as much increase in the deviations of manufacturing and service sectors as primary and value-added sectors. The greater dispersion of profit rates can perhaps be explained in part by the more severe underpricing of government utilities (to further subsidize industry) and in part by the increase in industrial concentration in the intervening period, a trend encouraged by the government. The state was eager to see the emergence of big trading companies along the lines of the Japanese *zaibatsu*. At the same time it had a policy of offering incentives to small firms to merge and make themselves stronger and more competitive internationally. One or two Korean firms now number among the world's top five hundred. The average number of employees per manufacturing establishment increased from 25 in 1966 to 69 in 1976 while enterprises with more than 500 employees employed 22 percent of the manufacturing workforce in 1963 and 45 percent in 1976 (with value added rising from 33 to 58 percent).[14] Between 1973 and 1978 the contribution to manufacturing GDP of the largest 10 chaebol grew from 14 to 23 percent and that of the largest 20 rose from 22 to 33 percent (Sakong, 1980).

There was a substantial decline in the (unweighted) average deviation of balanced growth outputs from 9.1 in 1966 to 5.4 in 1978 (see Table 4.2 Column 5 and Table 4.5 Column 4). This is to be expected since industrialization in the late sixties and seventies broadened the industrial base of the economy. One might have expected such a lessening of the deviation with the slowing of the growth of imports. As Table C.6 of Appendix C makes plain, the economy in 1978 was more heavily dependent on imported inputs especially capital goods imports.[15] Nevertheless, the figures confirm that structural change had become less rapid as

---

[14]These figures are from Youngil Lim (1981, pp44-51).

[15]Intermediate inputs were 17.9 percent imported in 1966 and 22 percent imported in 1978 (see Tables A.2 and A.3 of Appendix A) while the import value of stocks of machinery rose from 44.5 percent in 1966 to 78.7 percent in 1978 (see Appendix B).

one would expect of an economy leaving behind its industrial birth pangs. In their CGE model of the Korean economy for the early to mid-seventies, Adelman and Robinson found that quantities were much more stable than prices (1978, p185). Our results indicate that this relative stability of outputs depends on the degree of industrial development and is something which develops with industrial maturity.

Comparing 1978 actual with production prices we see that the broad pattern of 1966 had changed. No longer was underpriced agriculture subsidizing overpriced industry. In the case of grains the underpricing of the mid-sixties had been eliminated and the figures for agriculture suggest that these activities had become quite profitable.[16] Through the seventies, output of non-grain products - fruit, vegetables and livestock but not silk - had grown considerably faster than grains (ESY, 1981, p132). As we saw in Chapter 2, the trend towards increased agricultural prices was generally in accord with the change of government policy in the intervening period (in the third and fourth five-year plans) which aimed at giving a better deal to farmers, or rather, at encouraging agricultural productivity and self-sufficiency so as to minimize the foreign exchange losses due to mounting food imports. The government could do this through manipulation of the agricultural terms of trade over which it had a strong influence. Taking 1974 as a base (1974 = 100) the agricultural terms of trade (prices received by farmers divded by prices paid by farmers) rose from 78 in 1966 to 99 in 1978 with the main rises occurring in the 1969-72 period, in fact before the pro-agricultural Third Five-Year Plan (see Chapter 2, Section 5). It seems that the agricultural sector played its role as provider of surplus to manufacturing in the sixties; its subsequent share of gross output declined dramatically from 14.4 percent in 1966 to 7 percent in 1978. Note that the exchange rate in 1978 is not heavily influenced by the high level of foreign savings and that setting the latter to zero does not significantly influence the price results (Column 2).

There is still a tendency for sectors dependent on exporting to receive profits above those in other manufacturing sectors (although now no longer overpriced) - electrical machinery, lumber and ply, miscellaneous manufactures, leather, rubber, but less so in the textiles group which was in 1978 facing increased international competition. As we have argued, this does not necessarily mean that the exports were overpriced since our prices are averages of domestic and export sales. Some export industries (fishery, chemical fertilizers, steel products) were in fact substantially underpriced in 1978. Some have argued that there was such an excessive build-up of capacity for producing chemical fertilizers that surplus output had to be dumped on world markets. Big profits were now being earned in beverages and tobacco (possibly reflecting a change in the pattern of consumer demand and the government monopoly in tobacco products) and still in finance, insurance and real estate; but very big losses were being made in transport, electricity and water services reflecting the attempts by the government to keep prices low so as not to disadvantage export producers. This is in stark contrast to Brown's claim (1973, p101) that in the late sixties and early seventies the prices of utilities were moving closer to their 'correct', equilibrium levels.

On the output side, the still-high deviations in some sectors suggests that the

---

[16]It is still the case that, by construction, there is no profit generated by the self-employed sectors; value-added goes to self-employed income. The fact that we now have substantial overpricing, i.e. excess profits, in agriculture shows powerfully the general equilibrium nature of the solutions - they are not simply a reflection of the empirical construction of the SAMs.

Table 4-5: Output proportions and production prices 1978[a]

		OUTPUTS				PRICES	
	(1) Actual	(2) Base	(3) S_f=0	(4) (1-2)/1	(5) : (1-3)/1:	(6) Base	(7) S_f=0
1 Grain	3.55	3.61	3.60	-1.6	-1.5	0.93	0.91
2 Otherag	3.38	3.28	3.29	3.1	2.7	0.90	0.89
3 Forest	0.41	0.35	0.35	15.1	14.6	0.93	0.91
4 Fishery	0.93	0.92	0.94	1.6	-0.7	1.16	1.13
5 Coal	0.27	0.28	0.29	-6.9	-7.2	1.06	1.04
6 Othmin	0.36	0.38	0.38	-5.6	-3.4	0.97	0.95
7 Profood	2.90	2.85	2.87	1.5	0.9	1.00	0.99
8 Bevstob	1.84	1.84	1.84	0.2	0.2	0.95	0.94
9 Fibresp	1.48	1.47	1.55	0.4	-4.9	1.08	1.09
10 Textfab	1.51	1.47	1.54	3.0	-2.0	1.09	1.08
11 Fintext	2.43	2.35	2.47	3.3	-1.7	1.03	1.03
12 Lumply	0.71	0.71	0.71	-0.8	-0.9	1.00	1.04
13 Woodpro	0.13	0.13	0.13	3.1	1.0	1.03	1.03
14 Pulpap	0.59	0.59	0.60	-1.3	-1.8	1.03	1.03
15 Print	0.29	0.28	0.28	1.8	1.4	1.04	1.03
16 Leather	0.65	0.63	0.67	3.3	-2.3	0.97	0.99
17 Rubber	0.69	0.67	0.70	2.0	-2.1	1.03	1.04
18 Baschem	0.63	0.64	0.65	-1.6	-3.5	1.13	1.13
19 Othchem	2.27	2.29	2.33	-0.8	-2.6	1.02	1.03
20 Chfert	0.38	0.38	0.39	-0.1	-2.4	1.24	1.24
21 Petcopr	2.38	2.42	2.44	-1.7	-2.4	1.10	1.14
22 Nonmet	1.00	1.05	1.01	-5.2	-1.9	1.07	1.06
23 Irost	0.84	0.96	0.94	-14.0	-12.5	1.25	1.25
24 Steelpr	1.56	1.68	1.67	-7.7	-6.9	1.21	1.21
25 Nonferm	0.29	0.32	0.32	-11.4	-11.8	1.03	1.04
26 Fabrmet	0.80	0.78	0.80	2.3	0.0	1.09	1.10
27 Nonelm	0.82	1.11	1.04	-36.2	-27.1	1.05	1.06
28 Elmach	2.48	2.97	2.94	-19.6	-18.4	0.99	1.01
29 Transeq	1.70	2.20	2.14	-29.4	-26.0	1.04	1.05
30 Miscman	0.99	0.90	0.94	9.4	4.6	1.00	1.00
31 Build	5.02	5.32	4.98	-5.9	0.9	1.00	1.00
32 Trade	5.27	5.30	5.31	-0.6	-0.9	0.91	0.89
33 Transto	3.08	3.01	3.06	2.3	0.4	1.54	1.48
34 Fininre	2.55	2.35	2.36	7.7	7.6	0.87	0.85
35 Electr	0.88	0.90	0.90	-2.5	-2.9	1.83	1.74
36 Water	0.07	0.07	0.07	0.6	0.3	1.83	1.72
37 Commun	0.40	0.40	0.40	0.4	-0.3	1.10	1.06
38 Socserv	4.53	4.50	4.50	0.8	0.7	1.05	1.02
39 Other	1.30	1.34	1.35	-3.4	-3.8	1.10	1.08
40 Foreign	9.79	9.02	8.96	7.9	8.5	0.99	1.08
41 Labour	10.37	10.22	10.20	1.4	1.7	0.87	0.86
42 Selfem	7.75	7.55	7.57	2.5	2.3	0.83	0.81
43 Capscon	5.41	5.49	5.50	-1.5	-1.6	0.99	0.98
44 Govern	5.33	5.01	5.01	6.0	6.1	0.95	0.94
	Average percentage deviation			.5.4	4.7	11.8	11.6

a. For explanations of normalizations, column headings etc. see Tables 4.1 and 4.2.

economy continued to undergo significant structural shifts in 1978 although the overall output deviation had declined from 9.1 percent in 1966 to 5.4 percent in 1978. One notable feature is that those sectors which showed the biggest positive deviations (overproduction) in 1966 tended in 1978 to be producing more or less at their balanced-growth output proportions (with the exception of the still-overproducing miscellaneous manufacturing sector) suggesting that the imbalance due to rapid growth in particular sectors had mostly disappeared. The most marked change has been the big decline in the level of underproduction displayed by the capital goods-producing sectors (the three machinery industries and building) and concomitantly in their main supplying industries. This reflects the easing (but by no means elimination) of the foreign exchange constraint in the intervening period which accompanied export expansion. At the same time the computed undervaluation (overpricing) of the exchange rate had declined sharply from 37 percent in 1966 to 1 percent in 1978. The underproduction of the machinery sectors nevertheless remained severe.

Other mining became a significant underproducer in the intervening period as natural resource limits exerted themselves - there was in fact a sharp decline in copper production in 1978 while coal (underproducing by 6.9 percent) could not keep up with demand (FEER Yearbook, 1979, p225).

The severe underproduction of the building sector had declined a good deal (from -13.7 in 1966 to -5.9 percent) but the bottleneck had not been fully overcome. Although the construction industry was expanding very rapidly in 1978 (as it had been in 1966) - producing housing, industrial plants, dams, roads, ports and so on - it could not meet the demand pressures. The figures reflect continued long-run pressures on this sector. There continued in 1978 a serious housing shortage - 300,000 new homes were planned for that year (FEER Yearbook, 1979, p221) - and one of the first economic announcements of the new Chun government in 1980 was a promise to build more houses. The bottleneck was undoubtedly exacerbated by the export of construction teams, the numbers of which had expanded quickly since 1975; in 1978 around 75,000 Korean construction workers were employed overseas, mainly in the Middle East, while the industry at home employed around 820,000.[17] The difficulties of the construction industry affected the nonmetallic mineral products sector (underproducing by 5.2 percent) which depended on the former for 61 percent of its 1978 sales (I-O Table).

There is still a tendency for overproducers, such as they are, to be export-oriented industries while the underproducers tend to be heavily import-dependent once again (the summary measures below will reveal more on this). Some export producers (textiles, rubber, leather, fishery, and miscellaneous manufactures, but not electrical machinery or lumber and ply) overproduced in 1978 as the export producers did in 1966, indicating that these sectors were still in 1978 growing slightly faster than the rest of the economy. Stress on export production to overcome the foreign exchange constraint is still an essential feature of Korean industrialization although it is not as compelling as it was in the sixties.

We can repeat the 1966 exercise which provided summary measures of deviations with the non-agricultural productive sectors divided into the same three categories. In each case the cut-off point is again 10 percent. Export-oriented sectors exported 32 percent of their domestic product on average; sectors reliant on imported inputs did so to the extent of an average 25 percent of inputs imported;

---

[17]Figures are respectively from Sooyong Kim (1982, pp13-14) and ESY (1981, p272).

and sectors which imported a large share of total supply did so to an average extent of 29 percent.[18]

In Table 4.6, dealing with output deviations, A is once again the actual 1978 output proportion of this category, B is the weighted average deviation and C is the unweighted average.

Table 4-6: Summary output measures, 1978

		Export oriented I		Domestic oriented III
Domestic	A	5.82	A	25.49
inputs	B	+1.0	B	-0.4
	C	-0.2	C	-0.5
		II		IV
Imported	A	11.35	A	10.42
inputs	B	-8.8	B	-4.3
	C	-5.2	C	-7.7

		Export oriented I		Domestic oriented III
Domestic	A	9.13	A	24.19
supply	B	+1.2	B	-0.2
	C	+0.9	C	-0.2
		II		IV
Imported	A	8.04	A	11.72
supply	B	-13.0	B	-4.2
	C	-8.7	C	-7.2

In the top part of Table 4.6, quadrant I accounts for 26 percent of exports and quadrant II for 43 percent, and in the bottom part quadrant I accounts for 38 percent of exports and quadrant II for 31 percent.

The most notable result to emerge from these summary measures is that the pattern of 1966 has been reproduced for 1978 with very little change. It was still the case that sectors which relied on imported inputs or imported supply were underproducing to a significant (though reduced) degree, whether they were export-oriented or not. However, there does appear to have been some loosening of the restrictions on importation. Of the import-dependent sectors (those dependent on imported inputs or supply), there appears to have been greater underproduction in the export-oriented sectors. This is the reverse of the 1966 position and is indicative of the growing import dependence of export production. While the foreign exchange constraint was still biting, 1978 was a year in which foreign exchange limitations on industry were eased significantly in response to a developing inflationary danger

---

[18]For the detailed breakdown of sectors into these categories see Appendix C.

caused largely by remittances by overseas contract workers and government commitments to the grain stabilization fund. Trade restrictions were eased somewhat (although there was also something of a devaluation against the yen) for both consumer goods and industrial inputs.

What can be said about prices? As before we give the unweighted average of 1978 base-run relative prices according to the above classifications. These price averages all appear high because in 1978 the excluded labour, self-employed and agricultural sectors, all of which have heavy weights in the normalization, have low prices of production. The simple unweighted average of the prices of production of sectors 5-39 is 1.11.

Table 4-7: Summary price measures, 1978

	Export oriented	Domestic oriented			Export oriented	Domestic oriented
Domestic inputs	1.07	1.09		Domestic supply	1.07	1.20
Imported inputs	1.04	1.08		Imported supply	1.03	1.09

The results are not conclusive but it does appear that, as in 1966, products with a large imported component, whether intended for foreign or home markets, tend to be more profitable than those reliant on domestic inputs and supplies. Those using domestic inputs, or which were mostly domestically supplied, were in fact significantly underpriced if destined for domestic markets. These same conclusions were drawn for 1966. It would appear, then, that in 1978 there was still a premium to be had from importing, whether for export or domestic use, and a penalty to be paid for dealing in domestically produced goods. It should be pointed out that the underpricing of the domestic-input domestic-supply sectors is mostly a result of the underpricing and loss-making of government utilities (especially transport, electricity and water). The state was subsidizing the profits of export producers who imported their inputs.

One observation is clear from comparing the 1966 and 1978 solutions: there is no tendency for a sector's contribution to gross output to move against its level of over or underproduction - some do, some do not. In other words, an underproducing sector will not, *ipso facto*, come under pressure to produce more in order to close the gap with the optimal level of output. This confirms comment earlier that the balanced-growth output proportions cannot be interpreted as an equilibrium path towards which there is a tendency to converge.

Looking at the foreign sector it can be observed firstly that the weight of imports has grown substantially in the 1966-1978 period (from 7.0 percent of gross output to 9.8 percent, or from 16 percent to 24 percent of GDP, and this does not account for capital goods imports) confirming that in this case at least the 'overproduction' of imports in 1966 matched a real tendency for this sector to grow very fast. In 1978 imports were still growing more rapidly than the rest of the economy (with a positive deviation of 7.9 percent) but the deviation was much less than that of 1966 (18.8 percent). This decline is perhaps partly explained by the progress of import-substitution for several types of intermediate inputs (particularly steel, basic chemicals and synthetic fibres) but offset, a little out of the picture, by the ever-greater reliance on imports of machinery.

There has, however, been a significant decline in the 'overpricing' of imports - down from 37 percent in 1966 to 1 percent in 1978 - indicative of the dramatic improvement in the current account balance. As before, formally the overpricing of the foreign sector implies an undervalued exchange rate (the foreign sector is outside the country). In reality it is confirmed that the won had been getting progressively more overvalued since 1974 because inflation in Korea had been higher than in its main trading partners (USA and Japan) while the exchange rate was pegged rigidly to the US dollar. The won was not devalued against the dollar until January 1980, then by 16.5 percent, after which it was allowed to float against a trade-weighted basket of currencies so that by the end of 1980 the cumulative devaluation against the dollar stood at 36 percent.[19] The competitiveness and profitability of export industries had been declining with the overvaluation of 1974-1980, leading to the crisis of 1979 (and worse in 1980) when the current account deficit fell from just over US$1 billion to over US$4 billion (ESY, 1981, p204). It was reported at this time that 'export industry generally operated at a loss' (FEER Yearbook, 1981, p179). This leads to the same conclusion arrived at for 1966 - that export industry was profitable but exports themselves were not necessarily the cause of it. Rather, profits on imports and domestic sales made up for, if not losses then, small margins on exports. An econometric study for 1976-78 came to the conclusion that there was no correlation in this period between a firm's profitability and the ratio of exports to sales (Youngil Lim, 1981). This zero correlation may be an increase on a negative one for the mid-sixties. Continued export incentives in the mid-seventies (low interest loans, reduced taxes, rebates on public utility charges, and many more) appear, argues Lim, to have raised the quantity of exports but not necessarily the profitability of export activity. The former, after all, was the primary goal of the policy-makers, who took every measure to close the visible trade gap. Lim concluded that his results suggest that protected domestic markets have been more profitable than subsidized export markets. With this our results concur. Broadly one might say that export expansion did not drive industrialization but provided the foreign exchange essential for the imports which sustained industrialization.

Counterfactual experiments

We can see how Korea's dependence on foreign savings influenced the structure of outputs and relative prices - or rather we can observe how foreign savings affected balanced-growth outputs and prices of production - in the counterfactual experiment which sets foreign savings equal to zero (Column 2 of Table 4.1 and Column 3 of Table 4.2 for 1966). This is equivalent to a fall in the barter terms of trade since it requires more than one bundle of exports to buy a bundle of imports - imports become more expensive. Similarly we can see the effect of foreign aid on outputs and prices. Both of these operate in the same direction and their influence is more apparent if we examine the combined effect (Column 3 of Table 4.1, Columns 4 and 6 of Table 4.2, both for 1966).

---

[19]FEER Yearbook (1981, p179) and ESY (1981, p235). Between 1964 and 1980 the won was devalued against the US dollar by 158 percent; between 1960 and 1980 by 1220 percent (ESY, 1981, p235).

On the output side there are three striking facts for 1966. Firstly, the elimination of foreign aid and loans does not affect the optimal output proportion of the foreign sector significantly, which is to say that, while import ratios remain constant, there is a similar shift into more import-dependent and less import-dependent sectors. Secondly, Column 6 of Table 4.2 shows that most of the export-oriented sectors would have had to expand their shares of output significantly if balanced growth were to prevail when foreign savings and foreign aid are set to zero. Each of the textiles group, fisheries, other minerals, rubber, miscellaneous manufactures and transport and storage expand their optimal output shares substantially. In other words, positive deviations are turned into large negative deviations. This is no surprise since the payments gap must be spanned by additional exports. However there are some sectors that are significant exporters whose optimal outputs in fact decline in relative importance, in particular metal products and electrical machinery. This is easily explained, for these are the sectors which rely heavily on imports in their total inputs and supply. The export earnings of the latter sectors do not compensate for their drain on foreign exchange. In sum, exporting sectors expand while import-dependent sectors contract. The upshot of this is that, given the efforts to expand export production in the mid-sixties which implied that export industries were producing at a maximum, the growth of the economy was heavily dependent on inflows of foreign savings and foreign aid. Without these inflows and assuming the economy *could* make the structural adjustments necessary, the model's solution shows that the maximal growth rate falls from 10.58 to 7.65 percent without foreign savings and to 5.57 percent without foreign savings and foreign aid.

This brings us to the third point. The key building sector, which was shown to suffer from severe underproduction, now significantly overproduces compared with its optimal share on the long-run growth path. In other words, the demand for building would be much less on the optimal growth path if foreign savings were eliminated. Its deviation changes from -13.7 percent for the base run to +11.9 percent in the case of zero foreign savings and foreign aid, and the nonmetallic mineral products sector follows suit with its deviation rising from -9.5 to +5.1 percent. This is because the export sectors which expand under the new regime have lower-than-average capital-output ratios (see Appendix B, Table B.1). Overall the effects of the hypothesized changes on the output proportions indicate the profound influence which the external orientation of the Korean economy had on its internal structure both directly and indirectly.

The pattern to emerge from the changing prices of production in the case of zero foreign savings can be seen from Column 2 of Table 4.1. The production prices of primary products fall significantly - improving the agricultural terms of trade - while manufacturing production prices generally rise, with the biggest increases recorded in fibre spinning, textile fabrics, lumber and ply, rubber, iron and steel, steel products and fabricated metal products. All of these were heavily dependent on imported inputs and their rising production prices reflect the sharp increase in the production price of imports. They are also export industries (with the exception of iron and steel) and rising prices in these industries pay for the falling prices of agricultural products and the substantial falls in the optimal prices of services - especially trade, transport and various government services. Those export sectors which rely heavily on imports are in an ambiguous position for as foreign exchange earners their prices need to rise while as foreign exchange spenders their relative prices should fall. In fact the setting of foreign aid and savings to zero puts prices of production much closer to their long-run equilibrium levels with the average deviation of prices falling from 7.8 in the base run to 4.7 in the new situation. It must be said, however, that some of the 'equilibrating' occurs in the value-added sectors and the foreign trade sector in particular.

The price of production of imports rises sharply from .73 to 1.01 in the case of zero foreign savings since foreign savings are recorded as 'profits'. The 'undervaluation' of the exchange rate (imports 'too expensive') in the base run is thus eradicated when foreign savings are nil. The major impact of the setting of foreign aid to zero is on the government sector since the government, by assumption, must expand its deficit to accommodate the reduction in aid.[20]

In 1978 foreign aid was nil and foreign savings formed a much smaller portion of imports, so that the elimination of foreign savings (Columns 3, 5, and 7 in Table 4.5) has little impact on either balanced-growth output proportions or prices of production. So far as changes do occur they mirror almost exactly those for 1966 and discussed above, viz. production prices of agriculture and services fall while those of manufactures rise; export sectors expand their optimal output proportions while import-dependent capital goods-producing sectors decline relatively. The optimal output of the foreign sector remains more or less constant while the slight 'undervaluation' of the exchange rate is turned into an overvaluation when foreign savings are set to zero.[21] The average price deviation does not decline significantly with the elimination of foreign savings although the output deviation falls a little. On the whole, ending reliance on foreign savings would not have generated an optimal path much closer to that of the actual economy (unlike in 1968) and the long-run potential growth rate in 1978 falls from 11.20 in the base run to 10.03 when foreign savings are nil.

It has been suggested in the previous section that the Korean exchange rate in 1966 was 'undervalued' (by 37 percent) as against the long-run comparative dynamic growth path reflecting the intense pressure to export. In other words, imports were more expensive than necessary for the reproduction of the economy at its prices of production, and this result was due to the high level of foreign savings required to finance imports. There was also in this year a very substantial 'overproduction' of imports, indicative of the heavy reliance of domestic industries on imports of intermediate and capital goods.

---

[20]Since we have assumed that in the absence of foreign aid the government would have had to borrow the difference to pay its bills and that this borrowing would raise its indebtedness (a negative surplus), the 'price' of government services is now even further below its optimum (Column 3, Table 4.1). Moreover, the elimination of foreign aid means that its relative output declines substantially too.

[21]In the base run, actual prices of imports are marginally above their 'prices of production' partly reflecting the level of foreign savings. So from the perspective of the equalization of profit rates in every sector - including the foreign sector - imports are too expensive and the exchange rate is undervalued. Setting foreign savings equal to zero raises the price of production of imports so that actual prices are further from those necessary for profit equalization. This represent an imaginary revaluation.

4.2 Value-Added Sectors

We have argued previously that because of the construction of the SAMs used to solve the model and the nature of the price results for value-added sectors, we must approach the interpretation of the results for these sectors with great caution. On the basis of the output solutions of Tables 4.2 and 4.5, there was a slight underproduction of labourers in 1966 (-1.2 percent) indicating that the real economy was less labour-intensive than it would have been on the long-run optimal path so that on the latter there may have emerged some excess demand for labour. However, and particularly in the light of the huge levels of unemployment in the Korean economy at the time, we can conclude that there would have been essentially no labour constraint in switching to the optimal long-run path. But while this may have been so for labour in general, a disaggregation of labour by skill categories would reveal serious shortages of most types of skilled labour since optimal growth would have required major expansion of those industries which are relatively skill-intensive (the machinery and metal industries in particular). This effect would have persisted with 1978 technology though with lesser intensity because the output of the more skill-intensive sectors more nearly approached their optimal levels in that year. The slight excess of labour demand in 1966 on the long-run optimal path (an excess demand relative to the optimal demand not relative to the actual supply) is turned into a shortfall on the 1978 optimal path indicating a long-run decline in excess labour demand.

On the other hand, the optimal path would leave some numbers of self-employed workers redundant. The sectors which would expand greatly on the optimal path (the machinery and metal industries and the building sector) coupled with the decline of the labour-intensive export industries (the textile group and miscellaneous manufactures) would demand slightly more wage-labourers and fewer self-employed workers. In fact the distribution of labour of both types was changing rapidly in the mid-sixties with large-scale rural-urban migration transferring workers from the agricultural pool of underemployed to the industrial pool of factory workers and urban unemployed (see Chapter 2). Unemployment was endemic, but since our solutions reflect only labour demand this does not show up in the results. As a by-product of the fixed coefficients assumption and the bumper rice crop of 1966 the results do not fully reflect the relative decline of agriculture and (with wholesale and retail trade) the concomitant decline of the self-employed. Overstaffing appears small; but, given the greatly diminished role of the self-employed sector between 1966 and 1978, it is significant that this same level of overstaffing reappears in the 1978 results.

In the cases of the three value-added sectors (labour, the self-employed and capitalists' consumption) the price solutions for 1966 of Table 4.1 would be identical if the 'technology' for producing them, i.e. consumption patterns, were the same. In fact although we have made the empirical assumption that the distribution of consumption among the 39 productive sectors and imports is the same for each class of consumer, they differ in their consumptions of government services (taxes) and savings rates (see Appendix A, Table A.2). In part, labour is underpriced because of its negative savings rate, self-employed workers are overpriced because of their positive savings (which are allocated away in the solution process) and capitalists-as-consumers are underpriced because government services are underpriced (capitalists spend a quarter of their consumption fund on taxes). If savings and tax rates were equalized, each of these three sectors would be underpriced if the major items of consumption (grains, other agriculture, processed food, clothing, housing, domestic trade and social services) were underpriced in the optimal solution. If we do this experiment we find a price of production for each of the three consuming sectors of 1.025. The same comment applies to the pricing of the government sector although that underpricing in 1966 was mainly due to the underpricing of labour on which it spent a third of its income.

In 1978 the main items of consumer spending were the same as in 1966 with the addition of beverages and tobacco, and all of these are overpriced or nearly so (Table 4.5, Column 6). This fact (combined with the now significant levels of savings from the labouring and self-employed classes) brought about substantial overpricing of wage-labour and self-employed labour in 1978. On the optimal path wages and self-employed income would have been considerably lower.

Since imports did not form a large component of consumption in any of the three private consuming sectors, the direct effect of setting foreign savings equal to nil in 1966, and thus the elimination of the gross overpricing of imports, is limited (Table 4.1, Column 2). However, the production prices of the consuming sectors did fall a little as a result of the lower relative prices of major consumer items especially grain, other agriculture, housing and social services. The same effect is observable in 1978 (Table 4.5, Column 7) but operates with diminished force because of the decline of the contribution of foreign savings to investible surplus. In 1966 the effect of setting foreign savings to zero on the optimal price of government services is dominated by the fall in the production price of labour and this result is repeated in 1978 when wages still formed nearly a quarter of government spending.

4.3 Growth Rates

How do computed maximum long-run growth rates compare with the actual performance of the Korean economy in the base years? The computed growth rates of GDO can be compared with the official growth rates of GDP by first noticing the following points:

1. We must assume that intermediate inputs were growing in the base years at the same rate as GDP. This is probably an accurate assumption given the slow pace of technical change - not much happens in a year - although to the extent that intermediate input-saving technical change does occur our calculated growth rates will be less than the reported rates, ceteris paribus.

2. The model's growth solutions are calculated on the assumption that every sector grows at the same rate, so that the rates of growth of domestic output (i.e. excluding imports) of the 39 productive sectors are all equal to the maximal growth rate. This allows us to make a direct comparison with official growth rates of GDP (which of course exclude imports). On the other hand, since the model's foreign sector has a computed growth rate equal to that of the domestic sectors it is just as valid to compare the maximum growth rate with the actual growth rate of GDP plus imports. We do both.

3. Certain elements of consumption which were included in the model in

order to make the SAMs consistent are not apparent in the official estimation of GDP. These include taxes and government wage payments. However, these are in fact counted in government consumption and worker's consumption respectively as the receiving and then spending sectors.

Table 4-8: Computed and actual growth rates

	Maximum growth rate	Growth rate of GDP* - constant prices	Growth rate of GDP + imports - constant prices
1965	-	7.32	8.08
1966	10.58	12.85	19.08
1967	-	8.09	13.01
Average (weighted)		10.30	15.15
1977	-	10.05	14.01
1978	11.20	11.33	16.90
1979	-	7.09	7.61
Average (weighted)		10.40	14.48

* The 1965 growth rate is the percentage increase in GDP from 1964 to 1965, etc.

Sources: ESY, 1970, Table 6(II), p13; ESY, 1981, Table 148(II), p279.

4.4 Technical Change

We can use the model to analyse growth and structure by explaining changes in the growth rate and structure of outputs between 1966 and 1978 by reference to changes in technology which occurred between the two base years. The essential concept was developed and applied in detail by Carter (1970), and her application - which relies on straightforward input-output analysis rather than a general equilibrium model - is undoubtedly better for structural analysis than the one to be tried here. The reason is simply that her method compares actual outputs under various assumptions about technical change, while the present model generates optimal output proportions (under the same assumptions) and these may deviate considerably from actual proportions. Since part of our purpose is to explore the possibilities of the model we persist with the latter, and note that it has the advantage of allowing the direct breakdown of the growth rate into its technical components (albeit the optimal growth rate) as well as calculation of the impact of technical change on relative prices of production.

The method requires us first to revalue the 1966 flow and capital stock matrices in 1978 prices so as to eliminate the effects of price changes on technical coefficients. In theory we should account for price changes in each element of the matrices, particularly since each sector is an aggregate of industries and the output composition of sales to other sectors will change over time. However this is impossible in practice and we make the usual assumption that the price of the output of each sector changes uniformly for each purchasing sector. We have nevertheless been able to make one important exception to this; the price index of each sector's exports, in contrast to sales on the domestic market, is calculated separately. It was also necessary to calculate price indices for the import bundle, for wage-labour and self-employed labour, and for the dummy inputs government services and capitalists' consumption. In the case of labour, coefficient changes between 1966 and 1978 are due to three factors: i) changes in labour productivity, ii) inflation which alters the money level of wages relative to other products, and iii) changes in real wages. We want to capture the effects of changes in productivity and real wages separately and so we compute solutions for labour coefficient changes accounting only for productivity growth (i.e. 1978 real wages with 1966 productivity) and for both productivity and real wage changes together (1966 real wages with 1966 productivity). The prices indices for domestic and export sales of the 39 domestic sectors, for the foreign sector, for the government sector and the labour, self-employed and capitalists' consumption appear with explanation in Appendix C, Table C.4.

The procedure is then to calculate 1978 growth rates and output proportions (and production prices although these will not receive as much attention) on the assumption that various parts of the whole technology had not changed between 1966 and 1978. These assumed technical 'fossils' can be taken singly or together. We do not tamper with the 'technology' used in producing the 'final demand' outputs of the model since we are asking what levels (proportions) of sectoral outputs would be necessary to generate the 1978 levels of final demand under the various assumptions about technical change. For example one might ask what the 1978 growth rate would have been if the 1966 import coefficients, or the 1966 labour coefficients, or the 1966 intermediate technology had not changed between 1966 and 1978. By asking such questions we can see how the various components of technical change have contributed to the 1978 growth rate and to changes in the structure of outputs and relative prices. Care must be taken, however, to remember that we are dealing with *optimal* growth rates and *optimal* output proportions and prices of production.

Growth rate analysis

The maximal balanced growth rates under various assumptions about technical change between 1966 and 1978 appear in Table 4.9 below.

It should be no surprise to note firstly that the increased import dependence between 1966 and 1978 has, *ceteris paribus*, retarded the growth rate. The *ceteris paribus* condition is crucial, however, since clearly the whole progress of industrial development has depended on imported inputs and much of it would have been impossible without them. The next result shows an opposite effect and is more meaningful. Technical progress which has reduced markedly the relative contribution of intermediate inputs to production has been instrumental in sustaining rapid growth rates in Korea. Without such savings in intermediate inputs the 1978 optimal growth rate would have been more than halved to 5.14 percent. The fourth row of the table shows that this last-mentioned technical progress has outweighed the retarding effect of increased import dependence although the two are certainly related in that increased imports of certain

Table 4-9:   Effects of technical change on the growth rate

		Maximal growth rate in 1978
(1)	Base run	11.20
(2)	With 1966 import coefficients	13.94
(3)	With 1966 intermediate technical coefficients (domestically produced intermediate goods only)	5.14
(4)	(2) and (3)	8.15
(5)	(2) and (3) and with 1966 capital coefficients	11.38
(6)	With 1966 labour productivity & 1966 real wages	6.49
(7)	With 1966 labour productivity & 1978 real wages	-12.06

intermediate (and capital) goods have allowed the employment of technologies more sparing in their use of domestically produced intermediate inputs. The next result, in Row 5 above, takes this a step further in that it reflects in addition the increased capital-intensity of production which has in itself made high growth rates more difficult to achieve. Increases in fixed capital have been essential in that the new technologies embodied in new capital goods have permitted savings on intermediate inputs, but taken alone they have lowered the growth rate.

It is of interest to observe, comparing Rows 1 and 5 of Table 4.9, that the combined effect of technical changes in the application of material inputs, domestic and imported, intermediate and capital, to production has barely affected the optimal growth rate at all. Such has not been the case with human inputs into production. This is dramatically revealed in Row 6, from which we may conclude that, *ceteris paribus*, if the increases in labour productivity that marked the period between 1966 and 1978 had not occurred and if the real wage had stayed at its 1966 level then 1978 would have had a maximum balanced growth rate of 6.49 percent. If the levels of labour productivity had stayed at their 1966 levels but the real wage had risen to the 1978 level then the maximum balanced growth rate would have been negative and the Korean economy would not have been viable. Technical progress has been intermediate input-saving, fixed capital-using and import-using, but above all it has been labour-saving. It is not obvious to what extent rising wage costs have induced labour-saving technical progress and to what extent the latter has itself, by using more-skilled labour, caused wages to rise.

Structural change

The output and price results for the counterfactual experiments with technical change appear in Tables 4.10 and 4.11. Dealing first with outputs, we can see that the increased import dependence involved in the transition from 1966 to 1978 technology affected the optimal output structure significantly (see Column 2 of Table 4.10). In particular it caused declines in the output shares (i.e. with the 1966 import coefficients output in 1978 would have been higher) of the capital goods-producing sectors especially nonelectrical (general) machinery and building and the industries which supply these sectors (other minerals, nonmetallic mineral products, iron and steel products). The expansion of demand between 1966 and 1978 would have required these domestic industries to supply considerably more if it had not

Table 4-10: Experiments with technical change - outputs[a]

	(1) 1978	(2) m	(3) a	(4) a,m	(5) a,m,b	(6) labour
1 Grain	3.61	3.69	5.12	5.27	5.34	4.16
2 Otherag	3.28	3.31	6.99	7.03	7.09	3.72
3 Forest	0.35	0.35	0.60	0.64	0.64	0.37
4 Fishery	0.92	0.89	1.27	1.24	1.24	0.99
5 Coal	0.28	0.29	0.83	0.83	0.82	0.27
6 Othmin	0.38	0.41	1.60	1.72	1.67	0.31
7 Profood	2.86	2.87	2.81	2.82	2.85	3.21
8 Bevstob	1.84	1.87	2.03	2.08	2.10	2.06
9 Fibresp	1.47	1.32	0.91	0.78	0.75	1.40
10 Textfab	1.47	1.32	0.99	0.85	0.82	1.42
11 Fintext	2.35	2.12	2.10	1.83	1.78	2.31
12 Lumply	0.71	0.72	0.59	0.61	0.62	0.58
13 Woodpro	0.13	0.13	0.18	0.19	0.20	0.13
14 Pulpap	0.59	0.60	0.59	0.60	0.60	0.58
15 Print	0.28	0.28	0.33	0.33	0.33	0.30
16 Leather	0.63	0.56	0.56	0.48	0.47	0.60
17 Rubber	0.67	0.62	0.51	0.44	0.43	0.64
18 Baschem	0.64	0.62	0.42	0.41	0.39	0.62
19 Othchem	2.29	2.24	1.12	1.12	1.11	2.31
20 Chfert	0.38	0.37	0.17	0.15	0.15	0.40
21 Petcopr	2.42	2.43	2.35	2.37	2.35	2.36
22 Nonmet	1.05	1.14	0.85	0.96	0.99	0.82
23 Irost	0.96	1.00	0.29	0.29	0.28	0.74
24 Steelpr	1.68	1.75	0.89	0.90	0.88	1.32
25 Nonferm	0.32	0.33	0.51	0.52	0.46	0.27
26 Fabrmet	0.78	0.75	0.48	0.43	0.42	0.69
27 Nonelm	1.11	1.31	0.60	0.77	0.97	0.73
28 Elmach	2.97	3.10	1.77	1.81	1.55	2.50
29 Transeq	2.20	2.37	1.50	1.72	1.40	1.61
30 Miscman	0.90	0.80	1.20	1.10	1.09	0.87
31 Build	5.32	6.22	3.32	4.29	4.62	3.81
32 Trade	5.30	5.37	6.01	6.11	6.37	5.19
33 Transto	3.01	2.93	3.11	3.02	3.05	3.00
34 Fininre	2.35	2.39	1.78	1.80	1.79	2.48
35 Electr	0.90	0.91	0.54	0.54	0.53	0.88
36 Water	0.07	0.07	0.09	0.09	0.09	0.07
37 Commun	0.40	0.40	0.34	0.34	0.34	0.41
38 Socserv	4.50	4.58	4.79	4.89	4.86	4.83
39 Other	1.34	1.36	1.84	1.88	1.88	1.26
40 Foreign	9.02	7.35	6.93	4.94	4.67	7.97
41 Labour	10.22	10.49	10.36	10.69	10.72	13.54
42 Selfem	7.55	7.67	11.08	11.28	11.46	8.22
43 Capscon	5.49	5.58	5.17	5.28	5.30	5.26
44 Govern	5.01	5.11	4.46	4.57	4.54	4.83
Growth rate	11.20	13.94	5.14	8.15	11.38	6.49

a. Each of these six columns represents the output proportions which would have prevailed in 1978 under various assumptions about technical change: (1) with complete 1978 technology; (2) with 1966 import coefficients; (3) with 1966 (domestic) intermediate coefficients; (4) with 1966 import & domestic intermediate coefficients; (5) with 1966 import & domestic intermediate & capital coefficients; (6) with 1966 labour coefficients at 1966 real wages (i.e.) accounting for productivity changes but not changes in the real wage.

been for the growth of imports. Since these were the sectors which were underproducing to the greatest extent in 1978 (see Table 4.5) it is highly unlikely that domestic industry could have satisfied such an increase in demand.

On the other hand, several sectors would have had a diminished share of output if the lower 1966 level of imported intermediate inputs had prevailed in 1978. These were the textiles group, leather, rubber and miscellaneous manufacturing whose relative outputs would have been about 10 percent less. All of these were in fact overproducing a little in 1978. Their shares would have declined because they were important exporters in 1978 and exporting would have been much less important if import dependence had remained stable. The final major change to be noticed is in the foreign sector which shows that the relative share of imports would have been nearly 20 percent less under the old regime.

Changes in the structure of domestically produced intermediate inputs also had a major impact (see Column 3, Table 4.10). To begin with the obvious effects, the transition from 1966 to 1978 intermediate technology involved very large expansions (in some cases the doubling) of the relative shares of the chemical industries, iron and steel products, fabricated metal products, electricity, and finance, insurance and real estate. Many of these were in fact underproducing in 1978 (Table 4.5) thus reflecting the great increase in demand placed on them by the new technology and by the greater emphasis of industrial policy on heavy and chemical industries.

The new intermediate technology also had a major impact on the capital goods-producing sectors (including building), causing them to expand their output shares considerably in 1978. This is probably because those intermediate inputs suppliers which expand have higher capital-output ratios than those sectors which decline.

As for the declining sectors, there is an unexpected result here. Comparing Columns 1 and 3 of Table 4.10, by far the biggest falls in relative outputs caused by the transition to the new intermediate technology occur in the primary producing sectors - the shares of agriculture (Sectors 1 and 2) and forestry are halved while that of mining (Sectors 5 and 6) is reduced by three quarters. These are radical cuts indeed. In the case of mining this is due to the substitution of oil for coal in power generation and the fact that oil is imported. In the case of agriculture note only that between 1966 and 1978 there were not marked changes in the proportions of domestic product which went to intermediate rather than final demand (around 15 percent for grains and 36 percent for other agriculture in both years). The fall in their shares remains a puzzle.

The rapid fall in the agricultural share of output in response to changes in intermediate technology carried with it a large decline in demand for self-employed labour, predominantly farmers but also shopkeepers in the domestic trade sector which also declines.

The effect of changes in intermediate technology on the foreign sector is to increase its share substantially because of the increase in import dependence which is implicit in the technical change. In fact we can see (Column 4 of Table 4.10) that the combined effect of changes in intermediate technology and intermediate import requirements is almost to double the share of imports in gross output.

More generally, the combined effects of technical change in domestic and imported intermediate goods often reinforce each other, but when they operate in different directions the domestic changes are dominant (Column 4).

Technical change in fixed capital requirements does not have marked effects on the structure of outputs (Column 5, Table 4.10). Comparing Columns 4 and 5 of

Table 4.10 the biggest impact of the new capital coefficients is, not surprisingly, on the machinery sectors and less so on the building sector and the import sector. The shares of these sectors rise with the new technology reflecting higher capital-output ratios, except for building and, notably, non-electrical (general) machinery whose share perversely drops by a quarter. This cannot be explained by changes in the share of general machinery in sectoral total capital stocks since we applied the same proportions in 1978 to distribute sectoral stocks to each type of asset that were used in 1966 (see Appendix B). The reason for the falling share is firstly that domestic production provided only 35 percent of the 1978 total supply of general machinery (compared with 74 and 72 percent for electrical machinery and transport equipment respectively - see Table C.6) so that the increased capital requirements will not in themselves have had a major impact on the share of this sector. It may be that the rise in the share of imports with the new technology causes the shares of more import-dependent capital goods sectors to rise.

In the experiments with labour coefficients we have reported the output and price solutions only for the case of 1966 levels of productivity with 1966 levels of real wages. These appear in Columns 6 of Tables 4.10 and 4.11. The solutions with 1978 levels of real wages contain negative values which have no economic meaning.

The first influence of the rise in labour productivity is to reduce the share of labour in GDO from a hypothetical 13.54 percent to 10.22 percent and this is indicative of the labour-saving nature of this technical change. The second is to raise sharply the shares of the machine industries, the building sector and their supplying industries (sectors 22-29 and 31). This reflects the rising capital intensity associated with increasing labour productivity and the heavier demands for fixed capital relative to labour. This has follow-on effects on imports so much of which have been capital goods.

As in our experiment with intermediate inputs (Column 3) the sectors whose shares fall as a result of the technical change, this time labour-saving, are the agricultural (but not mining) ones and processed food. This is because the share of labour with the new, 1978, labour coefficients is much reduced and this is translated into reduced demand for consumption goods. This also affects beverages and tobacco, printing, finance, insurance and real estate and social services.

Price effects

The price results, reported in Table 4.11, throw further light on structural changes. Comparing Columns 1 and 2 we can see that the impact on relative prices of production of the increase in import dependence between 1966 and 1978. In some sectors the degree of overpricing declines substantially with the new import coefficients (i.e. the prices of production rise with the new import coefficients of Column 1 compared with the 1966 import coefficients used to calculate Column 2). This is especially so for leather products, petroleum and coal products, and processed food, and these are sectors which became much more reliant on imported inputs and were faced with bigger import bills which in turn ate into profits. Those which diminished their reliance on imported inputs due to the growth of import-substituting industries - especially fibre spinning, textile fabrics, rubber products and fabricated metal products - made up for their earlier underpricing (i.e. their prices of production fall with the new import structure). Once again, however, the *ceteris paribus* condition is crucial, for an increased reliance on imported inputs is

Table 4-11: Experiments with technical change - prices[a]

	(1) 1978	(2) m	(3) a	(4) a,m	(5) a,m,b	(6) labour
1 Grain	0.93	0.94	0.82	0.85	0.85	0.86
2 Otherag	0.90	0.89	0.71	0.71	0.71	0.83
3 Forest	0.93	0.95	0.91	0.94	0.95	0.99
4 Fishery	1.16	1.10	0.82	0.79	0.66	0.89
5 Coal	1.06	1.02	0.86	0.82	0.80	0.79
6 Othmin	0.97	0.96	0.65	0.66	0.61	0.68
7 Profood	1.00	0.89	1.27	1.18	1.16	0.96
8 Bevstob	0.95	0.91	1.63	1.60	1.63	1.02
9 Fibresp	1.08	1.42	1.04	1.37	1.44	1.19
10 Textfab	1.09	1.33	1.03	1.26	1.29	1.21
11 Fintext	1.03	1.14	0.83	0.87	0.87	1.10
12 Lumply	1.00	0.89	1.05	0.95	0.93	0.99
13 Woodpro	1.03	1.00	1.08	1.05	1.03	1.04
14 Pulpap	1.03	0.96	1.04	0.98	0.98	1.04
15 Print	1.04	1.06	1.17	1.19	1.16	1.18
16 Leather	0.97	0.62	1.04	0.68	0.67	0.96
17 Rubber	1.03	1.52	1.58	2.01	2.02	1.36
18 Baschem	1.13	1.00	0.80	0.81	0.79	1.09
19 Othchem	1.02	1.01	1.11	1.12	1.14	1.10
20 Chfert	1.24	1.15	0.76	0.73	0.66	1.16
21 Petcopr	1.10	0.64	1.10	0.64	0.54	1.03
22 Nonmet	1.07	1.03	1.09	1.06	1.04	1.00
23 Irost	1.25	1.38	1.45	1.56	1.51	1.20
24 Steelpr	1.21	1.26	1.00	1.02	0.96	1.19
25 Nonferm	1.03	0.92	1.97	1.89	1.87	1.05
26 Fabrmet	1.09	1.27	1.44	1.59	1.58	1.29
27 Nonelm	1.05	0.98	0.85	0.77	0.75	1.06
28 Elmach	0.99	1.04	1.90	1.90	1.90	1.30
29 Transeq	1.04	0.99	1.14	1.06	1.05	1.15
30 Miscman	1.00	0.95	0.72	0.67	0.65	0.99
31 Build	1.00	1.00	1.07	1.05	1.02	1.06
32 Trade	0.91	0.91	0.75	0.77	0.80	0.82
33 Transto	1.54	1.56	1.15	1.18	1.03	1.33
34 Fininre	0.87	0.86	0.81	0.80	0.81	0.87
35 Electr	1.83	1.85	1.73	1.80	1.64	1.68
36 Water	1.83	2.01	1.27	1.48	1.30	1.76
37 Commun	1.10	1.17	1.02	1.10	1.15	1.14
38 Socserv	1.05	1.08	0.96	0.99	1.16	1.03
39 Other	1.10	1.05	0.98	0.95	0.99	1.06
40 Foreign	0.99	1.02	0.99	1.01	0.99	1.02
41 Labour	0.87	0.87	0.87	0.87	0.88	0.85
42 Selfem	0.83	0.82	0.82	0.82	0.83	0.80
43 Capscon	0.99	0.99	0.99	0.99	1.01	0.99
44 Govern	0.95	0.95	0.95	0.94	0.97	1.00

a. For explanation of column headings see Table 4.10.

generally offset by a diminished reliance on domestically produced intermediate inputs (as in the cases of leather products and, less so, processed food and petroleum and coal products) (Column 4 of Table 4.11). The obverse is not equally true, i.e. those which are less reliant on imported inputs also save on domestic inputs (rubber products and fabricated metal products). These reflect respectively the process of substituting imported for domestic inputs when the latter are scarce and the general process of technical change which economizes on all intermediate inputs.

The sectors which appear to have profited most from the technical changes in intermediate inputs (domestic and imported) - those which have become more overpriced or less underpriced - are beverages and tobacco, rubber products, nonferrous metals and electrical machinery; those to have suffered most were fishery, other minerals, leather products, chemical fertilizers, petroleum and coal products, nonelectrical machinery and miscellaneous manufactures. Column 5 shows that if, in addition to technical change in domestic and imported intermediate inputs, we account for technical change in fixed capital and thus for all material inputs, the changes in sectoral over and underpricing discussed immediately above are only reinforced.

The price effects of the new levels of labour productivity are recorded in Column 6 of Table 4.11. Note first that there is little change in the production price of labour since the overall effect of price changes of consumption goods is neutral. The new levels of labour productivity cause the prices of production of capital goods to decline, especially that of electrical machinery, and this is indicative of the degree of labour-saving technical change in these sectors. Significant price falls are also recorded in rubber, printing, and fabricated metal products while those sectors which substantially increased their relative reliance on labour were fisheries, the mining industries and transport and storage.

4.5 Wage-Profit Frontiers

By varying the number of bundles of consumer goods necessary to produce one worker (i.e. the real wage, c_w) we can observe the response of the maximal profit rate and construct wage-profit frontiers for the base years (as discussed in Section 6 of Chapter 3). Since the computed maximal profit rates are very near the actual rates around 1966 and 1978, these frontiers are probably quite close to the actual trade-offs which characterized the Korean economy in those years. The frontiers appear below with the number of workers' consumption bundles on the vertical axis and the maximal profit rate on the horizontal axis. Since the composition of the workers' consumption bundles in 1966 and 1978 differed, strictly speaking the two frontiers should not be put on the same axes.

We can make the following observations.

1. The maximum attainable rate of profit, r(max) (i.e. the highest maximal profit rate when c_w is allowed to vary and $c_w = 0$) declines from 36.8 percent in 1966 to 24.2 percent in 1978. Put another way, if we evaluate aggregate capital and net output (here referring to wage and profit income only) at prices of production then the capital-net

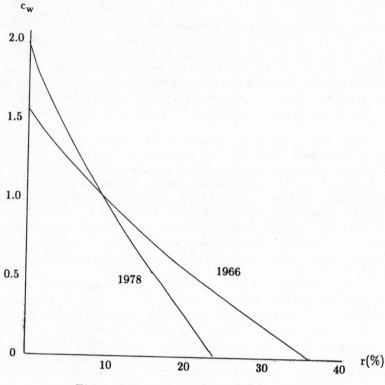

Figure 4-1: Wage-profit frontiers

output ratio rose from 2.72 to 4.13 between 1966 and 1978.[22] These profit rates are net of capitalists' consumption and refer only to earnings retained for investment.

2. The net output per worker, $c_w(\text{max})$ (i.e. when $r = 0$) rose from 1.54 in 1966 to 1.94 in 1978 when evaluated at prices of production. This reflects the marked increase in labour productivity in the intervening period and also indicates that, because in each case the real wage was one consumption bundle, workers were more exploited in 1978 even though the 1978 consumption bundle satisfied more of the workers' needs.

3. Putting the results of the above two paragraphs together gives us measures of capital-labour ratios. For 1966 the capital-labour ratio was 4.19 and this had risen to 8.02 in 1978.

4. In both years the curves are slightly convex so that we have a positive price Wicksell effect - the lower is the rate of profit the higher is the

---

[22]See Sekerka et al. (1970, pp188-89) on these relations.

value of capital per worker.[23]

4.6 The Results Summarized

Overall, several major conclusions emerge. While discussion of their more general significance will be deferred until the final chapter, it will be useful to provide a summary here. Firstly, the actual rate of growth was quite close to the long-run, balanced rate in both 1966 and 1978, although there were very substantial structural shifts and transfers of surplus occurring, especially in the sixties.

One of the essential points to emerge through analysis of the results is the importance of government manipulation of relative prices across the economy in order to influence the industrial structure in a particular direction. At the broadest level this took the form of squeezing agriculture to support and encourage manufacturing, and especially export-oriented industry. This reflected the primary emphasis of government long-run economic policy on the foreign sector and the fundamental importance of supplies of foreign exchange to continued growth.

The importance of exports to the economy often overrode the fact that export goods were not profitable for exporters unassisted by government subsidies. This was confirmed by the counterfactual experiments which demonstrated the heavy dependence of the growth rate and the industrial structure on continued flows of foreign savings and foreign aid, although this dependence (if not the dependence on imports) had diminished in the late seventies.

The growth process in South Korea was rapid and unbalanced, reflecting the great pace of structural transformation. Much emphasis was placed on the expansion of export sectors. Several key sectors had great difficulty keeping up with the growth of demand. This was particularly evident in the capital goods-producing sectors and those sectors which directly supplied them. These bottlenecks were indicative not only of the dependence of fast-growing manufacturing industries on capital goods *per se*, but also of the severe restrictions on importation. In an environment of serious rationing of foreign exchange, capital goods sectors which relied heavily on imports (for inputs and to supplement domestic supply) suffered the highest levels of underproduction. However, as industrialization progressed, these output 'distortions' lessened and the industrial structure became more stable.

The experiments with technical change reveal the very heavy reliance of continued growth and rising living standards on increasing labour productivity. The technologies associated with the big rises in labour productivity depended largely on imports of capital goods. Korea became increasingly dependent on imports of capital goods in the seventies. This meant that the rising expectations of the working class, associated with rising rural living standards, required continued export expansion, since only exports could provide the foreign exchange necessary to buy the capital goods essential to labour productivity growth.

---

[23]See Harcourt (1972, p41). Sekerka et al. (1970, pp195-98) derive for the 1966 Czech economy a frontier which is akin to the wage-profit frontier of a capitalist economy. The vertical axis represents the mark-up on wage costs and the horizontal axis the mark-up on fixed capital costs. Their curve is also slightly convex.

4.7 The Model Assessed

The process of construction and implementation of the model has revealed several serious limitations which must be recognized. They relate overwhelmingly to the foreign sector for it is there that the closure of the model is most artificial. It is very difficult to handle and interpret a foreign sector, the prices of which are inherently exogenous, as an endogenous industry with a produced output and a price determined largely within the domestic economy ('largely' rather than wholly because import and export prices enter into the determination of the coefficients which form part of the data of the solution process). In particular, the endogeneity of export prices (which in many economies differ from the domestic prices of the same commodity) is not easy to capture. We have ended up by calculating average prices. These can only be approximations. The iterative procedure of Appendix E, however, can largely overcome this problem and provide more precise solutions.

The second major problem that arises in the foreign sector concerns the treatment of foreign savings, for this has a major effect on the (endogenous) exchange rate which in turn has a big impact on relative prices. The structure of the reduced form model, which solves augmented matrices in an eigenequation (see Appendix E), compels us to treat the foreign sector as if it were a producing sector like the domestic industries - at least, the solution process treats the foreign sector this way. But, apart from the limitations associated with the assumption that there is only one (composite) imported good, we cannot consider imports to be produced commodities like others because they are produced outside the country. As a result the capital stocks which enter into the production of imports are not produced within the country, and their inclusion would upset the output solution of the model since, while in the closed model all inputs are treated as produced inputs, domestic sectors do not supply capital goods to the foreign sector. From the theoretical point of view, the device of considering imports to be produced commodities would be correct only if the model were applied to the world economy in which there are no imports.

The solution process does not recognize this problem and allocates foreign savings, like industrial profits, on the basis of fixed capital. The foreign sector has its savings entirely allocated away and this gives the impression of overpricing (actual exchange rate greater than optimal exchange rate). There does not appear to be any way around this problem, of economies with high foreign savings, as long as we allocate surplus on the basis of fixed capital alone. This basic problem applies to the value-added sectors as well. It is not as severe there, however, since the products of the value-added sectors are in some sense produced within the domestic economy. We could resolve the problem in the case of labour, in particular, by accounting for fixed capital used in the production of both basic labour (housing, durable consumer goods, perhaps health care) and skilled labour (education). This is empirically very difficult and would involve an additional estimation of the breakdown of the wage into its subsistence and surplus components (which in itself raises a serious conceptual quandary).

The awkwardness of the foreign sector impairs the applicability of this sort of model to a country such as South Korea which is so heavily integrated into the world economy. A closed model, which tries to endogenize everything, cannot closely reproduce an economy which is subject to powerful exogenous influences.

The final problem to be mentioned here applies to all applications of the model, and we refer to the difficulty of interpreting deviations of optimal prices and outputs from their actual values. We cannot know from the model whether a sector's overpricing is due to fast growth or to the effects of monopoly (including state intervention), nor whether underproduction is due to structural decline or bottlenecks. The solution does, nevertheless, alert us to something happening which additional information, from other sources, can help to explain.

How do the model's strong assumptions affect the results? In one sense, they do not affect them. It is usual to think of assumptions as approximations to reality, and model solutions are incorrect to the extent that these approximations are inaccurate. The assumptions of the present model - in particular, those of no technical change and balanced growth - are not meant to be approximations to reality. The results, expressed as deviations of actual prices and outputs from hypothetical optima, will reflect two sets of forces, those which are due to the artificiality of the assumptions and those that would occur even if the assumptions were accurate representations of the real economy. The two effects can be distinguished only by observation of the real processes at work in the economy.

It would be possible to change the model's assumptions so that they more nearly reflected real economic processes. This would involve incorporating differential sectoral growth and profit rates, and perhaps even taking account of technical change, although empirically the latter is very difficult. Abandoning the balanced growth assumption would require a different and far more complex solution procedure. The end result of the 'more realistic' model would probably be only to obscure the distinction between the effects of the remaining assumptions and other influences on the deviations of actual oputputs and prices from their optimal levels.

Other CGE models have not been explicitly oriented towards the analysis of economic structure and the implications of economic structure for the form of industrialization. They have been more interested in the influence of policy choices on direct welfare criteria such as income distribution, employment and growth. The present model is not well-suited to these sorts of policy experiments because of its necessarily artificial assumptions in the value-added sectors. It has, nevertheless, proven itself to be extremely informative as a device for exploring the economy-wide impact of particular economic strategies. Comparison of the model's base years with the actual base years gives a measure of the structural 'distance' the economy would need to travel to get onto a hypothetical turnpike. Relative sectoral distances can alert us to structural pressures operating in the economy, and patterns of these can tell us a good deal about the sectoral ramifications of the industrialization process. In the case of South Korea, the influence of the integration of the economy into the world market has been exposed in detail. The various experiments conducted using the model have provided insights into the fundamental importance of supplies of foreign exchange and rising labour productivity to continued growth in South Korea and the industrial form that that growth has taken. The price solutions of the model locate centres of accumulation and identify patterns of surplus transfer. Moreover, the wage-profit trade-off helps us to interpret the place of distributional questions in the accumulation process.

It is true that most of the conclusions drawn from the interpretation of the model's solutions could be derived from other, less elaborate sources. The power of the present model lies in its ability to combine various and diverse statistical indicators so as to provide a coherent explanation of the industrialization process.

CHAPTER 5
The Theory of Development

The essence of the process of industrial development lies in the production and allocation of an investible surplus. The social relations on which the production of an investible surplus are based are almost invariably taken as given. We search in vain in most accounts of Third World industrial development for an analysis of the processes whereby the social relation of private capital coupled with wage labour becomes dominant. But if one fails to study the development of the social basis of accumulation in general, one cannot understand the particular forms of these social relations and the ways in which they influence the form which the industrialization process itself takes. For instance, if we fail to study the emergence of the dominance of capitalist industry over peasant-proprietor agriculture in South Korea, then we cannot understand how capital was able to profit from low agricultural prices in the sixties; nor can we understand the relationship between industrial capital and the state. The influence of the state's policies on agriculture-industry terms of trade will still be apparent, but we cannot answer *why* such a policy was pursued and why it had the effects it did. Chapter 2 is an attempt to set this right by putting the form of the development of capitalist social relations at the centre of the explanation of South Korean industrialization. However, while providing the foundations and broad structure of it, the class analysis of that chapter is not nearly adequate to explain the details of the industrialization process. The model of structural change of Chapters 3 and 4 set out to do this using only one particular empirical technique, but one which, for all of its limitations, has the convenient property of giving answers to several key questions at once. We might say that whereas the class analysis could tell us *why* capitalist industrialization in South Korea took place and what its general form was, the model can help to explain the pace of accumulation, its international context and the sectoral interrelations that characterized it.

5.1 The Role of Prices in Industrial Development

The production and allocation of investible surplus are, respectively, revealed in the dual output and price solutions of the model of Chapter 3. The price system in a capitalist economy conditions the investment process on the one hand by allocating funds to those who are able to invest and on the other hand by rewarding that investment so that it will be repeated. These are really two aspects of the same process. Prices of production in effect reallocate investible surplus so that the rewards to investment are equalized among sectors, and these are the prices relevant to a state of competitive equilibrium. There is no reason, however, to imagine that the conditions of competitive equilibrium in price markets correspond to the social structure of accumulation on which production and distribution are based. In South Korea, as we have seen, the government has intervened in a variety of important ways to usurp the ability of the price system to allocate surplus.[1] Firstly, the state has had an often determinant role in the allocation of investible surplus directly through the distribution of investment funds via cheap bank loans to favoured sectors. Of equal significance has been the influence of the state over relative prices so as to carry through by indirect means a planned pattern of investment and sectoral growth. In particular this has applied to the fixing of low agricultural prices in the sixties which were translated into higher industrial profits and investment, and to the encouragement of domestic industry (especially export industry) by allowing superprofits on sales of imported and certain domestic goods on the home market. The desired form of industrial growth, that which necessarily involved heavy integration into the world economy, has required this. The price system has been used explicitly to drive export production which has often been unprofitable, and more recently to induce expansion of heavy and chemical industries which could not compete unaided. In the case of export industries it has not been possible to use the price mechanism directly to drive up profit rates because high prices for exports would have made them uncompetitive. This has been tackled by lowering costs through subsidies, through compensatory profits on sales to the domestic market and through lowering prices of inputs by means of keeping food prices low, giving rebates on imported inputs and setting low prices for government utilities.

What does this say about the nature of prices in this sort of industrial development? If the importance of the price system is its allocative function - the placing of investible funds in certain industries - then the intervention of the state has brought about a different pattern of investments. In industries that would not have been privately profitable without state encouragement, especially exporting industries, the price mechanism has been used as an *ex post* validation of investment decisions taken on other criteria, most powerfully for reasons of foreign exchange. Far from this sort of activity dying out, our results show that price deviations increased markedly between 1966 and 1978, although the emphasis was away from draining agriculture to draining taxpayers through providing discounted utility services to industry. Although some of this increase in price deviation may be due to the growth of monopoly, it is inconsistent with the claim of neoclassical writers that government interference has been declining over the years since the early sixties.

This is not to argue that the price system has been a mere accounting tool. Apart from the fact that much investment activity has been undertaken in response to relatively uninhibited price formation, this is because in a capitalist economy which responds to financial reward the validation, *ex post* or otherwise, of investment decisions is a social necessity. The government is much less the opponent of capitalism than the prisoner of social conditions. Under centrally planned socialism where rewards can be other than financial the price system (in fact, money) can function as no more than an accounting measure, and the output

---

[1]The effectiveness of government regulation through the price mechanism is confirmed by the results of Adelman & Robinson (1978, p185) which consistently show that 'the economy adjusts to policy interventions mainly through changes in wages and prices'. They go on to observe: 'In view of the scope for substitution in both consumption and production in the model, it is surprising that wage and price effects are so dominant' (*ibid.*).

primal predominates.[2]   There may be a hint of this ultimate emasculation of the price system in Korea insofar as industrialists have been rewarded with the status of national hero for outstanding export success, although capitalism's Stakhanovites did not go profitless.

As for the function of the price system in the process of Third World development in general, one can only say that the formation of prices will reflect the features of the socio-economic structure and both influence and be influenced by changes in that structure. This view is inconsistent with a conception of societies as made up of individual utility maximizers. In practice there is nothing neutral about the price system and it is false to claim, as some neoclassical economists do, that free markets will bring about industrial development.[3]   The main effect of free markets is to reinforce, but also to change, the socio-economic structure which lies at the base of price formation, and the socio-economic structure may well be inimical to industrial development. This is the case in most Third World countries. For instance, the structure of prices may reinforce plantation agriculture, or enrich a landlord class, or put potential industrial capital into the hands of money-lenders. A radical intervention in the process of price formation may be necessary in order to strip these non-industrial classes of their control over economic assets and their political power. Moreover, a free market in labour, especially skilled labour, may drive real wages to the point where many types of industrial production become unprofitable. The intervention of the state in price formation, therefore, cannot rob the price structure of its social neutrality, since it is not neutral to begin with, but can only influence the evolution of the socio-economic structure in a direction different from that of unfettered markets. As for which direction can be judged more desirable, that depends on particular circumstances and on the class position of the judge.

The question now becomes this: Has the state's planned pattern of investment produced faster growth than the one which would have resulted if investible funds had been allocated by prices uninfluenced by the state? In the light of Korean experience, it would be difficult to justify a negative answer to this question. Rapid growth is achieved by allocating investment funds to those sectors with the highest potential productivity growth and, given the social structures and technological conditions of Korean agriculture and tertiary industries in the early sixties, this meant favouring manufacturing industry.   The government's intent is reflected in the results of Chapter 4 where the relative prices calculated for 1966 show agriculture and utilities subsidizing industry, especially export industry.

What does the relation between the price system and investment allocation tell us about the relationship between the state and capital? Does the opposition between planning and the free market represent an opposition between the state and private capital in the South Korean context? Here we must account for the conflicts between sections of capital and between the latter and other classes. We saw in Chapters 2 and 4 how industrial capital has been in danger of domination by financial capital and how industrial capital profited from the draining of

---

[2]The economic reforms in Hungary and Czechoslovakia in the sixties can be seen as the conversion of the price system into a means of validation.

[3]Others conform to the logic of the doctrine of comparative advantage and argue that there is no reason to believe that Third World countries would necessarily be better off if they industrialized.

agricultural surplus. The exertions of the state in these conflicts of interest were, broadly speaking, interventions in favour of industrial capital. The unfettered operation of the free market, insofar as larger amounts of investible surplus would have accumulated in the hands of money-lenders and peasants and thence used for further short-term lending, trading, consumption and agricultural investment, would have inhibited the accumulation of industrial capital. It should be borne in mind that the suppression of agricultural prices was not simply an intersectoral transfer of investible surplus but a suppression of the incomes and living standards of farmers and an expansion of the incomes of capitalists in manufacturing. In other words, the agricultural terms of trade are very much a class issue and reflect the configuration of class power at certain conjunctures. As was argued in Chapter 2, peasant proprietors were politically weak in the sixties and the state under Park used its strength (which it derived partly from its relative independence from particular classes) to encourage the accumulation of industrial capital.

Historically, almost every process of industrialization, capitalist and socialist, has been achieved in greater or less degree at the expense of agriculture, and this has been reflected in fierce class struggles such as those over the Corn Laws in Britain and the kulaks in the Soviet Union. The level of exploitation of the Korean peasantry has probably been fairly mild by historical comparison,[4] and quite short-lived since industrial expansion began in earnest in the early sixties and the results of Chapter 4 show that by 1978 agriculture was significantly overpriced along with industry, reflecting the changes in the agricultural terms of trade discussed in Chapter 2. This suggests that the relationship between industry and agriculture had changed. That was indeed the case, for the circumstances which conditioned the relationship had changed. In the earlier period the effects of low agricultural prices on farm output could be tolerated by industry because food imports were cheap in terms of foreign exchange and did not squeeze out industrial imports. By the early seventies, however, the phasing out of PL 480 food aid from the US, by requiring full payment for grain imports in hard currency, imposed a substantial check on the availability of foreign exchange to pay for the imports of intermediate and capital goods that were essential for continued industrial production. By 1970/71 rice imports accounted for 20 percent of total rice supply whereas no rice was imported in 1964-66 (Brown, 1973, Table 12, p119) and food imports as a proportion of the value of total imports rose from 13 percent in 1964-66 to 16 percent in 1970-72 (KSY, 1979, Table 128, p231). This did not *necessarily* mean that the interests of farmers and industrial capitalists would coincide since there are ways of expanding agricultural output which do not benefit the cultivator. However, it was decided that the most efficient way to achieve bigger output was through the price mechanism, and the results have confirmed that petty proprietors will respond to price incentives by raising output and marketed product. In the short run the latter is very important.[5] The constraint that had influenced the decision to set low agricultural terms of trade in the sixties - the need to keep industrial wages low especially in export industries - had been eased to some extent with increases in labour productivity and skill levels and changes in consumption patterns. Direct

---

[4]We refer only to the modern period of industrialization. There was nothing mild about the exploitation of the peasantry under the Japanese or the latter part of the Yi dynasty.

[5]'Because of this high degree of sensitivity of [Korean] farmers' decisions to eat or sell their rice to relatively small changes in the rice price ... a modest change in the rice or barley price produces a major change in the quantity of rice marketed' (Brown, 1973, p118).

price incentives were supplemented by continuous provision of cheap inputs, especially fertilizer, and capital works, mainly irrigation. In other countries more drastic measures have been applied including collectivization, consolidation of plots, enforced mechanization, the development of capitalist production relations on the farm through dispossession, and compulsory purchase. While elements of some of these measures have appeared in South Korea - development of wage-labour, pressure to lift the three hectare limit on land ownership, inducements to productivity improvement through intense use of fertilizers and mechanization - undoubtedly in the social and political conditions of South Korea in that period price incentives were the most effective means of boosting agricultural output.

The influence of the Korean state over the savings and investment process has extended further than the direct manipulation of prices. It has attempted by various means to gain influence over the collection of savings not only so that more private savings would be made but also so that these savings would find their way into the hands of industrial investors. The prohibition of most imports of consumer goods has deliberately aided this, but more important has been the state's control over the commercial banks and the organized money market in general, and the attempts over the years to draw the unofficial money market into organized channels. The importance of this is not simply in encouraging savings but in the control which the state, through the banks, then has over the distribution of investible funds. This led one international institution to complain of 'excessive government intervention' in industry by a system of 'directed credit operated through the financial system' (FEER, May 21, 1983, p54). 'In other words', comments the FEER correspondent, 'banks were compelled to lend large sums of money to industries centrally targeted to lead South Korea's growth drive'. We might also mention in this regard the activities of the state in inducing foreign savings in the form both of aid and loans. The state has, on the other hand, used measures other than direct price manipulation to allocate investible funds. These have taken the two main forms of distribution of bank loans at low interest rates to favoured industries and, critically, the allocation of foreign exchange to selected investors. In recognition of the importance of the latter to industrial growth, the government has required exporters to deposit all foreign exchange earnings with the central bank.

5.2 Imperialism and Capitalist Development

The debate over the effects of imperialism on Third World development has been vigorous in recent years. On the one hand the basic notion of dependency analysis is that the form of integration of peripheral countries into the world economy limits and distorts development in the periphery and makes underdeveloped countries dependent on economic activity in the centre. The periphery is underdeveloped because of this integration and lacks the capacity for autonomous growth. The more sophisticated *dependentistas* argue that the mechanism by which this works is through its effects on the domestic class structure, in particular through the creation of a comprador bourgeoisie. In a similar vein the unequal exchange theorists see underdevelopment as a process in which the centre draws investible surplus out of the periphery through trading relationships and thus renders the latter physically incapable of industrial growth. On the other hand, Warren (1980) argued that imperialism does bring about industrial development and improvements in living standards because it imposes on its colonies capitalist social relations which contain their own dynamic of accumulation. The thrust of most neoclassical arguments is that international trade and specialization is the cause of industrial development, in the newly industrialized countries at least, and that everyone profits from economic integration.

Several of the concepts used in the above are vague, not least the concept of imperialism. From the start one needs to differentiate between the forms of imperialism - direct colonial rule, neocolonialism or indirect influence through economic and political contacts, and the 'imperialism' of trade. As we will see, even this is not enough. The argument here is that despite the polar conclusions reached by the forementioned schools of thought their error is a common one. The last wish here, incidentally, is to propose a compromise between the 'impossibilists' (dependency, unequal exchange) and the 'inevitabilists' (Warren, neoclassicism),[6] but rather to attack both on the same score and to counterpose a different view. The conception they share is one of method; they each see the (non-socialist) world as a global system, in which certain real forces determine the fate of each country. For dependency these forces are the centre-periphery links which connect up all parts of the world; for neoclassicists it is the technological and resource endowments which determine the outcome through trade; for unequal exchange theorists it is again the conditions of production in the form of (socially determined) wage levels which, via trade, impose international inequality; for Warren it is the spread of capitalist social relations and the revolutionizing of productive forces which goes with it. The problem with all of these is that they employ concepts to analyse the whole world which only have practical meaning when they grow out of particular, country-specific circumstances. In other words, the concepts employed are not at a sufficient level of generality to allow a general analysis of the effects of imperialism and trade. They are unaware that the concepts they employ are at too high a level of abstraction to explain historical events; these abstractions are essential tools of analysis, or rather, this level of abstraction is essential, but to make concrete use of them they need to be interpreted in particular historical contexts. The concepts of imperialism, capitalism, class, accumulation and exchange must all be employed in the study of development but they are, as it were, only chapter headings which need to be elaborated upon in each individual study. For instance, if we want to specify the effect of direct colonial domination we need to understand the purpose and method of colonial rule by a certain country over its colonies. The aims of colonialism vary widely and while we can make the general statement that colonialism is exploitative in the sense that the colonial power profits from it, the effects on the colony can vary widely. It may or may not reinforce or transform existing social relations, destroy domestic industry or encourage agricultural productivity. Equally, the form of integration of an economy into the international division of labour will have a determining influence on the impact of trade - it depends on such things as commodity-types of exports and imports, the size and diversity of the economy, the level and form of penetration of foreign capital, the ability of the local state to influence the conditions of production and the terms of trade, and the domestic class structure. Knowledge of these is essential to decide whether in a given country (peripheral or otherwise) a certain trading pattern will

---

[6]If these characterizations appear too strong then we reply that all of these writers argue that the essential *tendency* is for imperialism either to inhibit development or to cause it.

generate internal accumulation and development.[7]

Initially, Japanese colonialism had specific designs for its Korean colony; it was to provide an agricultural surplus for export. Later it became profitable as a base for certain types of industrial production. But there were several ways by which these could have been provided each with different effects on the Korean economic and class structure. It emerged that the most efficient method of ensuring rice exports was to regularize the system of land tenure, acquire a large proportion of cultivated land for Japanese landowners, and extract rice from Korean farmers by trade and taxation. The development of industry as well as the changes in the rural economy introduced to Korea the foundations and accoutrements of capitalism while not overturning the precapitalist agricultural social relations. Wage-labour developed on a fairly wide scale; notions of private property in land, which had been underdeveloped traditionally, were imposed; exchange relations spread to all corners of the country; modern industrial facilities were established and some workers acquired factory skills; many thousands of workers became accustomed to the discipline of factory work and the obligations of the employee; international trading relations were thoroughly developed; and, not least, a centralized state authority with the power to impose its decisions throughout the land became a part of daily life.

But here was a contradiction. While Japanese colonialism created the conditions of capitalist development, it was at the same time compelled to suppress the indigenous offspring of these conditions. Korean moneyed classes saw opportunity in the expansion of exchange, industry and international trade which accompanied the Japanese and were persistent in their attempts to exploit them. Since this represented a threat both to Japanese capital operating in Korea and Japanese trade with Korea the colonial administration took measures to limit it. The events were similar in Formosa, especially in the sugar refining industry which the colonial government wanted to be dominated by the Japanese monopolies. Insofar as colonialism does introduce capitalist social relations, which is by no means certain (and if it does we still need to know the extent of them and the conditions in which they exist), the question arises as to whether, as Warren maintains,[8] Third World capitalism develops its own 'increasingly vigorous internal dynamic'. This is the antithesis of the dependency position, even of the more sophisticated writers such as Cardoso and dos Santos who write of 'dependent development'. To answer the question we must first ask whether this refers to the

---

[7]Cardoso & Faletto stress this in their book:

We conceive of the relationship between external and internal forces as forming a complex whole whose structural links are not based on mere external forms of exploitation and coercion, but are rooted in coincidences of interest between local dominant classes and international ones, and, on the other side, are challenged by local dominated groups and classes (1979, p xvi).

[8]'Direct colonialism ...acted as a powerful engine of progressive social change, advancing capitalist development far more rapidly than was conceivable in any other way, both by its destructive effects on precapitalist social systems and by its implantation of elements of capitalism. Indeed, although introduced into the Third World externally, capitalism has struck deep roots there and developed its own increasingly vigorous internal dynamic' (Warren, 1980, p9).

period of direct colonial rule or after formal independence is achieved. In the Korean case, capitalism in the Japanese period certainly had a vigorous dynamic but its internal engine, if this is meant to refer to capital accumulation in indigenous hands, was subordinated to an external one in the double sense that it was in foreign hands and that accumulation was geared to foreign trade. More generally, it cannot be maintained that even vigorous indigenous capitalist accumulation will induce industrial expansion if local capitalism is for one reason or another not established in industry but on plantations or in mines, or indeed services of various sorts as was largely the case in British-occupied Singapore.

Does colonialism introduce capitalist social relations? In Korea, we have argued, Japanese control brought deep penetration of capitalist forms of production and exchange but did not do so directly in agriculture. Warren expounds on Marx's view that colonialism has conserving tendencies and that colonial powers have at times taken measures which have inhibited the development of the productive forces, but he insists that the forces tending to destroy pre-capitalist modes would 'far outweigh' their opposite (Warren, 1980, p153). But, notwithstanding the powerful rhetoric of the *Communist Manifesto*, capitalism does not always and everywhere sweep everything before it. A more measured view appears in the *Grundrisse*:

> In all cases of conquest, three things are possible. The conquering people subjugates the conquered under its own mode of production ...or it leaves the old mode intact and contents itself with tribute ...or a reciprocal interaction takes place whereby something new, a synthesis arises ... (Marx, 1973, p97).

Imperialism needs to be understood in the way it structures classes and the means by which the colonizing and colonized societies reproduce themselves. It simply may not be in the interests of invading capital to transform all social relations. Such a transformation may occur despite this, and there does appear to be a historical tendency for capitalism to spread by osmosis. However, Japanese colonialism in Korea and Formosa showed that colonial capital can regulate as well as foster the spread of capitalism.

If Japanese colonialism kept in check the development of indigenous capital accumulation, did it 'underdevelop' Korea? There is no doubt that the transformation of social relations and the construction of industry laid some foundations for the later transition to industrial capitalism in South Korea. Moreover, although colonialism is exploitative this does not necessarily imply that it will leave its colonies worse off, particularly if colonial policy emphasizes advances in agricultural productivity and industrial growth. While the mass of Korean peasants suffered under the Japanese (whether more than they would have under the old regime is unanswerable) they would benefit later from improvements in productivity, the growth of industry and various infrastructural developments. This does not sit easily with Korea's unquestioned 'dependence' if the latter is understood to mean that Korea's expansion was conditioned by the expansion of the Japanese economy. On the other hand, there is no question that industrial development, distorted and dependent as it was, advanced infinitely further than it could have under the old regime. Moreover, in relation to internal social and economic conditions one could with some justification call Korean industry under the Japanese overdeveloped.

Warren's critique of dependency (Warren, 1980, especially pp162-70) was necessary and powerful but nevertheless failed to attack it for its failure to study the specific effects of forms of imperialism on class relations. Even the less crude *dependentistas* like Cardoso *begin* with the idea of dependency and ask how it affects class structure rather than beginning with the form of foreign penetration and the form of integration into the world market and asking how this affects class structure and the position of the national state, and then making conclusions about the level of dependency at a certain point in history. It is trivial to attack dependency theory for its unsubstantiated predictions (by reference to formerly underdeveloped countries such as South Korea and their records of industrial growth and welfare) if it is not accompanied by an analysis of growth as a process of class formation, for it is in the latter that the criticism of dependency lies buried. Class formation in underdeveloped countries takes place in an international context. The dependency position is that integration into the world economy is inimical to autonomous development, while the neoclassical position holds the reverse. The argument here, that it depends on the form of integration including the social structure on which production and trade are based, does not permit unconditional conclusions. Japanese colonialism in Korea brought about an enormous degree of integration through trade: it made it possible for indigenous accumulation to flourish but at the same time suppressed it. US neocolonialism in South Korea, which exercised detailed and extensive economic and political control there in the three decades after the Second World War, was central in the promotion of the process of indigenous capital accumulation. But Korean industrial development under US tutelage was autonomous in the crucial sense that it was undertaken almost entirely by Korean capitalists.

The study of US neocolonialism in South Korea strongly reinforces the earlier insistence that the form of imperialism - in all of its complex internal ramifications - determines the effects of foreign domination on the colony. The purpose of US policy in South Korea was decidedly not to make it an extension of US economic territory, nor to exploit that country for its own financial advantage, but to sustain it as a front-line state in its battle against Soviet and Chinese power. It was not an economic imperialism, except insofar as US prosperity in general depended on the security and stability of its spheres of influence, but a political and strategic one. Economic stability and strength in South Korea were important to this so as to minimize the risk of its 'fall' and US policy increasingly favoured national industrial development. The capitalist foundations had already been laid by the Japanese and the political obstacle in the shape of Syngman Rhee fell out of favour and collapsed when it became clear that the regime could not deliver the US requirements. From the outset indigenous capital, merchant and industrial, were succoured by the US presence and in the sixties achieved a vigorous internal dynamic. This development, to be sure, was 'dependent' on US aid but this very fact can dispel two of dependency's most cherished notions. The first is that although aid was massive in the fifties and sixties, it was instrumental in generating the process of industrial development which enabled the Korean economy to achieve *independence* from aid. This dependence was self-cancelling. Secondly, we have argued that aid was essential (primarily to cover the foreign exchange deficit) to industrial development in the fifties and sixties. This immediately challenges the persistent but often only implied claim of *dependentistas* that the alternative to dependence, even 'dependent development', is a superior autonomous development. This is usually supported by the argument that growth at the periphery is faster when the centre is at war and cut off from the periphery. If one can conceive of some alternative independent capitalist path for South Korea it would have been impossible to compensate for US aid from domestic sources, and without such a ready supply of imported inputs industrial growth would have been slower. All of these comments apply with near-equal force to Taiwan.

Notice, finally, that the critique of dependency has to this point accepted its perception of the importance of imperialism and argued that the impact will vary according to circumstances and cannot be judged *a priori*. The position can be reinforced by returning to the argument that the primitive accumulation of industrial capital (its occurrence and non-occurrence) is as much a political process as an economic one. Whatever may be the international laws of accumulation (surplus drain, unequal exchange, trade and specialization, export platforms and so on), and whatever may be the influence of imperialist powers on political processes in Third World countries, politics are above all a *national* question.[9]   When dependency does talk about classes they are discussed in terms of international economic laws (compradors, labour aristocracy, peasants whose tribute finds its way to the centre) so that even dependency's best case is economistic. This helps to explain the political position of dependency as the ideology of the national bourgeoisie since if the Third World malaise is attributed to international forces then the solution lies with nationalist forces and not domestic class struggle.[10]

5.3 Class Formation and Industrial Development

It has been argued above that the form of production and allocation of investible surplus, and thus the path of development or underdevelopment, is a class issue and that industrialization is predicated on the transformation of the whole class structure. This latter is a turbulent and often violent process and not one that can be decreed by government. In many Third World countries the greatest obstacle to industrial development is the entrenched position of rentier interests, particularly landlords. If wealth from surplus-producing (or potentially surplus-producing) activities is kept on the land then industrial development is impeded. If this economic predominance is translated into political power for the landlord class, the inherent difficulty of industrial accumulation may be intensified by actively discriminatory measures particularly relating to the trade regime.

Historically, the first big step in some countries towards capitalist industrialization has been the conversion of agricultural social relations from feudal or semi-feudal ones into capitalist relations. In South Korea the development of capitalist agriculture never seemed historically likely. Wage-labour in agriculture did not have an opportunity to take deep root partly because consolidation of plots did not appear technically feasible under the Japanese or politically feasible after independence. Landlords were not, then, converted into capitalist farmers. Their economic hold was broken by the land reforms, although their political power had been severely weakened in the Japanese period and the subsequent events of

---

[9]The idea that the trend towards the internationalization of capital is making the concept of the nation-state irrelevant (eg. Murray, 1971) cannot stand up to historical scrutiny and is subject to the same criticisms levelled at other theories of the world economy.

[10]Australia, whose mining, manufacturing and financial industries are heavily foreign-controlled, has a Left which is excessively influenced by dependency thinking.

independence. A remarkably similar process occurred in Taiwan, that other miracle of East Asia, where the land reforms of 1949-53 laid the social foundation for the rapid capitalist industrialization which began in earnest in the early sixties. The Taiwanese land reform was a product of the populist streak in Chinese nationalism, and the Kuomintang leadership was not averse to such a change partly because they attributed their defeat on the mainland to the inequality of land ownership and partly because they themselves were no longer tied to the land (many had been landlords). Taiwanese landlords, like their Korean counterparts, had been weakened politically under the Japanese. They were not closely affiliated with the new, invading, ruling elite and, to add to their vulnerability, the US AID mission gave its imprimatur to this 'modernization'. The three-stage reform programme began in 1949 by substantially reducing rents and giving tenants greater security, and in 1952 the government sold off public lands to landless farmers. The final stage required private owners to sell to the government all holdings above three hectares (as in Korea) in exchange for government bonds and shares in state enterprises. The government subsequently sold the land to the tenants at purchase price. In fact many landlords sold up before the third stage as the rent reductions cut deeply and expropriation on poor terms appeared imminent. Whereas in 1952 owner-cultivators comprised 38 percent of agricultural households, by 1965 this had risen to 67 percent.[11] Business speculators travelled the countryside to buy the dispossessed landlords new share-wealth cheaply, but it was mainly the smaller landlords who suffered in this way. The essential point is that after the land reforms it was no longer profitable or safe to invest in rural land and there began a shift into industry and commerce.

The importance of these processes, which tend to place the whole structure of class relations into a fluid state, is in the destruction of agriculture as a principal arena of asset-holding, investment and accumulation. The extent of the direct conversion of landlords into capitalists is likely to be highly variable and difficult to assess, but ultimately it is not very important since the key process is the transformation of society from one based on precapitalist production relations to one in which capitalist production relations assume the leading and dynamic role. The destruction of agriculture as the focus of wealth-expansion is important to industrialization not only for its economic and political effects on the landlord class but also because it can open up the countryside to exploitation by industry through the state's taxation and pricing policies. Atomized and individually weak, petty proprietors are less able to resist this exploitation than the organized and united class of wealthy land-owners. We should not fail to mention that in South Korea and Taiwan the reorganization of the agrarian ownership structure was a significant contributing factor in the provision of large numbers of farmers to the new industrial factories.

The making of agriculture unattractive for idle wealth cannot itself provide the stimulus to the building of industry. The expansion of industrial investment may take the form of the transformation of commercial and financial capital - involved in domestic and foreign trade, urban property ownership and money-lending of various sorts - into industrial pursuits. It was stated above that the transformation of the class structure cannot be decreed by the state. Government

---

[11]Liu (1969, p65). Jacoby (1966, p81) says that owner-operated farms rose from 59 percent of the total in 1951 to 87 percent in 1965. For a fuller discussion of Taiwan see Hamilton (1983).

policy can, however, exercise a great influence by making industrial investment more attractive and commercial pursuits more difficult. This was certainly the case in Korea with the closing off of many avenues to windfall profit-making via trade and access to foreign exchange, and then the encouragement of industrial investment with cheap loans, tax concessions, control of labour, allocation of foreign exchange and so on. The necessity of the transformation of capital was even more consciously articulated in Singapore, a city-state which had been more or less created as a trading centre by British interests. The decision to break from mainland Malaya, from which Singapore had drawn most of its traded commodities, left the newly independent state in a position where economic viability required trade to have a higher level of domestic value-added.[12] It became increasingly necessary for local capital to be transformed from a merchant to an industrial circuit. The state took a leading role in this although on the whole indigenous capital took a position subordinate to foreign companies. Local investors, mostly involved in trading ventures, were accustomed to making short-term investments with quick returns. Moreover, few bankers had the experience to assess the value of industrial assets which could serve as collateral for industrial loans. The government's Economic Development Board attempted to overcome this difficulty by itself offering medium and long-term loans for industrial investments and by underwriting the issue of shares and bonds by industrial enterprises.[13]

The recent history of South Korea, and of Singapore and Taiwan, identifies the central role of the state in the formation of a class of industrial capitalists and the dominance of industrial accumulation.[14] In Korea, industrial capital is, in a sense, the creature of the state. This contradicts the usual explanation of the relationship among those who consider class important. But the state cannot be taken as some neutral societal decision-maker standing above the material forces which surround it. We need to comprehend the social basis of the state's policies. Why is it that the state promotes industrial capital, and why is it effective in doing so? This is the reason for devoting space to an attempt to explain the forces which brought about the emergence in South Korea of a state sympathetic to capitalist industrialization. These sympathies cannot be taken for granted, and in practice most Third World states are sympathetic only to the *idea* of industrialization. There is no attempt here to develop a theory of the state because the state under capitalism is conditioned by the dominant mode of accumulation, the requirements of social reproduction. The state does not have the same theoretical status as accumulation. Theories of the state end up by interpreting the accumulation process, the means of social reproduction, in the context of the activities of the

---

[12]In Hong Kong, the Chinese hinterland which had been the fountain of its great entrepot trade was closed off by the US ban of 1950 and the UN embargo of 1951, and local capital was forced to go beyond its traditional trading environment to survive. Much of the new industry in Hong Kong in the fifties was in effect transferred from China, especially from Shanghai and in the textile business.

[13]Bankers in Hong Kong were less hidebound, and by lending against the insubstantial collateral of personal standing helped lay the foundation of the textile industry, the main force behind industrialization there.

[14]'...the history of capital accumulation is the history of class struggles, of political movements, of the affirmation of ideologies, and of the establishment of forms of domination and reactions against them' (Cardoso & Faletto, 1979, p xviii).

state. This is an inversion of the correct analytical approach.[15] The purpose here is decidedly not to propose that the state is the product of the form of accumulation, still less of the dominant social class, nor that its principal resolve is necessarily to foster the accumulation of capital except in the widest sense of ensuring the reproduction of society; the purpose is only to argue that the state must be analyzed and understood in relation to accumulation, even though this will leave some of its activities and relations, from this but not other points of entry, 'undetermined'.

5.4 Trade and Industrial Development

Trading patterns are conditioned by the form of development, and the form of integration into the international division of labour conditions development. The results for growth and structure in Chapter 4 show consistently that the pattern of South Korean industrial development has been very heavily influenced by dependence on imports, imports of both intermediate inputs (including raw materials) and capital goods. The viability of many industries - their domestic efficiency let alone their international competitiveness - would have been undermined without these imports. The rapid growth of imports and the increased dependence on them were strongly reflected in the results of the model. There is nothing unusual, for underdeveloped and developed countries, in being heavily dependent on imports, but its significance in the process of Korean industrialization has been largely ignored. The argument here is that it lies at the very heart of the process and that the progress of industrialization including government policies can be interpreted as a process of trying to ensure that the indispensible flow of imports continued unimpeded.

The rapidity of Korean industrial growth necessitated increased reliance on imported inputs since domestic import-substituting industries could not have provided the essential inputs so readily. One of the strongest results of the model solution was that the domestic capital goods sectors, in those commodities that were competitive, had great difficulty keeping up with demand. This imposed a severe constraint on industrial growth - the availability of foreign exchange - and it was this that dominated economic planning, especially in the sixties. This explains the intense emphasis on export performance, a stress which became more acute as US aid petered out in the mid to late sixties.[16] The form of export production had a direct impact on the structure of industry as a whole. When imports are paid for with exports of *manufactured* goods this itself intensifies dependence on imports since manufactured exports tend to be more heavily import-dependent than other types of export such as mineral and agricultural products. This in turn limits the possibilities for import substitution because export production cannot afford the more expensive domestically produced inputs which would be necessary while infant

---

[15]One of the essential oppositions between capitalism and socialism, particularly socialism as it is practiced in Eastern Europe, is that under the latter it is quite valid to interpret the reproduction of the economic basis of society in the context of the state.

[16]Roxborough (1979, p33) has observed that 'for many underdeveloped countries, the export sector functioned as a quasi-capital goods sector'.

industries grew up. Under the whip of international competition, Korean exporters, as we have seen, had no margins to play with. As the price results suggested, it often required state intervention to provide the incentives to export, and indeed the incentives to import substitution. The latter occurred in the late sixties and the seventies in intermediate inputs such as chemicals and steel products and in capital goods although the latter have been mainly simple parts for machinery. Finally, it has been argued that the promises of welfare gains which industrial growth held up were delivered through improvements in labour productivity. The latter was in turn heavily dependent on the growth of imports of capital goods embodying more advanced technologies.

Insofar as imports are financed by manufactured exports and this in turn intensifies reliance on imports, a Third World country would do better to export traditional, resource-based, mineral and agricultural products. But we know that there is more to it than that. There are several good reasons why reliance on traditional (often colonially established) exports has been inimical to industrial development. Firstly there is the influence of primary exports on the exchange rate (the Dutch disease) which tends to make manufactured imports cheaper and import-substitution more difficult. Secondly, the structure of trade will reinforce the position of export producers who will not invest in industry but expand profitable mining and cash-crop operations. These activities appear more prone to foreign control so there is the additional problem of the outflow of investible surplus through profit repatriation. The corollary to this is that those groups around which accumulation is centred, in the export industries, tend to wield disproportionate political power and often use it to stifle attempts at indigenous industrial development because the latter would increase costs and diminish export earnings. Thirdly, if capitalism is underdeveloped, the orientation of the exchange economy around traditional exports may limit the spread of capitalism since it has historically been industrial capital which has carried the burden of spreading wage-labour deeply into society.

Warren (1980, pp146-51) has successfully discounted on empirical and logical grounds the usual reasons for criticizing reliance on primary exports, viz. that relative to manufactures they suffer from fluctuating and declining terms of trade, that they lack extensive linkages and that their productivity grows more slowly. The common feature of these usual reasons, and which immediately exposes them to attacks such as Warren's, is their technological nature. They attach to the technical rather than the social aspect of production. We prefer to emphasize the influence of the export pattern on the class structure and the ways in which this may inhibit industrial growth.[17] From this perspective, the central importance of the nature of exports - which is a product of both resource endowments and the social relations of production and the influence over class structure of colonial policy - is diverted away from purely technical considerations to the nature of the accumulation process in which technical considerations find their meaning.

The economic conflict between exporters and importers (which is often expressed in political conflicts which bedevil Third World countries) has been cunningly mitigated in Korea by tying foreign exchange spending (importing) directly to foreign exchange earning (exporting). As a rule, foreign exchange

---

[17]Warren does not take this step, although he does stress that the emergence of an independent state in post-colonial societies is crucial in abolishing the obstacles to diversification from a primary export base (1980, p150).

spenders have no direct interest in the way in which foreign exchange is earned - consumers of imports and manufacturers for domestic markets who rely on imported inputs generally have no direct connection with the mining companies and cash-crop producers who earn foreign exchange. Korea's dearth of natural resources has been a blessing in that it has put exporters into the same manufacturing boat as importers, so that their interests over trade have become more aligned. Of all aspects of economic planning in Korea perhaps the most critical, and certainly the least understood outside Korea, has been the Foreign Exchange Demand and Supply Plan which has, at least since the late sixties, annually set out in detail sectoral requirements for earning and allowances for spending foreign currency.[18] The level of detail of the Plan is unclear, but it is based on reports to the Ministry of Finance by industry associations of the imports planned by that industry for the year. When the Plan is finalized, industry associations are informed of the import limits and firms within the industry duly adjust their production plans to fit the restrictions on imports (including restrictions on so-called automatic approval items). The government also uses the banks as an executive instrument by instructing them to issue licences only for specified types of imports to a specified value. Korean sources have referred to the Plan's 'absolutely binding force' (Korea Annual, 1971, p169).

The Foreign Exchange Plan has been necessary because of the difficulty of earning foreign exchange and the ease of spending it. Trade policies have reflected this by carefully limiting imports to essential industries only and favouring those which will convert them into exports. This shows up in the model results and has been confirmed in other studies (Luedde-Neurath, 1983). Exports have been not so much promoted as demanded by the state and our model results have been consistent with the view that it has been necessary to compensate for losses on exports by allowing windfall profits on imports and high prices for domestic market sales. Schemes such as the export-import link system and the wastage allowance tried to ensure that the windfalls fell to exporters although a barrage of export-subsidizing measures were necessary too. The foreign exchange constraint persisted into the late seventies although more export industries were then profitable, and despite greater import dependence the constraint had been eased. The policy of promoting export production even at a loss was based on the abandonment of the notion that the value of a foreign exchange dollar should be equal to its domestic cost in exports. If a dollar can buy imports which are essential to the continued expansion of industry then it pays to spend more won earning that dollar than the exchange rate suggests. This discount for overseas buyers is a means of cheapening exports without raising the domestic cost of imports which accompanies the alternative method, devaluation. It also contradicts the conception of international trade as a process of exchange and confirms it as an interaction between changing systems of production. This strategy is not to be recommended for Third World countries in general since it pays to import at this price only if those imports augment the productivity and growth of an already dynamic domestic manufacturing base.

To reinforce the connection between class structure and the pattern of trade we can point to the severe restrictions on consumer goods imports in Korea. These

---

[18]I am endebted to Richard Luedde-Neurath for pointing out the significance of this. The information which follows is from Luedde-Neurath (1983) where can be found more details about the Plan and a discussion of its significance.

restrictions have been imposed both to conserve foreign exchange and to protect domestic producers. Large quantities of grain imports were permitted in the sixties because they did not represent a major drain on foreign reserves (imported grain was cheap under PL 480) and the domestic producers who suffered as a result, the small owner-cultivators, were at the periphery of the industrialization drive and were politically weak. Restrictions on imports of consumer goods mostly affected urban professionals and moneyed classes since it was they who could afford them. In most Third World countries the moneyed classes, including landlords and government officials, hold political sway often in alliance with foreign interests. Sometimes domestic manufacturers are sufficiently influential to restrict competing imports but the unity of moneyed classes and their sense of their own interests as a group are usually too underdeveloped to overcome their personal consumption habits and to recognize the potential industrial development that could be gained from saving foreign exchange for productive rather than consumption ends. Here the independent strength of the Korean state, beholden not even to the industrialists, has been a powerful force since only a state with autonomy from particular class interests and with a strong central bureaucracy could strictly control imports and eliminate the abuses and corruption which as a rule accompany this sort of restriction. The Korean trade regime as a whole - based on the protection of domestic industry, the promotion of exports, the regulation of foreign exchange flows, restrictions on consumer imports, reliance on grain imports, the inducement of particular forms of foreign loans and foreign investment - reveals that in the eyes of the state the promotion of indigenous industrial capital has been the centre of economic policy.

All of this stands in direct contrast to the neoclassical view of the relation between trade and industrial development in Korea. The orthodox view,[19] which has a great deal of uniformity, begins with the division of modern Korean economic history into the 'easy phase' of import substitution in the fifties followed by export-oriented or outward-looking industrialization in the sixties and seventies. The import substitution of the fifties - in processed foods, beverages and tobacco, finished textile products and other light, non-durable consumer goods - filled the gap in consumer-goods production left by the disruption of war. These industries had some degree of natural protection reinforced by high tariffs and could be quickly developed because of their low capital and skill-intensity. The exchange rate was biased against manufactured exports, and foreign exchange earnings (so far as foreign exchange was earned) were made with traditional primary exports. The key to the success of Korean industrial development, in the orthodox view, lies in the transition around 1963-65 and subsequent years to export orientation. The fundamental change which marks the transition according to all of the neoclassical writers is a significant change in government policy in the direction of liberalization; prices were allowed to approach more closely their equilibrium levels.[20] These prices included the exchange rate (which was unified and devalued by about 50 percent in 1964), interest rates and, above all those of traded goods which were

---

[19]In particular Westphal (1978), Little (1979), Balassa (1971), Kwang Suk Kim (1974), Frank et al. (1975) and Ranis (1983). Hong (1979) is much more detailed in his knowledge of import controls and is much more reluctant to draw the neoclassical conclusions.

[20]See for example Balassa (1971, p55), Westphal (1978, pp349-50), Frank et al. (1975, Chapter 4). Ranis (1983, p10) repeats the claims but without the qualifications of the more careful neoclassicals.

influenced by the liberalization of import restrictions. The freeing of markets allowed the economy to achieve specialization according to a new comparative advantage, one reflected in a shift away from land-based primary exports to labour-intensive manufactured exports. Some of these writers do not put so much emphasis on government policy as the initiator of the new period, preferring to stress the 'natural' transition to the new trade structure. Rapid industrial growth led by the export sectors and an expanding domestic market followed the transition. The thrust of the entire argument is that industrial growth and prosperity has come about through the operation of relatively free markets (relative to other Third World countries which mistakenly stuck to import substitution) and the pursuit of Korea's natural comparative advantage. None of these writers denies the existence of substantial protective measures and subsidies to exporters, but all of them appeal to empirical calculations which purport to show that 'on average' the effective rates of protection, defined as the percentage difference between domestic value-added and the value-added component of world market prices, on manufacturing have been close to zero and, in particular, export production has operated more or less under a free-trade regime.[21] The political implications of this analysis are immense, for it is this vindication of the invisible hand which provides the rationale of World Bank policy today.

The response to the orthodox view begins by questioning the assertion that there was significant liberalization of trade restrictions in the sixties. Recent detailed work based on a thorough study of the whole system of import controls concludes that there is no basis for claiming that there was any significant loosening of the restrictions on imports and that in fact as the decade progressed Korean planners and officials became more skilled in imposing restrictions so as to exclude foreign competitors with more discrimination.[22] This study further argues that quantitative controls, including a range of subtle and largely unnoticed (by academics) methods such as the foreign exchange plan and 'voluntary' self-regulation carried out by industry associations, have been a critical element of the trade regime. These measures have probably had a substantial influence on investment and resource allocation.

There are further problems with the interpretation of the neoclassical story. Firstly, serious doubts must be expressed about the conclusion that the system of incentives was 'neutral' with respect to exporting. This is taken to imply that the existing exporting activities were naturally profitable and therefore efficient, and expressed Korea's comparative advantage. This is contradicted by several studies, referred to in Chapter 4, which suggest that many exports were sold at a loss. Our own calculations tended to support this. Moreover, if we consider export subsidies (which were necessary to make exports profitable at world prices according to the orthodox studies) to be *ex post* validations of decisions made on other criteria then the final export price is not indicative of efficiency. These other criteria included

---

[21]See Frank et al (1975, Chapter 10), Westphal (1978, pp9-12), Kwang Suk Kim (1974, pp28-34). Ranis (1983) is a notable exception preferring to interpret the state of affairs as liberalization unalloyed. They also argue that the import substitution which occurred in the sixties, to the extent that it was inefficient (and not much of it was), substituted for imports directed at the domestic market and not for imported inputs used in export production (Suk Tai Suh, 1975, p262).

[22]Luedde-Neurath (1983). Nam (1981b, p209) comes to the same conclusion from within the orthodox perspective.

many forms of government coercion, for as we know from Chapters 2 and 4 the price of doing business in Korea has been to export. As a rule, to export was not a private decision taken on the basis of profitability. This is clear even from the orthodox calculations; Westphal (1978, pp11-12) acknowledges that in many export sectors there were much greater incentives to domestic sales than to export sales, yet export sales were large and growing. This 'inconsistency' Westphal explains away by reference to cartels, but the real response is to recognize that the price system did not operate in a neoclassical fashion. Rather than the price system expressing the natural pattern of economic efficiency, the state used the price system to mould the economy so that accumulation would take place in the sectors deemed important in the plans. This conclusion is reinforced when we realize that the government not only influenced the structure of prices (and thus the direction of investment) by indirect means, but directly through price control measures. In Nam's words:

> ...price controls have been widely applied to a number of commodities in Korea with varying intensities over time ...[and in inflationary 1978] prices were strictly controlled for commodities that were subject to government price stabilization and fair trade laws or other special laws (Nam, 1981b, p203).

In his price comparison survey for 1978, Nam found that no less than one third of surveyed commodities were under price-control. This figure does not include the artificially low prices for the products of key industries owned by the government - industries such as coal, iron and steel, fertilizer and oil refining. For instance, in 1978 coal was sold in Korea at 40 percent less than the world price, cement at 20 percent less, and petroleum products at 3 percent less (*ibid.*).

Most of the orthodox writers acknowledge the fact of compensatory profit-making and we have seen that several studies agree that many export productions were unprofitable in the sixties and seventies. Export subsidies of various kinds, although the core of the neoclassical argument is that they were as a rule only enough to counterbalance the increased costs of inputs due to protection, are admitted in certain case to have gone 'too far' and thus to have distorted market signals. Balassa (1971, p72), who adheres to the view that 'the average rate of export subsidy does not exceed that of import protection', draws attention to the case of electrical machinery (mainly radios) in which sector the total domestic cost in 1966 of earning a dollar through exports was 600 won, while the exchange rate was only 271. An exceptional case one might think, but 'similar results are shown for plywood and knitted products' and subsidies for some textile products are also too high according to Balassa. But these three items were Korea's major export earners in the mid-sixties. In 1966, electrical machinery, plywood and knitted goods made up 33 percent of manufactured exports and 20 percent of total exports (ESY, 1970, Table 150).

Secondly, to refer to the low effective rate of protection on manufacturing as a whole as indicative of a general policy in Korea of balanced protection which gives manufacturing 'no preferential inducement' (Westphal, 1978, pp456-57) is misleading and directly contrary to the result of the model of this study which shows agriculture subsidizing industry in the sixties. Differences in domestic and world prices matter only if there is competition with the world product; in import-competing industries the effective rates of protection have been very large, over 90 percent in 1968 according to Westphal (1978, Table 5) and Kwang Suk Kim (1974,

Table 7). In no sense have import-competing industries (including those engaged in exporting) operated in anything approaching free-trade conditions (something the orthodox writers are careful to avoid saying). The general conclusion is that without the various forms of government interference the structure of the Korean economy would have been quite different - many export industries would not have developed as they did and many industries could not have survived international competition.

The claim that South Korea's success is attributable to the impersonal and largely uninhibited operation of the laws of comparative advantage is the broad conclusion of the neoclassicists. Thus Westphal:

> ...assuming that its comparative advantage lies in labour-intensive activities, Korea provides an almost classic example of an economy following its comparative advantage and reaping the gains predicted by conventional economic theory (Westphal, 1978, p376).

One of the difficulties with this conclusion is that it is by no means obvious what it was that changed between the fifties and the sixties which caused Korea's comparative advantage to shift from land-based to labour-intensive exports. Ranis's position on this is peculiar. He maintains that the basis for comparative advantage shifts gradually from land to unskilled labour *after* the decision to pursue 'primary export substitution' (1983, p9). This suggests that the new basis for production was imposed by the government until the conditions of production and factor-intensity caught up. But Ranis is very reluctant to attribute such a causative influence to public policy preferring to let the latter only 'facilitate' the shift into primary export substitution (*ibid.*, p10). In fact Ranis uses the same tautological argument as the others, viz. that since exports were by the end of the sixties intensive in unskilled labour therefore comparative advantage must have shifted to this factor. In the fifties the productivity of agricultural land had been increasing respectably (Ban et al., 1980, Table B.6) and as we have seen in a previous chapter hundreds of thousands of potential industrial labourers who were accustomed to factory work were available.

All of the above has attacked the neoclassical argument on its own terms, within a vision that cannot see beyond technological facts and government interference. Even if we accept the version of events of the orthodox school - that there was a liberalization and relatively free trade in exports and that specialization grew out of the pursuit of comparative advantage - even then this could not explain the process of Third World industrialization. Many countries, such as Chile, have swallowed the World Bank pill and their conditions have deteriorated. The explanation of the transition from preindustrial society to industrial capitalism lies in the process of class transformation, in the emergence of the classes of industrial capitalists and factory workers and the political domination of the former.

There is a final point to be made about the interpretation of the events of the sixties and seventies and this relates to the characterization of Korean industrial development as 'export-led' i.e. that the essence of the growth process lay in the expansion of exports. None of the orthodox scholars denies the empirically obvious fact that throughout the period there was continuing and substantial import substitution in many sectors.[23]   There was a contradiction in this though, in that while the state pursued policies of import substitution (in heavy and chemical industries as well as durable consumer goods) by protecting import-competing capital, export expansion required more and more imported inputs so that the economy became more import-dependent over the industrialization period. But the fundamental point is this: Korea did not import in order to export but exported in order to import. Industrial expansion was not 'export-led' or driven by exports; in fact to ask which sectors were pulling or pushing is not the right question.[24] Export expansion was the essential means to the end of acquiring the foreign exchange necessary to buy the imports which were indispensable to the continued growth of industry in general - export, import-competing and naturally protected. Korean industry was built with imports - in 1978, 22 percent of intermediate inputs and 79 percent of machinery stocks were imported - and our model results showed that foreign exchange has been the severest constraint on growth. It could not be otherwise. Export industries were a means of converting unskilled labour into sophisticated imports.

Trade, then, in Kravis's terminology (1970), was not the engine but the handmaiden of growth. The burden of the argument of Chapter 2 was that the essential explanation of industrial growth and development in Korea lies in the transformation of the domestic class structure and the economic conditions which accompanied this, even though external forces were powerful in this process. The Korean state has used trade to direct industrial development and build indigenous capital, and changes in the trade regime reflect changes in the domestic structures of classes and industries.

The implications of this interpretation of export expansion are considerable. It casts serious doubt on the notion that the development of the Korean economy was a response to its developing natural comparative advantage. The nature of import substitution in the sixties and seventies revealed that the purpose of the state was to protect and build domestic industrial capital and it planned import substitution with this in mind. On the one hand it was necessary to chip away at the reliance on foreign exchange earnings, on the other it was necessary to avoid imposing extra costs on export producers. In practice this has proven extremely difficult. The conceptualization of continued import substitution in the neoclassical story is that it was a natural and passive response to market signals reflecting further shifts in factor intensities - even, presumably, to the point where ships, automobiles and advanced chemical processes could be efficient. The argument here is that export production and import substitution were forced; many export industries were marginal and would never have survived without government support and coercion, and many import-competing industries (at least for their initial years of operation)

---

[23]None of them, however, stresses Suh's conclusion to the detailed study of import substitution that substitution 'was achieved most rapidly during the period of export expansion rather than during the period of import substitution in the early periods' (Suk Tai Suh, 1975, p275). Ranis (1983) puts it all down to the 'Secondary Import and Export Substitution' phase which did not get under way until the early-to-mid seventies. This import substitution, he argues, was in response to market signals (rising real wages) and not government policy (despite the Third Five-Year Plan).

[24]Thus the irrelevence of those statistical studies which break down the growth rate into various 'sources' (eg. Westphal, 1978, pp17-20). One might just as well divide the economy into city-based and country-based sectors and conclude that growth was 93 percent city-led.

would not have been viable without very high levels of protection. What is extraordinary - in the knowledge of the detailed economic planning, the extensive and direct control over key resources and the ability to influence pricing, marketing and investment decisions by the Korean state - is that the accepted view of Korean industrial development attributes it largely to the free play of market forces.

Appendix A
Augmented Flow Matrices (SAMS)

The augmented flow coefficient matrices which are used in computing the model's solutions each form a kind of social accounting matrix (SAM), but one in which the usual distinction between production accounts and institutional accounts is not adhered to. This does not mean, however, that there is an assumption of one-to-one correspondence between the classification of economic agents by ownership of 'factors of production' and receipt of the matching 'factor income', which is simply to say that workers and the self-employed receive a return to their savings (capital ownership) as well as wages and income from self-employed labour.

The cores of the SAMS for 1966 and 1978 are provided by the input-output (I-O) tables for those years. We refer to the tables of domestic transactions at producers' prices where all imports are aggregated into a single sector and no distinction is made between competitive and non-competitive imports. This last is necessary in order to provide an 'import-producing' sector, and it would be a simple matter to account empirically for differences in competitive and non-competitive imports by changing the coefficients of total imports used in the calculations. For instance, if competitive imports were arbitrarily cut to zero, then the domestic inputs coefficients would rise to make up the difference. The sectoral classifications of the 1966 and 1978 I-O flow tables were made to conform by aggregating up to 39 sectors (4 agricultural, 26 mining and manufacturing, and 9 service). Sectoral correspondences are given in Table A.1. Note that the 1978 Sector 55 ('government services', covering administrative services) is a dummy value-added sector and in our classification is added to the final demand category 'government consumption expenditure'.

The 1966 and 1978 SAMS with the 39 industrial sectors aggregated into one productive sector appear as Tables A.2 and A.3. They are presented in this way in order to emphasize the value-added sectors. We have omitted the row sums but, by definition, these must equal the corresponding column sums.

Foreign Sector

Total imports of intermediate, consumer and investment goods = Total exports + Foreign aid + Foreign savings.

The first task was to record the value of imports used in each sector broken into two parts: one part which goes to the overseas producer as a flow of foreign exchange and one part which goes to the government in the form of customs duties and commodity taxes on imports. Imports then enter into each sector at c.i.f. value.

Table A-1: Sectoral correspondences[a]

		1966 I-O	1978 I-O	1978 MMC
1	Grain	1	1	
2	Other agriculture	2	2-4	
3	Forestry products	3	5	
4	Fishery products	4	6	
5	Coal	5	7	21
6	Other mining	6	8-9	23,29
7	Processed food	7	10-14	311-312
8	Beverages and tobacco	8-9	15-16	313-314
9	Fibre spinning	10	17	3211
10	Textile fabrics	11	18	3216,3217,3219
11	Finished textile products	12	19	3212-3215,322,324
12	Lumber and plywood	13	21	3311
13	Wood products and furniture	14	22	3312,3319,332
14	Pulp and paper	15	23	341
15	Printing and publishing	16	24	342
16	Leather and leather products	17	20	323
17	Rubber products	18	33	355
18	Basic chemicals	19	25-26	3511
19	Other chemicals	20	28-30	3513,352
20	Chemical fertilizers	21	27	3512
21	Petroleum and coal products	22-23	31-32	353,354
22	Nonmetallic mineral products	24	34	36
23	Pig iron and raw steel	25	35	37101,37102
24	Primary iron & steel products	26	36	37103-37109
25	Nonferrous metal products	27	37	372
26	Fabricated metal products	28	38	381
27	General machinery	29	39	382
28	Electrical machinery	30	40-41	383
29	Transport equipment	31	42	384
30	Miscellaneous manufactures	32	43-44	385,39
31	Building and public works	33-34	45-46	
32	Wholesale and retail trade	40	49	
33	Transportation & warehousing	39	51	
34	Finance, insurance and real estate	36	53-54	
35	Electric power and gas	35	47	
36	Water & sanitary services	37	48	
37	Communications	38	52	
38	Social and other services	41	50,56-57	
39	Other	42-43[b]	58-60	

a. The first column refers to the 1966 I-O classification, the second to the 1978 I-O classification and the third to the 1978 MMC classification. We use the last-named in the calculation of capital coefficients in Appendix B.

b. Plus 'business consumption'.

Note that the 'final demand' sectors also have their domestic purchases differentiated from their imported consumption spending, and the same goes for purchases of investment goods.

The 'output' of the foreign sector is the basket of imports and the 'inputs' are exports. The latter represent inflows of foreign exchange into the economy and are augmented by foreign aid (T_f), a component of government revenue. The balance comprises foreign savings (S_f) which includes net (short and long-term) capital inflows and changes in foreign reserves. It is calculated as a residual.

The values of exports and imports are taken from the I-O tables; in 1978 foreign aid was nil, but stood at 35,530 mw[1] in 1966 (see the explanation under government revenue).

Labour Sector

Wages from productive sectors (ΣW_j) + Wages from government (W_g) = Consumption of domestic goods (ΣC_w) + Consumption of imports (M_w) + Taxes on imports (T_{mw}) + Income taxes (T_w) less transfer payments (G_w) + Savings (S_w) less profit income of workers (Π_w).

1978 SAM

Total income of the labour sector is derived from four sources: wages paid by the 39 industrial sectors, wages paid by the government sector, transfer payments from the government, and profit income i.e. interest payments on workers' savings. However, since we only want to attribute to labour the returns to the performance of labour (the input into the production process), we consider the last two items to be negative consumption items.

Wages paid by the 39 producing sectors are taken from the category 'compensation of employees' in the I-O tables, and wages paid by the government are also from the I-O tables and are extracted from government value-added activity (see under government expenditure). Government transfers to the labour sector $(G_w = 120900.0 \text{ mw})$ will be explained in the government accounts section.

Calculation of labour's profit income (Π_w) was more indirect and relied on surveys of household income and expenditure. In 1978 average monthly earnings by regular employees in all industries was 111201 won (KSY,1979,p82). Looking at the income and expenditure distribution of the average salary and wage earner's household (i.e. those in the 110000-129999 won bracket) we see (KSY,1979,p436) that interest, dividends and rent add 2,350 to average monthly earnings of 112740 won (i.e. .0208). Therefore we estimate that labour's total 1978 profit income was

$$\Pi_w = (\Sigma W_j + W_g) \times .0208 = 172121.7 \text{ mw}.$$

In the household expenditure survey, the remaining elements of 'other income' (i.e 'gifts and assistance' and 'others') are more or less covered by transfer payments.

---

[1]'Million won' is abbreviated to 'mw' throughout.

We now have total labour income for 1978 (8550238.6mw). From the household expenditure survey (KSY,1979,p436) we see that the average household 'spends' .01462 (or 1750/119700) of its total income on taxes and public charges i.e. $T_w = .01462 \times (\Sigma W_j + W_g) = 125004.5$ mw. Similarly the savings proportion (given by income less expenditure plus interest on personal debts) is .15263 (or 18270/119700) so that $S_w = .15263 \times (\Sigma W_j + W_g) = 1305022.9$ mw. Total workers' consumption we calculate as the residual when savings and taxes are subtracted from total income. Total consumption is 7120211.2 mw and this is divided into the following categories: purchases of domestic goods (divided into 39 sectors), purchases of imports net of customs duties, and that part of the value of imports made up of customs duties.

These consumption proportions - the division of consumption expenditure between 39 domestic, one foreign and the government sector - are assumed to be the same for labour, the self-employed and capitalists-as-consumers and are calculated from the aggregate figure in the I-O table for private consumption expenditure on domestic commodities, imports net of customs duties and customs duties. The proportions are for 1978:

domestic commodities	.97571
imports net of duties	.02020
customs duties	.00410

1966 SAM

The same procedure was used here as for 1978. Average monthly earnings of regular employees in all industries were 6753 won (KSY,1970,p322) scaled up from 'manufacturing' to 'all industries' using the average scale factor for 1971-73 from KSY (1979,p82). We use the income and expenditure pattern of wage and salary earners in the 6000-8000 won per month group (KSY,1967,p201). In this average group 'interest, dividends and rent' add 70 won to monthly earnings of 6510 (i.e. .0108). Thus $\Pi_w = (\Sigma W_j + W_g) \times (.0108) = 3455.5$ mw, and total labour income for 1966 was 329802.9 mw (of which government transfers were 3455.5 mw). Using the same reasoning as for 1978 and employing the household expenditure survey (KSY,1967,p201) $T_w = (\Sigma W_j + W_g) \times .0145 = 4765.0$ mw and $S_w = (\Sigma W_j + W_g) \times (-.0309) = -12868.0$ mw.

Total workers' consumption, calculated as the difference between total income and spending on taxes and savings was 337905.9 mw, and was divided in the I-O tables between the domestic, foreign and government sectors in the following proportions:

domestic commodities	.98360
imports net of duties	.01524
customs duties	.00116

Table A-2: Simplified 1966 SAM

	Productive sectors	Foreign	Labour	Self-employed	Capitalists consumption	Government	Investment
Productive sectors	604469.0	113507.9	332363.8	381359.0	936640.0	96465.9	125710.3
Foreign	131806.6	0	5148.7	5907.7	1450.6	7983.2	56628.6
Labour	270079.8	0	0	0	0	51277.6	0
Self-employed	412496.4	0	0	0	0	0	0
Capitalists consumption	126188.4	0	0	0	0	0	0
Government	14422.0 54107.1 11990.0 2987.6	35530.1	393.4 4765.0 -4990.0	451.4 7769.0 -6400.0	110.9 30986.0	461.7	0
Savings	126455.2	59887.5	-12868.0	24451.7	0	-3604.3	0
Total Output	1747516.8	208925.4	321357.4	412496.4	126188.4	152584.1	189824.4

* See Table A.3 for explanation of some of these values.

In millions of won.

Table A-3: Simplified 1978 SAM

	Productive sectors	Foreign	Labour	Self-employed	Capitalists consumption	Government	Investment
Productive sectors	19989.9	7113.3	6947.2	4907.5	2939.8	2835.1	4147.2
Foreign	5650.8	0	143.8	101.6	60.9	177.8	1659.2
Labour	7285.3	0	0	0	971.9	0	0
Self-employed	6165.9	0	0	0	0	0	0
Capitalists consumption	4306.1	0	0	0	0	0	0
Government	969.1(T_m) 1126.4(T_x) 399.8(T_π) 361.7(T_{π_1})	0	29.2(T_{mw}) 125.0(T_w) -120.9(G_w)	20.6(T_{mv}) 84.9(T_v) -90.2(G_v)	12.3(T_{mc})	30.2(T_{mg})	0
Savings	3205.2	679.3(S_f)	1305.0(S_w) -172.1(π_w)	1188.0(S_v) -46.5(π_v)	0	226.2(S_g)	0
Total Output	48880.0	7792.0	8257.2	6165.9	4306.1	5806.4	

* For definition of the symbols see text.

In billions of won.

Self-Employed Sector

Income from self-employed labour (ΣV_j) = Consumption of domestic goods (ΣC_v) + Consumption of imports (M_v) + Taxes on imports (T_{mv}) + Income taxes (T_v) less transfer payments (G_v) + Savings (S_v) less profit income (Π_v).

The statistical problem here is that the self-employed sector is composed of two disparate parts: peasant proprietors from the agricultural sectors, and workers in family businesses mainly in the wholesale and retail trade sector. In the I-O tables the incomes of all non-wage-earning classes are lumped together under 'other value added'. We need to separate 'other value added' produced capitalistically by wage-labour (i.e. profits) from that produced by independent producers (on farms and in small businesses) with their own family labour.

The procedure is this. We discover from various sources the proportion of total output in each sector attributable to the self-employed and, on the assumption that the ratio of value added to total output within each sector is the same for self-employed and capitalist production, we apply this proportion to sectoral value added to determine the income of the self-employed in each sector. Table A.4, Column 1 shows that proportion of 'other value added' recorded in the I-O table which is attributable to production by the self-employed, assumed to hold equally for 1966 and 1978.

The figures for Sectors 1-3 are assumed on the basis of the ownership structure of Korean agriculture, which is based overwhelmingly on owner-cultivation. In 1978 less than 1 percent of farm workers were employed labourers (KSY,1979,p98). We assume therefore that all of 'other value added' in these sectors accrues to the agricultural self-employed.

Sectors 4-39 are more difficult to get at accurately. In their study of income distribution in Korea in the late sixties, Adelman and Robinson used a category of self-employed defined as the smallest firm size - those with fewer than 5 workers - and for want of more precise and up-to-date figures we assume that, except for wholesale and retail trade, they still held in 1978. The proportions are taken from Adelman and Robinson (1978, Table D.5, p262) which shows the value of output by sector attributable to the self-employed in 1968. We make the assumption, therefore, that there have been no marked shifts in industrial concentration at the lower end since 1968.

For the wholesale and retail trade sector, Sector 34, we give in brackets an updated figure. This sector is by far the most important in generating income for the non-farm self-employed. This bracketed figure (from KSY,1979,p222) shows the proportion of 1976 total sales in the wholesale and retail trade sector attributable to firms with 1-4 workers (including owners). Table A.5 shows that the self-employed are heavily concentrated in a few sectors. We can now derive our figures for 1978 and 1966.

1978 SAM

Total self-employed earnings within the 39 productive sectors (ΣV_j) were 6165920.2 mw (of which 3935603.4 mw came from the agricultural sectors and 2230316.8 mw from manufacturing and services). The value of government transfers $(G_v=90200.0$ mw) will be derived in the government sector.

Profit income (Π_v) provided problems again. For the non-farm self-employed we assume that the proportion of income received as interest, dividends and rent is

Table A-4:   Self-employed income shares and capital stocks

		Proportion of output due to self-employed	Capital stocks owned by the self-employed (mw) 1966	1978
1	Grain	1.00	367,519	4,192,521
2	Otherag	1.00	270,071	3,980,896
3	Forestry	1.00	40,141	482,573
4	Fishery	.31	27,498	832,932
5	Coal	.01	163	2,065
6	Othermin	.01	55	2,352
7	Profood	.11	3,109	96,178
8	Bevstob	.02	262	6,749
9	Fibrespin	.01	522	10,981
10	Textfab	.01	156	7,901
11	Fintexpro	.15	1,516	97,793
12	Lumply	.03	105	7,649
13	Woodpro	.36	885	22,933
14	Pulpaper	.06	440	12,999
15	Printpub	.06	199	9,252
16	Leather	.06	38	6,564
17	Rubber	.06	141	11,810
18	Basichem	0	0	0
19	Otherchem	0	0	0
20	Chemfert	0	0	0
21	Petcopro	.05	738	105,365
22	Nonmetmin	.02	411	12,821
23	Irosteel	0	0	0
24	Primispro	.04	283	46,270
25	Nonfermet	.04	185	5,720
26	Fabmetpro	.04	135	12,038
27	Nonelmach	.06	342	23,948
28	Elecmach	.01	32	5,403
29	Transpeq	.02	167	12,833
30	Miscman	.06	255	17,312
31	Building	.02	827	25,398
32	Wr trade	.68(.61)	66,921	1,452,516
33	Transtor	.05	22,400	704,209
34	Fininre	.42	11,173	365,035
35	Electric	0	0	0
36	Watersan	0	0	0
37	Communic	0	0	0
38	Socserv	.04	7,600	227,474
39	Other	0	0	0
	Total		824,289	12,800,490

Source: see text

the same as that for wage and salary earners. The same assumption applies to savings propensities and tax rates. This assumption is made necessary by the absence of figures but is probably not too far from the truth.

Total agricultural household income is comprised of farm and non-farm income. In 1978 the latter made up 25 percent of the total in the average farm household. Nearly all of this will appear elsewhere in the SAM; 5 percent as small

Table A-5:   Proportions of total self-employed income
arising in certain sectors (percent)

	1966	1978
Agriculture (sectors 1-3)	76	64
W'sale & retail trade (sector 34)	18	26
Finance and real estate (sector 36)	3	7
The rest	3	3
	----	----
Total	100	100

business income, 10 percent as wage-earners income, perhaps 8 percent as government transfers (KSY,1979,pp100,108). These would be difficult to separate sensibly so we leave them where they lie.

Interest, dividends and rent to farm households are negligible and are ignored (so that for farm households, $\Pi_v = 0$). We calculate the average farm household tax and public charges rate and the savings rate (income less expenditure plus interest on personal debt). From KSY (1979,p100) for farm households only, $T_v = 3935603.4 \times .0133 = 52343.5$ mw and $S_v = 3935603.4 \times .2154 = 847595.2$ mw.

The savings and tax payments for the self-employed sector as a whole are the sums of its components, farm and non-farm self-employed. Thus for the sector as a whole $\Pi_v = 46491.0$ mw, $T_v = 84950.7$ mw and $S_v = 1188008.5$ mw.

Total self-employed income in 1978 is thus 6302611.2 mw. Consumption of the self-employed is given by total income less taxes and savings (5029625.0 mw) and this is divided between domestic commodities, imports net of duties and duties in the same proportions as for labour.

1966 SAM

Using the same procedures and assumptions as in 1978 we calculate our figures from KSY (1967,p82). Note that in 1966 non-farm income comprised 21 percent of total agricultural income on average. Total self-employed earnings for the 39 sectors was 412496.4 mw of which agriculture accounted for 315551.5 mw and manufacturing and services 96944.9 mw, with government transfers 6400.0 mw. We get $\Pi_v = 1042.4$ mw, $T_v = 7769.0$ mw and $S_v = 24451.7$ mw. Total self-employed income in 1966 was thus 419938.8 mw and total self-employed consumption was 387718.1 mw.

Capitalists' Consumption Sector

Capitalists' consumption fund allocated from profits (ΣC_j) = Consumption of domestic goods (ΣC_c) + Consumption of imports (M_c) + Taxes on imports (T_{mc}) + Taxes on capitalists' income (T_c).

These represent the funds deducted from net profits and used for the purposes of capitalists' consumption. Capitalists do not save out of this fund by definition - all savings are assumed to stay within the firm as retained earnings. Capitalists do, however, pay taxes on this consumption expenditure - income taxes - while company taxes are paid out of retained earnings.

The figures for this sector are calculated in an order opposite to the previous two, i.e. we first calculate capitalists' consumption and from this we know how much income to deduct from profits net of taxes.

1978 SAM

First we note the total consumption of the labour and self-employed sectors as calculated in the previous two sections from the household expenditure surveys. The difference between that total and total private consumption expenditure in the I-O tables we allocate to capitalists' consumption. This way of dividing up private consumption expenditure in the I-O tables preserves the additivity of the I-O tables, which is the touch-stone of all calculations. We assume that capitalists divide their consumption expenditure between domestic goods, imports less duties and duties in the same proportions as labour and the self-employed. Total expenditure by capitalists on these was 3013024.8 mw in 1978 which was 19.9 percent of total private consumption. The assumption is of course quite unrealistic, but since the Korean statisticians do not single out capitalists as consumers (or as anything else) there is little alternative. There are no government transfers to capitalists as consumers. They do pay taxes on income (total in 1978, 1293100.0 mw) - see the section on government revenue for the derivation. Total income, therefore, of the capitalists' consumption sector in 1978 was 4306124.8 mw.

Sensitivity analysis shows that this way of treating capitalists' consumption does not have a major effect on the results. However, output proportions are sensitive to variations in the absolute level of capitalists' consumption while prices are not, and relative prices are sensitive to variations in sectoral contributions to the consumption fund while outputs are not.

Now it remains to distribute this total fund among the 39 producing sectors and we do so on the unavoidable assumption that every sector allocates a fixed proportion of its surplus to the consumption fund. We calculate total available surplus from the I-O table by adding together 'other value added less self-employed earnings' plus 'consumption of fixed capital' (depreciation). Total surplus available in 1978 was 7692547.5 mw. The proportion of this allocated to the consumption fund in each sector was 0.5598. Note also that taxes on profits were subtracted from total available surplus in the same way and allotted to the government revenue account (taxes on profits were derived from national income figures - see the government sector - and assumed to fall equally on the sectors).

1966 SAM

Exactly the same procedure was used for the 1966 figures. Expenditure on domestic goods, imports less duties and duties was 95202.4 mw and taxes on capitalists' consumption amounted to 30968.0 mw. The total fund for capitalists' consumption was thus 126188.4 mw which was 14.4 percent of total private consumption. Total available surplus in 1966 was 260135.9 mw so that the proportion of this allocated to capitalists' consumption in each sector was 0.4851.

Government Sector

Indirect taxes less subsidies (ΣT_{xj}) + Customs duties on intermediate, capital and consumption goods $(\Sigma T_{mj} + \Sigma T_{ij} + T_{mw} + T_{mv} + T_{mc} + T_{mg})$ + Taxes on profits (T_{π}) + Foreign aid (T_f) + Taxes on income less transfer payments $(T_w + T_v + T_c - G_w - G_v)$ = Consumption of domestic goods (ΣC_g) + Consumption of imports by government (M_g) + Government wage payments (W_g) + Government savings (S_g).

This sector proved most difficult to put into consistent order because of the need to resort to government accounts and the consequent requirement that these conform to the I-O figures. Where it was necessary to choose between the two, the I-O figures were assumed correct so that some of our numbers may not match those in the national income statistics.

Government revenue is derived from taxation of all sectors. On the 39 productive sectors these are customs duties (T_m), indirect taxes less subsidies (T_x) and taxes on profits (T_{π}). The consumer sectors paid customs duties on the consumer goods they imported (T_{mw}, T_{mv}, T_{mc}) as well as income taxes (T_w, T_v, T_c). The government pays customs duties to itself (T_{mg}). The government also receives foreign aid (T_f).

Government expenditure is made up of purchases of consumption goods *and* government fixed capital formation (the latter being added to consumption as a government investment activity which does not, by assumption, leave it with accumulated capital stocks - these passing to the community). Some of these purchases are imports. The government also pays wages to its employees (W_g) and makes transfer payments to the labour and self-employed sectors (G_w, G_v). The difference between total expenditure and total revenue is government savings $(S_g$, negative for a deficit).

1978 SAM

1) Receipts from indirect taxes less subsidies are from the I-O table; customs duties are calculated from the imports tables of the I-O tables. Note that the *sum* of customs duties and indirect taxes is quite close to the sum of the national income categories 'taxes on goods and services' and 'taxes on international trade and transactions' (ESY,1981,p79), although the deviation of the individual components therein is due to differences in the system of classification in the two sources. In the I-O tables, customs duties and commodity taxes on imports are added together.

2) Taxes on profits are made up of the national income items 'company, corporate and enterprise taxes' and 'social security contributions by employers', and total 399800 mw (ESY,1981,p79). This amount was subtracted from total available surplus in a fixed proportion (.0520) from each sector. [Note that having subtracted capitalists' consumption and taxes on profits from available surplus in each sector we are left with investible surplus in each sector - the amount that appears as a residual after all deductions (but not interest payments on the savings of labour and the self-employed since these flow straight back to the investors in the form of personal savings) are made.]

3) Taxes on labour and the self-employed: we have already seen how these are calculated from the household expenditure surveys and total wage and self-employed income.

4) Taxes on capitalists' consumption. This category, which like others in our

SAMs we create as a composite of more usual categories, is also calculated as a residual. It is the difference between the sum of taxes paid by labour and the self-employed and the sum of government revenue from the following five national income categories:

a) taxes on individuals
b) other taxes on net incomes and profits
c) other taxes
d) taxes on property
e) non-tax revenue except administrative fees and charges
    and non-industrial sales.

For details of figures see ESY (1981,p79). Note that 'capital revenue' is assumed to have been deducted from government fixed capital formation in the I-O tables.

5) Foreign aid was nil in 1978.

The basis for government expenditure is the sum of the 1978 I-O final demand categories 'government consumption' and 'government fixed capital formation', but this is augmented from the government accounts (ESY,1981,p81). In the 1978 I-O table, however, government 'value-added activity' is recorded in the dummy Sector 55 ('administrative services'). Unfortunately, this covers only government wage payments etc. for administration and not for government services such as education and health. The latter appear in Sector 56 ('social services') mixed up with privately run services. The fiction of the I-O table is that the government 'purchases' its administrative and social services from these sectors. We cannot feasibly net out private services from Sector 56 so we go along with the fiction, but Sector 55 is added to the government consumption column so that purchases from that sector are eliminated. The treatment of Sector 56 outputs as sales to the government means that government wage payments to teachers, for example, will not be recorded as government wage payments but as part of government purchases of the output of Sector 56. Government workers thus receive their wages from the government 'mediated' through Sector 56. Also the big government revenue category 'administrative fees and charges and non-industrial sales' (amounting to 425900 mw in 1978) is already accounted for in private consumption expenditure of Sector 56 output. As such it will be netted out of government purchases from that sector.

We have tried to allow for all this in using the government accounts statistics. In particular, note that according to the government accounts, total government outgoings for wages and salaries in 1978 were 1290000 mw while we have recorded in our SAM only 971882 (wages paid in Sector 55); the difference (318118 mw) appears in government purchases from Sector 56 and amounted to 860281 mw (Sector 56 had a total wage bill of 976030 mw).

Government expenditure on transfer payments (G_w and G_v) is taken from ESY (1981,p81) the total being divided between labour and the self-employed in proportion to their total income.

Government savings are made up as below, the second, third and fourth items being derived from ESY (1981,p81) with the deficit a residual (total revenue less total expenditure including savings).

1966 SAM

Details of the national income figures are given in Tables A.6 and A.7. It was necessary to add together central government and local government figures from the national accounts.

other value added in Sector 56	19834.3
transfers abroad	14200.0
interest payments, domestic and foreign	216100.0
capital transfers, domestic and foreign	147900.0
government deficit	-170275.3
	----------
total government savings	227759.0

1) Customs duties are calculated from the I-O tables. Contrary to 1978 practice the 1966 I-O tables record commodity taxes on imports under 'indirect taxes' levied on the wholesale and retail trade sector rather than added to customs duties (i.e. it is a row rather than a column item) - see BOK, *Compilatory Report* (1978,p158). Indirect taxes less subsidies are taken directly from the I-O table. Note the near equality between the national income category 'taxes on production and expenditure' and the sum of the I-O categories 'customs duties' and 'indirect taxes less subsidies' (KSY,1971,pp270,298).

2) Taxes on profits correspond to 'taxes on income of corporations' (see Table A.6).

3) Taxes on labour and the self-employed have been derived from the household expenditure surveys and total wage and self-employed income.

4) Taxes on capitalists' consumption are calculated as the difference between the sum of taxes paid by labour and the self-employed and the sum of government revenue from the following categories:

a) taxes on household income
b) other current transfers from households
c) income from ownership of property
d) taxes on capital
e) other capital transfers from the private sector.
See Table A.6.

5) Foreign aid is made up only of 'transfers from abroad' (Table A.6). Government borrowing from abroad appears along with private overseas borrowing in the foreign savings catogory of the SAM.

In the 1966 I-O tables, government wage payments in the general administrative sector do not form a dummy sector but are considered to be the value-added portion of 'government consumption'. However, it remains true that a large part of government wage payments (those for teachers etc.) are hidden in government purchases from Sector 41, 'other services' (mostly education). The 1966 I-O tables record government wage payments as 51278 mw while the national income figures list wage and salary payments by local and central government as 80030 mw (see Table A.7). In 1966 government consumption from Sector 41 was 27209 mw, not enough to fill the gap. The balance is buried somewhere in government purchases from other sectors.

The tables below are condensed from KSY (1971, Table 136, p270 & Table 143, p298) which contain the economic classification of central and local government transactions. Note that in South Korea the financial (fiscal) year is the same as the calendar year.

To calculate government savings and the net deficit, we first form the category 'net lending':

Net lending =   domestic loans and subscriptions - repayments
of direct loans - net domestic borrowing
- other net capital receipts.

Government savings (in billion won) are made up as follows:

5520	Domestic capital transfers
820	Current transfers abroad
1080	Interest payments
6780	Net lending

14200	Total
-17804.3	Government deficit (= total government income - total government expenditure including the savings items above)

-3604.3	Government savings

Table A-6: Government receipts, 1966 (billion won)

	Central govt	Local govt	Total	Corresponding figure/symbol from I-0 or SAM
Net profits from govt enterprise	9.01	1.65	10.66	Accounted for elsewhere in I-0
Income from ownership of property (rent, interest, dividends)	5.38	0.47	5.85	T_c
Taxes on production and expenditure	62.56	9.76	72.32	72.924 (ind. taxes + customs duties)
Taxes on income of:				
Households	20.83	5.21	26.04	T_w, T_v, T_c
Corporations	11.01	0.98	11.99	T_π
Other current transfers from households	5.13	5.64	10.77	T_w, T_v, T_c
Current receipts	113.92	49.79	163.71	
Saving	11.13	14.09	25.22	
Depreciation of fixed capital	3.05	-	3.05	Assumed netted out of fixed capital
Taxes on capital	0.75	-	0.75	T_c expenditure
Other capital transfers from priv sector	0.11	-	0.11	T_c
Transfers from abroad	35.53	-	35.53	T_f
Repayment of direct loans (domestic)	0.70	0.08	0.78	S_g
Net borrowings	8.09	1.18	9.27	
of which:				
Abroad	5.76	-	5.76	S_f
Home	2.33	1.18	3.51	S_g
Other capital receipts	6.37	1.07	7.44	S_g
Savings and capital receipts	65.73	24.70	90.43	

Source: KSY (1971, pp270, 298)

Table A-7: Government expenditure, 1966 (billion won)

	Central govt	Local govt	Total	Corresponding figure/symbol from I-O or SAM
Wages and salaries	46.31	23.72	80.03	51.278
Other current expenditure	18.76	10.31	29.07	4904.6 (incl. business cons.)
Interest payments	1.02	0.06	1.08	S_g
Subsidies	0.02	-	0.02	T_x
Domestic current transfers:				
Private	9.78	1.61	11.39	G_w, G_v
Local/central govt	(26.08)	-	(26.08)	
Current tranfers abroad	0.82	-	0.82	S_f
Current expenditure	102.79	35.70	138.49	
Saving	11.13	14.09	25.22	
Gross capital formation	32.31	17.00	49.31	52.950
Domestic capital transfers:				
Private	4.70	0.82	5.52	S_g
Local/central govt	(8.28)	-	(8.28)	
Capital transfers abroad	-	-	-	S_f
Loans and subscriptions:				
Home	18.29	0.22	18.51	S_g
Abroad	-	-	-	
Capital expenditure	63.58	18.04	81.62	

Source: as for Table A.6

Appendix B
Capital and Inventory Coefficients

Capital Coefficients, 1966

The matrix of capital coefficients is derived, for mining and manufacturing sectors (5-30), from that in Adelman (1969, Table 1, p120). The total coefficients appear in Table B.1, Column 1. These coefficients were constructed for the end of 1965 and here it is assumed that they apply in 1966. Estimates of capital stocks by type of asset (including imported machinery) were made by South Korea's economic planners in preparing the Second Five-Year Plan. They were based on profiles of firms compiled by the Korean Reconstruction Bank from its loan application files and extended through the work of industry committees set up by the planners to gather data on various aspects of Korean industry. The sampled firms were generally among the most modern in their sectors. The coefficients are the required marginal capital coefficients.

Where aggregation was necessary to convert Adelman's (and below Han's) figures to the sectoral classification used here, 1966 sectoral outputs were used as weights. Note that Adelman's figures were calculated using purchasers' prices (see later).

Capital coefficients for non-manufacturing sectors (1-4 and 31-39) are derived from two sources. The total coefficients for each sector are from Kee Chun Han (1970, Table 7.2, pp337-343). These apply to 1968 and were calculated from the National Wealth Survey data. The totals for each sector are distributed among the supplying sectors using the figures compiled by Byung-Nak Song for 1970 and presented in Yoon Hyung Kim (1977, Annex Table 2, pp88-99). The sectoral totals appear in Table B.1, Column 3. The value-added sectors for 1966 are discussed with the 1978 figures.

Capital Coefficients, 1978

Mining and Manufacturing Sectors (5-30)

For 1978 it has been necessary to construct capital coefficients especially for this study. The basis for the sectoral capital stocks is the *Report on the Mining and Manufacturing Census (Survey)*, available for the years 1968-1978 (hereafter MMC or Census). The statistics available allow accurate calculation only of average and not marginal capital coefficients and it is assumed that there was not significant difference between them in an era when Korea had passed the period of capital widening, i.e. it is assumed that the capital stock was not growing much faster than output.

The 1978 Census records sectoral capital stocks by type of asset at book values. It is necessary to convert these book values into replacement values by taking account of i) changes in the prices at which stocks are valued, and ii) the difference between financial depreciation and actual deterioration of capital assets.

Preliminary calculations using the perpetual inventory method produced total coefficients which were well below expected levels and well below those calculated by others for earlier years. It is possible that this is due to serious underestimatioon of rates of depreciation, or more probably due to understatement of levels of investment in the Census. In Table B.1 we present the sectoral total capital coefficients for South Korea reported in other sources; in the last column are the total coefficients finally computed for this study.

Below we construct a net-to-gross conversion factor which is applied to book values of 1978 capital stocks which still employs the understated investment series but avoids the aforementioned problem. As will become apparent, we now rely not on the absolute values of investments but on their relative values. In other words, the investment series are treated as indexes. The same investment series, for each asset in each sector, occurs as both numerator and denominator in calculating the conversion factor so that the only constraint is that the errors of the figures be consistent. A net-to-gross conversion factor (F) is computed for each asset in each sector and this factor is applied to recorded book values (K_b) to arrive at replacement costs (K_r). Stocks of unimproved land are ignored, and $K_r = K_b$ x F. This is the method of Kahn & MacEwan (1967). The modification introduced here is in the calculation of investment indexes for machinery and buildings.

The conversion factor for asset i in sector j is given by

$$F_{ij}^T = \sum_{t=T-L-1}^{T-1} I_{ij}^t P_i^t r_{ij}^t \Big/ \sum_{t=T-L}^{T-1} I_{ij}^t d_{ij}^T$$

where

F_{ij}^T = net-to-gross conversion factor for asset i in industry j at the end of year T; T is 1978

I_{ij}^t = investment in asset i by industry j in year t

P_{ij}^t = price index of asset i in year t

r_{ij}^t = survival factor indicating proportion of capital good i in industry j installed in year t which is still in service in year T

d_{ij}^t = financial depreciation of asset i in industry j installed in year t

L_{ij} = average life-span of asset i in industry j

L_{ij} = vintage of the oldest piece of asset i in industry j.

Note that the investment series I_{ij} may be actual investments or simply an index of investments. The capital-output coefficients are calculated from

Table B-1: Total capital-output coefficients for South Korea

		(1) Adelman 1965	(2) Song 1970	(3) Han 1968	(4) Hamilton 1978
1	Grain		1.465	.567	
2	Other agric		1.465	.122	
3	Forestry		1.465	.602	
4	Fishery		3.618	2.486	
5	Coal	1.057	2.069	.525	.962
6	Other mining	.361	1.550	.467	.815
7	Processed food	.285	.362	.258	.379
8	Bevs & tobacco	.230	.270	.192	.231
9	Fibre spinning	1.000	1.282	.751	.934
10	Textile fabric	.364	.726	.518	.656
11	Fin.text. prod	.164	.357	.255	.337
12	Lumber & ply	.155	.295	.211	.454
13	Wood prod/furn	.360	.397	.283	.598
14	Pulp & paper	.389	1.192	.709	.464
15	Print & publ	.217	.593	.423	.676
16	Leather prod	.075	.403	.287	.211
17	Rubber prod	.160	.921	.629	.359
18	Basic chemical	.922	1.564	1.055	.926
19	Other chemical	.378	.855	.234	.385
20	Chem. fert'zer	1.430	1.816	.987	1.470
21	Pet &coal prod	.406	1.150	.507	1.150
22	Nonmetmin prod	.908	1.196	.873	.811
23	Iron & steel	.863	1.278	.672	1.278
24	Steel prod	.446	1.151	.554	.932
25	Nonferr. metal	.850	1.354	.756	.619
26	Fab.metal prod	.279	.782	.535	.473
27	General machin	.507	.804	.567	.614
28	Elect machine	.209	.338	.229	.274
29	Transp equip	.335	.791	.409	.475
30	Misc manuf	.204	.368	.390	.367
31	Building		.317	.189	
32	Trade		.567	.567	
33	Transp & stor		5.769	4.737	
34	Finance & real		.429	19.244[a]	
35	Electric & gas		8.074	3.528	
36	Water & sanit		7.008	3.533	
37	Communications		2.770	2.428	
38	Social service		1.572	3.019	
39	Other		0	.378	

a. Clearly there are differences of classification here and we use Song's figure.

Sources: (1) Adelman (1969, p120), (2) Yoon Hyung Kim (1977, pp88-99), (3) Han (1970, Table 7.2, pp337-43).

$$k_{ij}^T = K_{ij}^T / Y_j^T u_j$$

where

k_{ij}^T = the capital coefficient for the ith capital good in industry j at the beginning of year T

K_{ij}^T = replacement cost of the ith capital good in industry j

Y_j^T = gross output of industry j in year T

u_j = reciprocal of the level of capacity utilization in industry j

The sources and application of the data are descibed next.

Survival factors The survival factor r is the percentage of the relevant capital good installed in year t still in service in year T and its particular form is taken from Evans (1972, p167). It is derived from a survival function $R(\tau)$ in which τ is the number of years since the capital good was installed and which for discrete time has the form

$$R(\tau) = 1 - [1/\sqrt{2\pi L}] \sum_{t=0}^{\tau-1} \exp[-(t-L)^2/2L] .$$

This function is based on a probability distribution around the average life L, as in the figure below:

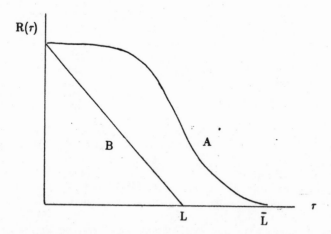

The cut-off point for L is taken to be two standard deviations $(2\sqrt{L})$ from the average life L. A survival function with this shape reflects the fact that new assets do not, as a rule, deteriorate as rapidly as old assets.

Depreciation rates The financial depreciation function d_{ij}^t is assumed to be a straight line (curve B in the figure above) for want of accurate data on financial depreciation rates in South Korea. Curve B can be written $R(\tau) = 1 - \tau/L$. The complexity and obscurity of depreciation rules in Korea have led to the assumption that depreciation is of straight-line form. This assumption is also applied in the International Management Institute study cited below, and is made in the model of the Korean economy built by Adelman & Robinson (1978, p207). To make some allowance for the favourable provisions of the tax laws we have assumed that the depreciable life of buildings and structures is 25 years while that of the other assets remains equal to assumed life-spans (see below).

Capacity utilization We assume that for the year 1978 there is full capacity utilization in all sectors. According to official figures, manufacturing industry operated above capacity in 1978 at a level of 111.1 taking the 1976 capacity level as 100. This was the highest level in the 1974-1980 period (ESY, 1981, Table 100). This was the case in nearly all industry groups. See also the industrial production indexes which reveal that all indicators were rising in 1978 to their peak in 1979.

Life-spans The estimated life-span for each asset is assumed to apply equally in all sectors. They are taken from International Management Institute (1972, pA-5-159).

Asset	Average serviceable life (years)
Buildings and structures	50
Machinery and equipment	10
Vehicles and delivery equipment	5

These correspond closely to the average service lives of buildings, machinery and vehicles for Japan reported in OECD (1983, Tables 2-5).

Investment series The basic source here is the collection of mining and manufacturing censuses and surveys for the years 1968-1978 (census years were 1968, 1973 and 1978). Investment by sector is only available from 1968 so that it was necessary to attempt to estimate the replacement cost of the stock of each asset in each sector which existed in 1968 and which still survived in 1978. Clearly this is unnecessary in the case of vehicles in which category the oldest surviving asset in 1978 was bought in 1968 $(L + 2\sqrt{L} = 9.5)$.

One method would be to construct an estimate of the investment series for each sector prior to 1968. This was the preferred method in the case of machinery and equipment where the pre-1968 tail of the investment series accounts for a very small proportion of the 1978 stocks as a consequence of the rapidity of deterioration of machines after ten years (the average life-span). It was decided to apply a common tail to each sector, one derived from figures for aggregate investment in machinery and equipment - the 'machinery and equipment' component of gross domestic capital formation from KSY (1967 & 1979) and ESY (1967).

How much error is likely to be introduced into the calculation of machinery stocks as a result of choosing a particular year (here 1968) to splice the industry-specific body with the common tail? In the following example the errors are exaggerated to indicate the maximum likely deviation. Suppose that the common tail underestimates actual pre-1968 investment in industry j because of i) the deviation of the actual pre-1968 investment profile from the hypothesized profile, and ii) the choice of splicing year, which has an uncharacteristically low value. Assume that the real level of undeteriorated (accumulated) investment is an evenly-distributed 100 both before 1968 and since 1968. Because of the shape of the survival function, after deterioration the pre-1968 part of total investment will stand at only one ninth of the level of post-1968 investments. If the actual undeteriorated tail in fact represents one third rather than one half of total undeteriorated investments (representing perhaps an upper limit for Korean development) then only $1/2 \times 1/9 = 1/18 = 5.5$ percent of the error will be carried through to final deteriorated stocks.

The common tail (J) appears in Table B.2 along with the price index and deterioration function for machinery and equipment. We now have for each sector an index of investment in machinery and equipment for 1960-1977 and can apply the formula for the conversion factor.

Table B-2: Investment and price indexes for machinery

	J	P	r
1977		1.040	1.00
1976		1.085	.99
1975		1.163	.98
1974		1.400	.96
1973		1.669	.93
1972		1.713	.87
1971		1.897	.79
1970		2.009	.69
1969		2.294	.57
1968	(100.0)	2.349	.44
1967	65.0	2.637	.32
1966	59.7	2.879	.22
1965	23.4	3.371	.14
1964	17.3	3.890	.09
1963	14.9	4.866	.05
1962	10.8	5.311	.04
1961	7.3	5.384	.03
1960	5.5	5.538	.02

In the case of buildings and structures, use of the method described above would not give results of acceptable accuracy because of the importance of the pre-1968 tail for this asset. The assumption of a uniform or common pre-1968 investment index would be spurious because of i) the fact of bunching in investments in construction, and ii) the related inaccuracy due to the choice of 1968 (or any particular year) as the date for splicing the common with the sector-specific indexes.

Instead, we use a method which adds investments in the 1969-1977 period to the *stock* of buildings in 1968 in each sector. These sectoral stocks are given as book values in the 1968 Mining and Manufacturing Census (but see later). The apparent problem raised here is the variable age distribution of 1968 stocks of buildings since this will influence the proportion of 1968 stocks that survives into 1978.

However, this difficulty is avoided by reference to the fact that nearly all of the buildings existing in 1968 were built subsequent to 1953 - 87 percent of real value in fact, and 67 percent subsequent to 1962 (see Table B.3). Observe that, using our survival function, assets with an average life-span of 50 years do not deteriorate at all for the first 25 years. As a result, the stocks of buildings in 1968 do not deteriorate significantly in the years to 1978, and we assume that they do not deteriorate at all. We can thus treat the stock of 1968 buildings as if it were a block of *investments* in that year.

Table B-3: Indexes of building investment and prices, 1913-68

Index of investment (cur.price) / Price index / Survival factor

Year	J	P	r		Year	J	P	r
1968	414,363	1,000,000,000	1.00		1939	1.23	1,305	.99
	268,215	885,841,000	1.00			.939	1,113	.99
	209,185	871,224,000	1.00			.788	931	.99
1965	148,706	803,027,000	1.00			.601	799	.99
	79,365	666,134,000	1.00		1935	.500	752	.99
	78,767	560,388,000	1.00			.340	682	.99
	57,853	551,123,000	1.00			.326	672	.99
	39,225	548,341,000	1.00			.256	605	.98
1960	28,723	505,588,000	1.00			.208	610	.97
	30,126	475,710,000	1.00		1930	.231	758	.96
	25,554	499,846,000	1.00			.269	869	.95
	25,328	499,267,000	1.00			.262	900	.93
	15,821	431,066,000	1.00			.249	918	.91
1955	14,146	379,760,000	1.00			.247	981	.89
	5,908	270,495,000	1.00		1925	.221	1,082	.86
	3,712	140,205,000	1.00			.206	1,020	.82
	2,341	83,923,000	1.00			.192	947	.78
	930	48,448,000	1.00			.183	960	.74
1950	125	9,809,000	1.00			.162	965	.69
	133	7,393,053	1.00		1920	.192	1,284	.64
	69.1	4,374,296	1.00			.188	1,238	.59
	32.2	2,757,796	1.00			.118	988	.53
	16.4	1,185,595	1.00			.070	724	.47
1945	8.80	42,728	1.00			.049	521	.41
	4.49	2,972	1.00		1915	.045	446	.36
	3.83	2,714	1.00			.024	475	.31
	3.13	1,724	1.00			.023	503	.26
	2.30	1,643	1.00					
1940	1.54	1,393	1.00					

Sources: the current-price index of investment in buildings and structures, J, is made up of proxies from various sources. The 1913-1940 period is measured by 'gross output of manufacturing industry' and is from Hong (1979, Table B.1). The difficult war years have been represented as follows: 1941-1942, 'employment in manufacturing industry' × 'wage index' from Hong (ibid. Table B.12) and BOK, Chosen (1948, Table 6); 1943-1945 'total loans by banks etc' from BOK, Chosen (1948, Table 6). The period 1946-1953 is represented by an index of production of major commodities x wholesale price index for the relevant years taken from, respectively, Kim and Roemer (1979) and BOK, PSS (1970, p162). The years 1954-1968 are represented by the 'non-residential buildings' and 'other construction and works' components of gross domestic capital formation from KSY (1967 & 1979). The price index, P, is from Han (1970, Appendix B), 'glass clay and stone products'.

Note that the above method for buildings could not be used for machinery and equipment because the shorter life-span of machines requires that we know the age-distribution of 1968 stocks. Different age-distributions would leave different proportions of 1968 stocks intact in 1978, whereas we have argued that in the case of buildings the age-distribution is given by the newness of building investment. The key assumptions of this method, therefore, are 1) that we can estimate the replacement cost of building stocks in 1968, and 2) that industrial development has been so recent that the great bulk of buildings existing in 1978 are less than 25 years old.

How do we estimate the replacement value of 1968 stocks of buildings? There are two possibilities: 1) Adjust the sectoral book-values of stocks given in the 1968 MMC by applying a crude net-to-gross conversion factor. This would of necessity be an economy-wide conversion factor using aggregate data on investments and prices. These indexes appear in Table B.4. The computed conversion factor would be applied to each sectoral book value to get replacement value. 2) Apply actual capital-output coefficients for buildings in 1968 from another source. Coefficients for 1970 have been prepared by Yoon Hyung Kim (1977, pp88-99) and these are based on the coefficients derived by Byung-Nak Song (1975?). We assume that the 1970 coefficient values do not deviate markedly from 1968 values. The second method has been used here.

We now have sectoral investment series for 1968-1977 and, applying the price series, deterioration and depreciation functions, we can calculate our conversion factors for buildings and structures. Our final conversion factor is given by

$$F^{78} = \Sigma_{68}^{77} I^t P^t / \Sigma_{68}^{77} I^t d^t$$

remembering that $r^t = 1$ for all relevant years. Although we have chosen the second method for calculating investments in 1968, as a matter of interest the calculation of 1968 investment from book values of stocks in 1968 would use the formula

$$I^{68} = K_B^{68} \times F^{68}$$

$$= K_B^{68} \times (\Sigma_{10}^{67} J^t P^t r^t / \Sigma_{10}^{67} J^t d^t)$$

where K_B^{68} is the book value of stocks in 1968 and J^t is an index of total investments in buildings over the period. In fact $F^{68} = 1.7503$.

Price indexes For each type of asset, price indexes are taken from KSY (1967 & 1979), and BOK, PSS (1967 & 1970). In the case of buildings and structures, the pre-1968 price index appears, with sources, in Table B.3. Price indexes for the 1968-1978 period appear in Table B.4.

The net-to-gross conversion factors for the three types of asset in the mining and manufacturing sectors appear in Table B.5.

Capital stocks and their valuation Book values of capital stocks by industry for the three asset groups 'buildings and structures', 'machinery and equipment' and 'vehicles and ships' are from the 1978 MMC. These are recorded in purchasers' prices so it was necessary to convert to producers' prices to conform to the valuation of outputs in the input-output tables from which we take values of sectoral outputs. (The I-O tables do not give alternative values of outputs in

Table B-4: Price indexes of capital goods, 1968-1978

	Buildings & structures	Machinery & equipment	Vehicles & ships
1978	1.000	1.000	1.000
1977	1.067	1.040	1.026
1976	1.172	1.085	1.067
1975	1.248	1.163	1.126
1974	1.498	1.400	1.367
1973	2.087	1.669	1.586
1972	2.355	1.713	1.584
1971	2.563	1.897	1.849
1970	2.600	2.009	1.986
1969	2.993	2.294	1.986
1968	3.136	2.349	1.986

Table B-5: Net-to-gross conversion factors

		Buildings & structures	Machinery & equipment	Vehicles & ships
1	Coal	2.7353	1.9414	2.2358
2	Othermin	3.2757	1.9299	2.0857
3	Profood	2.5080	1.8608	2.2533
4	Bevstob	2.3586	1.9370	2.1470
5	Fibspin	2.2380	1.8626	2.5568
6	Textfab	2.1937	1.8524	1.9727
7	Fintexpr	2.3478	1.9576	2.0924
8	Lumply	2.4997	2.7899	2.0855
9	Woodfurn	3.3212	1.8501	1.7940
10	Pulpaper	2.7153	1.8249	2.0455
11	Printpub	2.4252	2.0235	2.3909
12	Leather	1.8800	1.5108	1.7389
13	Rubber	2.2257	1.8163	1.7078
14	Basichem	2.1832	1.8102	1.8921
15	Othechem	1.9303	1.8142	1.9947
16	Chemfert	2.1727	2.7299	1.9924
17	Petcopro	3.1835	2.2896	1.9845
18	Nometmin	2.3961	1.8761	1.7505
19	Irosteel	2.1142	1.5516	1.8861
20	Irostpro	2.0522	1.6956	2.2021
21	Nofermet	2.5263	1.9939	2.1569
22	Fabmetpr	2.0718	1.6699	1.8820
23	Noelmach	1.7280	1.3724	1.7351
24	Elecmach	1.5768	1.5918	2.1502
25	Transpeq	2.1815	1.5437	2.0302
26	Miscman	2.2304	1.6032	1.6962

purchasers' prices.) In the I-O tables over several years, the proportion of private fixed capital formation due to 'wholesale and retail trade' and 'transportation and storage' has hovered around a fairly stable 6 percent. We assume that the trade and transport margins for building and construction are negligible so that the whole of these costs are applied to machinery. Applying the weight of machinery in total capital stock (.6609) to this 6 percent we get factors for converting our capital stocks of buildings and machinery from purchasers' prices to producers' prices of, respectively, 1.0 and .9092. The same method was used to convert 1966 capital stocks to producers' prices, here taking the trade margin to be 6 percent and the weight of machinery in total capital stocks to be .5925, giving a conversion factor for machinery of .8987.

Reclassification of assets Once we have the conversion factors for each of the three assets in each of the manufacturing industries we can calculate the replacement value of capital stocks and thus the capital-output coefficients. However, our crude data do not divide stocks of machinery between nonelectrical and electrical machinery, and, more importantly, do not distinguish imported machinery (including transport equipment) from the domestically-produced article. This is of the utmost importance in the case of Korea. As far as I am aware there are no figures which indicate or approximate the value of machinery imports by destination for 1978 or thereabouts.

As a rough approximation, we distribute the sum of stocks of machinery and equipment and vehicles in each industry between the domestic categories (nonelectrical machinery, electrical machinery, and transport equipment) and imported machinery (imports undifferentiated) in the same proportions as those which were applied in Adelman's 1965 coefficient matrix (Adelman, 1969, Table 1, p120). We could make some adjustment to these proportions, however, on the basis of the trade figures which indicate the composition of imports by sectoral origin. Table B.6 shows the proportions of total investments in machinery and transport equipment which have been imported, for the period 1955-1980. Clearly there has been a substantial increase in import content of machinery stocks. We can estimate the extent of this increase by taking a weighted average of import coefficients over the 18 years prior to 1978, 18 being the age of the oldest vintage of machinery still in use in the base year with our chosen survival assumption for machinery. The weights are the survival factors. Data were not available prior to 1955 so we had to be content with the 11 years prior to 1966. This would not have an appreciable effect on the results. The averages are for 1978 .787 and for 1966 .445.

In fact, on the basis of Adelman's coefficients and 1966 outputs the total stock of imported machinery forms .737 of the total stocks of machinery in 1966 - very close to the 1978 figure calculated from the trade figures. Hong (1979, Table 7.3, p154) suggests on the basis of I-O tables for the years 1960-73 that the import content of inputs of machinery was, apart from 1960, around 70 percent. The high figure in Adelman is due to two facts: 1) her coefficients refer to manufacturing industry only in which imported machinery has played a proportionately greater role, and 2) Adelman's method of compiling the figures emphasized the most modern factories which were more import-dependent. In the end, then, we made no adjustment to Adelman's 1965 distribution between imported and domestically-produced machines in our calculations for 1978.

Summary
In summary, the procedure for calculating 1978 capital coefficents is as follows:

1. find net-to-gross conversion factors for each asset in each industry using investment and price series, financial depreciation and deterioration functions;

Table B-6:   Import content of machinery investment

	Investments in machinery(b won)	Proportion imported
1955	3.40	.482
1956	6.01	.356
1957	6.94	.306
1958	6.72	.273
1959	7.00	.299
1960	8.51	.306
1961	12.03	.458
1962	17.25	.526
1963	26.33	.571
1964	27.96	.637
1965	39.61	.503
1966	95.56	.489
1967	126.37	.670
1968	180.75	.817
1969	222.16	.813
1970	233.53	.799
1971	308.48	.827
1972	374.38	.812
1973	560.93	.820
1974	890.78	1.004
1975	1,381.89	.669
1976	1,411.83	.818
1977	1,908.37	.737
1978	3,081.98	.777
1979	3,948.07	.751
1980	3,783.87	.878

Sources: Total investment in machinery is the sum of the 'machinery and other equipment' and 'transport equipment' components of gross domestic capital formation from ESY (1981, Table 153) and BOK, NIK (1982, Table 6). Imports of 'machinery and transport equipment' are from ESY (1981, Tables 124 & 130), and ESY (1970, Tables 142 & 147), ESY (1967, Tables 149 & 156), and ESY (1960, Table 117).

2. calculate capital stocks by applying conversion factors to book values;

3. convert capital stocks into producers' prices;

4. reallocate capital stocks to imported capital goods and domestic capital goods (nonelectrical and electrical machinery, and transport equipment);

5. calculate capital coefficients using total outputs; and

6. validate the results against the investment figures in the base years.

The final capital-output coefficients appear in Table B.7 below and for convenient comparison the totals for each sector appear in Table B.1.

Table B-7: Capital-output coefficients, Korea 1978

Sector		5	6a	7a	8	9	10
Noelmach	27	.0167	.2562	.1234	.0368	.0129	.0884
Elecmach	28	.0773	.0369	.0190	.0153	.0020	.0051
Transpeq	29	.0463	.0854	.0029	.0078	.0034	.0047
Building	31	.6695	.3349	.1886	.1063	.2552	.2286
Imports	40	.1526	.1012	.0449	.0665	.6600	.3290
Totals		.9624	.8146	.3788	.2327	.9335	.6558

11a	12	13	14	15a	16a	17	18a
.0512	.0258	.0060	.0133	.0425	.0004	.0358	.0663
.0112	.0123	.0102	.0190	.0042	.0380	.0165	.0280
.0022	.0252	.0102	.0052	0	.0051	.0041	.0103
.1531	.1386	.2989	.1760	.2552	.1147	.1016	.2420
.1195	.2516	.2724	.2507	.3742	.0531	.2010	.5792
.3372	.4535	.5977	.4642	.6761	.2113	.3590	.9258

19a	20a	21b	22	23b	24	25	26
.0338	.0065	.0049	.0573	.0517	.1679	.0318	.0746
.0223	.0013	0	.0365	.2444	.0149	.1337	.0153
.0041	.0366	.0805	.0035	.0357	.0056	.0029	.0012
.1419	.1628	.4502	.3044	.3380	.2320	.2121	.1717
.1829	1.2628	.6145	.4094	.6082	.5113	.2388	.2097
.3850	1.4700	1.1501	.8111	1.2780	.9317	.6193	.4725

27	28	29a	30a
.1084	.0240	.0334	.0192
.0100	.0187	.0087	.0375
.0052	.0014	.0123	.0061
.2698	.0973	.1940	.1823
.2210	.1321	.2261	.1218
.6144	.2735	.4745	.3669

a. Where there are large differences in sectoral gross outputs between the I-O tables and the MMC, due to differences in classification and the base for compiling figures (the Census excludes some establishments), the Census has been taken as the divisor for calculating coefficients. This ensures that capital stock and gross output figures refer to the same set of establishments.

b. In the cases of these two industries there are irrecon- cilable differences in classification between the I-O tables and the MMC. Instead we have used the coefficients in Song, the totals of which appear in Table B.1.

Other Productive Sectors (1-4, 31-39)

Coefficients for Sectors 1-4 and 31-39 are as for 1966, i.e. total coefficients from Han (see Column 3 of Table B.1) distributed among supplying sectors using the proportions from Yoon Hyung Kim (1977).

Labour, the Self-Employed and Capitalists' Consumption (41-43)

We must account for capital stocks used in (re)producing labour and the self-employed and capitalists as consumers. It would prove too difficult to attempt a reasonable assessment of the resources put into the production of skilled labour, i.e. the education costs of the average wage-worker and self-employed worker. We could, however, estimate the average stock of housing necessary to reproduce these workers, this capital being (besides skills) the most important fixed asset in these sectors.

However, we find that the 'depreciation' on housing which is embodied in workers etc. is already accounted for in the I-O category 'private consumption expenditure' since this current expenditure includes imputed rent on owner-occupied dwellings as purchases from the real estate sector (see BOK, *Compilatory Report*, 1975, p160). Moreover, in the case of labour, the wages row of the transactions table covers not only the needs of simple reproduction (subsistence) but also a return to the skill component of labour and therefore 'profits' on capital used in producing labour-power. Consequently, fixed capital used in these sectors is zero.

As a matter of interest, we can calculate the average unit cost of dwellings in rural and urban areas in 1978 from Korea Housing Bank, *Twelfth Annual Report* 1978, (p26):

Urban housing unit cost   5.9687 m won
Rural housing unit cost   3.1359 m won.

For the labour sector we know that on average in each city household of wage and salary earners there are 1.26 earners (KSY, 1979, p420). Thus our capital coefficient for labour is

cost of housing per worker = 5.9687 x 1/1.26 = 4.7371.

For the self-employed sector we first assume that the coefficient for the urban self-employed is the same as that for labour. For farms, the number of farm workers engaged in agriculture in 1978 was 4,713,000 (KSY, 1979, p72) and the number of farm households was 2,223,807 (KSY, 1979, p95) giving 2.12 farm workers per household, so that

cost of housing per farm worker = 3.1359 x 1/2.12 = 1.4797.

For the self-employed sector as a whole we take an average of the coefficients of the farm and urban components weighted by the number of workers in each. The number of non-farm self-employed (including working family members) was 2,547,000 (KSY, 1979, p73). The coefficient for the self-employed sector as a whole is therefore

cost of housing per self-employed worker = 2.6225.

Inventory coefficients, 1966 & 1978

These proved difficult. For 1966 we chose to accept the inventory coefficients computed by the Economic Planning Board for 1967 (Jo & Park, 1972, p273) and reported in Table B.8. They were preferable to those compiled by Kee Chun Han for 1968 and reported in Y.H. Kim (1977, p54) also reproduced in Table B.8, although the latter have been used for sectors 31-39. There is no reason to believe that the figures chosen will closely reflect actual 1966 inventories; we can only say that they are closer than anything else available.

For 1978 the best source for inventory coefficients appears to the BOK's *Financial Statements Analysis for 1978* (1979), which reports results for all sectors except agriculture (1-3), water and sanitary (36) and other (39) - see Table B.8. These latter are taken from Han's 1968 figures for want of an alternative. The FSA figures, it should be noticed, have 'net sales' as the divisor for computing coefficients, but it was felt the consistency in the compilation of the FSA figures outweighed the formal correctness of dividing by total outputs from the I-O tables.

We have assumed that inventories held in each industry are in the form of own-products; in other words, all inventories are assumed to be finished or semi-finished goods. According to the 1978 FSA, these two categories accounted for 39 percent of total inventories held by manufacturing industry while raw materials (38 percent) and others (24 percent) accounted for the rest (*ibid*. p96). The 1978 breakdown of inventories is inadequate for the allocation of raw materials and others to the sectors which supplied them (including the foreign sector). Nor was it thought appropriate to adopt the method of some statisticians of distributing inventories in the same proportions as the flows of intermediate goods. The error due to the own-product assumption will be quite small when inventories are added to capital stocks.

Table B-8: Inventory coefficients[a]

		EPB 1967	Han 1968	FSA 1978
1	Grain	.0547	.063	
2	Otherag	.0564	.063	
3	Forestry	.0547	.063	
4	Fishery	.0619	.018	.131
5	Coal	.0860	.088	.097
6	Othermin	.0885	.083	.180
7	Profood	.1110	.085	.090
8	Bevstob	.0866	.200	.087
9	Fibspin	.0957	.291	.176
10	Textfab	.0957	.238	.176
11	Fintexpr	.0347	.103	.143
12	Lumply	.0976	.161	.099
13	Woodfurn	.0601	.196	.100
14	Pulpaper	.0704	.109	.111
15	Printpub	.0520	.096	.047
16	Leather	.2692	.187	.242
17	Rubber	.0820	.295	.139
18	Basichem	.0812	.097	.118
19	Othechem	.0812	.141	.125
20	Chemfert	.0812	.253	.139
21	Petcopro	.0549	.156	.133
22	Nometmin	.0994	.186	.130
23	Irosteel	.0776	.159	.186
24	Irostpro	.0776	.223	.186
25	Nofermet	.0776	.054	.127
26	Fabmetpr	.0867	.205	.158
27	Noelmach	.1389	.126	.155
28	Elecmach	.0110	.149	.145
29	Transpeq	.1044	.181	.207
30	Miscman	.0580	.245	.125
31	Building		.023	.086
32	Wr trade		.347	.067[b]
33	Transpor		.012	.036
34	Fininre		.001	.129[c]
35	Electric		.012	.097
36	Watersan		.017	
37	Communic		.010	.051
38	Socserv		.016	.086[d]
39	Other		.254	

a. Where aggregation was necessary the weights used were total outputs from the I-O table for the nearest year.

b. This value conforms quite closely with the coefficient calculated from the 1978 figures on wholesale and retail trade in KSY (1979, p216).

c. 'Real estate' only.

d. Comprising 'hotels' and 'other services'.

Appendix C
Further Data

Returns to Self-Employed Capital

To calculate the return-to-capital component of the income of the self-employed sector we first assume that the self-employed own the capital they employ in the labour process. In the case of the agricultural sectors we thus assume that all capital is owned by the self-employed farmers. In the case of the non-agricultural sectors (mainly domestic trade) we assume that the self-employed own a fraction of the total capital in each sector equal to the fraction of total output attributable to the self-employed. The values of capital stocks owned by the self-employed by sector are recorded in Table A.4 of Appendix A and were calculated by applying the total capital coefficients compiled for 1966 and 1978 which appear in Table B.1 of Appendix B. For each year, 1966 and 1978, we apply the real interest rate to the capital stocks owned by the self-employed in each sector to arrive at the return to capital owned by them.

To calculate the real interest rate for each year we subtract the rate of change of the wholesale price index from the (actual) nominal interest rate on 6 month time deposits at deposit money banks (DMBs). Note that there was a drastic increase, by fiat, in interest rates on time and savings deposits in September 1965.

Table C-1: Real interest rates, 1966 & 1978

	Nominal interest rate	Rate of change of wholesale price index	Real interest rate
1966	24.0	8.8	15.2
1978	15.5	11.7	3.8

Sources: Nominal interest rates from ESY (1981, Table 15) and ESY (1970, Table 34). Wholesale price index from ESY (1981, Table 136) and ESY (1970, Table 156).

Applying these real interest rates[1] to the total value of capital stocks owned by the self-employed, our estimates for the return-to-capital component of the

---

[1]Compare with those calculated in Hong (1979, Table 7.7). Hong calculates real interest rates on DMB loans rather than DMB deposits.

161

income of the self-employed are 125292mw for 1966 and 486419mw for 1978. These represent, respectively, 30 percent and 8 percent of total self-employed income in those years, and 109 percent and 20 percent of the total investible surplus retained by capitalist enterprises (but see the following).

The returns-to-capital component of self-employed income is merely an imputed category and is not distinguishable as a separate part of flows of self-employed income. On the other hand, the 'interest, dividends and rent' component (returns to personal savings) is separable and is separated in our accounts. We have thus made a distinction between returns to physical capital used in production and returns to financial capital (personal savings).

We also need to know the total number of self-employed workers and employees in the capitalist sectors, from which we can calculate 'wage' rates.

Table C-2: Distribution of workforce (thousands)

	1966[d]	1978
Self-employed:		
Agriculture[a]	5,013	4,713
Non-agriculture[b]	1,347	2,547
Employees[c]	2,299	6,230
	-------	-------
Total employed	8,659	13,490

Source: KSY (1979, Table 28) and KSY (1970, Table 199).

a. Includes all working members of farm households engaged in agriculture, forestry and fishing, as well as the small number of wage-workers in these sectors.
b. Includes the self-employed and family workers in non-farm households (capitalists are also lumped into this group, but only their number and not their income etc).
c. Includes employees (regularly and temporarily employed and daily workers from non-farm households (5,406,000 for 1978) plus wage-workers from farm households (887,000) less wage-workers from farm households who worked in agriculture (63,000).
d. Employment figures for 1966 are not broken down by status in the official figures so it was necessary to extrapolate backwards from the figures for 1970-78. In 1978 the ratio of non-farm self-employed to the total non-farm employed was .320 and this had declined fairly smoothly from .360 in 1970. Linear regression (with a correlation coefficient of .922) suggests that in 1966 the ratio was .396. This is a measure of proletarianization.

Using these figures for numbers of wage-labourers (L) and self-employed (N) with the total incomes (except returns to savings) of these groups calculated in the SAMs for 1966 and 1978 we can find the annual average wage rate of wage-earners and the average annual 'wage' rate of the self-employed.

There is a problem, however, in that we have assumed that total self-employed income (other than returns to savings) is a return to the labour of the self-employed and not a return to the capital used in the relevant sectors. In the self-employed sectors of the economy there is no capital-wage labour relation and

Table C-3:   Average annual wage rates (won)

	1966	1978 current prices	1978 constant prices[c]	Compound growth rate 1966-78[d]
Self-employed[a]	64,858	849,298	178,720	8.8
Wage-labour[b]	139,781	1,325,393	278,907	5.9
Total	84,750	1,069,170	224,989	8.5

Source: Price indexes - KSY (1979, Table 250) and KSY (1970, Table 210).

a. We can calculate a rough 'wage' for the self-employed in 1978 from official figures by taking an average (weighted by the numbers of agricultural and non-agricultural workers) of the wage rate in agriculture (by occupation) and in wholesale and retail trade (the industry). The result is 1,123,808w. *Source*: EPB, Social Indicators (1981, Tables 3.7 & 3.9).

b. These compare with the official figures: annual earnings of regular employees in establishments of 10 or more persons in all industries except agriculture, forestry, fishing and hunting were 80,911 in 1966 and 1,334,412 in 1978 (KSY, 1979, Table 34 & KSY, 1970, Table 217). We have assumed that the ratio of wages in manufacturing to wages in all industries was the same in 1966 as it was over 1971-73.

c. The CPI increased over 1966-78 by a factor of 4.752.

d. Here the growth rate r is given in the formula

$$A(1+r)^t = B$$

where t=12 and A is the 1966 wage level and B is the (constant price) 1978 wage level.

this is why the words 'wage' and 'profits' must be used guardedly. The purpose of separating them at all is simply to try to get at the notion of an economic surplus, potentially investible, so that we can generate within the model a growth rate which corresponds to the usual one of the growth rate of value-added or GDP. Any 'profit' income may be considered to be a part of the investible surplus, even though in the case of the self-employed sectors the largest part of such income is spent on consumption goods and is required as part of the necessary costs of reproducing the labouring ability of the self-employed.

We could therefore calculate a wage for the self-employed by dividing their total income (except returns to savings) less returns to capital by the total number of self-employed workers. In fact, this wage in current won would have been 45,158 for 1966 and 782,298 in 1978 with the latter translating into 164,621 won at constant 1966 prices by the method above. This gives a growth rate of the wage paid to the self-employed for their labour alone of 11.4 percent. The rise in the growth rate of the wage rate for self-employed labour is due to the fall of the real interest rate over the period. In practical terms this distinction between what we might call the total rate of income and the wage rate of self-employed labour is not of much use if we want to examine the effects of income redistribution on the growth rate because the wage rate of self-employed labour is no more than an accounting relation, an imputation, which has no real analogue in terms of flows of money. The self-employed merely sell their products and the proceeds form their income. In practice then we talk of the 'wage' of the self-employed as the total rate of income, v.

Observe that with an official wage rate for the self-employed in 1978 of 1,123,808 (see note a to Table C.3) - 32 percent higher than the one calculated here from the I-O data and the total numbers of self-employed - if we calculate the return to capital ownership by the self-employed we will get a negative rate, that is, negative 'profits'. At the official rate total self-employed income is 8,158,846mw giving a real return on self-employed capital of -15.6 percent. This of course explains why there can remain large sectors of the economy under noncapitalist forms of production, since it would not be profitable for capital to penetrate them under given conditions of production. Capital can, however, transform these conditions of production in, for instance, the wholesale and retail trade sector (especially the wholesale side) and thereby make it profitable. In agriculture, while the imputed return on fixed capital is not as negatively large because of the fact that the official wage rate is lower than in other self-employed sectors, the limitations on the transformation of the conditions of production and mode of production are political rather than technical. Most particularly we refer to the upper limit of 3 hectares on the ownership of land; in recent years powerful interests have been pressing for the abolition of this limit.

Price Indices

Notes to and sources for Table C.4 Columns 1 and 2: In order to construct the domestic price index it was necessary to extract the imported component from the reported price indexes. To do this we calculated a separate price index for imported goods and used the proportions of imported goods in each sector's total supply (see Tables C.5 and C.6) to calculate the domestic price index. Throughout the compilation of the price indexes (domestic, imported and exported), there were problems with mismatching classifications and incomplete series. The most detailed sectoral breakdown of import prices is in PSS (1977). This breakdown only applies to the years 1971-76 inclusive. The indexes for 1966-70 and 1977-78 were taken from often more aggregated categories and found, respectively, in ESY (1974, Table 133) and KSY (1979, Table 256). We calculated separate import price indexes only for those (22) sectors which imported more than 5 percent of their total 1978 supply.

In the calculation of export price indexes similar limitations applied here as for the import price indexes. However, prior to 1971 export price indexes were not separately published so we have used the general (domestic plus imported) wholesale price indexes for the closest category in the 1966-70 period. This means that the rise in export price indexes will very likely be overstated a little since we know from later years that export prices do not rise as quickly as domestic prices. We have calculated separate export prices only for those (26) sectors which exported more than 5 percent of their total domestic product in 1978.

The price indexes for capitalists' consumption and government presented a

Table C-4: Price indexes 1978 (1966 = 1) and export/domestic price ratios, 1968 & 1978

	(1) Domestic sales[a]	(2) Export sales[b]	(3) Export/domestic price 1968	(4) 1978
1 Grain	7.446	7.446	.884	.592
2 Otherag	10.345	10.345	.902	.994
3 Forest	4.896	1.557	.947	.904
4 Fishery	10.972	5.714	1.000	.992
5 Coal	6.810	6.810	.911	2.049
6 Othmin	16.787	9.702	.992	.933
7 Profood	4.247	3.026	1.454	.770
8 Bevstob	2.761	2.761	1.114	.985
9 Fibresp	2.104	2.591	.956	1.014
10 Textfab	2.202	2.266	.823	.890
11 Fintext	3.583	3.189	.852	.903
12 Lumply	3.531	2.648	1.000	.956
13 Woodpro	3.310	2.648	.978	.729
14 Pulpap	3.389	3.389	.892	.896
15 Print	2.661	2.661	1.000	.970
16 Leather	6.866	2.437	.930	.534
17 Rubber	1.230	3.152	1.000	1.721
18 Baschem	4.524	1.346	.828	.915
19 Othchem	2.388	1.387	.753	.796
20 Chfert	5.411	1.032	.952	.761
21 Petcopr	9.823	9.823	1.355	1.038
22 Nonmet	4.106	1.929	.963	1.098
23 Irost	2.620	2.620	.877	1.024
24 Steelpr	3.718	3.302	.707	1.104
25 Nonferm	2.762	3.347	.779	.869
26 Fabrmet	1.904	3.650	.802	.874
27 Nonelm	5.141	1.015	.763	.778
28 Elmach	1.540	1.033	.595	.682
29 Transeq	3.072	0.839	.810	.975
30 Miscman	5.773	2.422	.991	.834
31 Build	3.670	3.670	1.000	1.000
32 Trade	4.993	2.584	.978	.912
33 Transto	5.133	2.584	.978	.912
34 Fininre	3.670	3.670	1.000	1.000
35 Electr	2.103	2.103	1.000	1.000
36 Water	3.221	3.221	1.000	1.000
37 Commun	3.352	2.584	1.000	1.000
38 Socserv	3.948	3.948	1.000	1.000
39 Other	4.264	1.955	1.000	1.000
All commodities	4.982	2.584		
40 Foreign	2.552	2.552	1.000	1.000
41 Labour	9.482	9.482	1.000	1.000
42 Selfem	13.095	13.095	1.000	1.000
43 Capscon	5.888	5.888	1.000	1.000
44 Govern	5.629	5.629	1.000	1.000

a. Prices of goods produced domestically and sold domestically.
b. Prices of goods produced domestically and sold overseas only.

problem since there is no real object which has a measurable price. We employ the fiction that capitalists-as-consumers and the government provide some sort of service necessary to production. To arrive at price indexes for these two sectors we first assume that there is no change in the 'productivity' of the services they provide so that changes in the total values of their flows of services between 1966 and 1978 are due to price changes alone. We assume that these price changes simply reflect the increased money costs of reproduction of capitalists-as-consumers and government, so that their new prices represent the average rise in prices of goods they consumed in 1966 weighted by their consumption coefficients. Since the government 'sells' to capitalists' consumption (taxes) and since the government 'buys' from itself (customs duties on government imports) we first solve for the government price iteratively (it converges to 4 decimal places in 3 iterations) and then for capitalists' consumption. *Sources for Table C.4 Columns 1 and 2*: Imports: KSY (1979, Table 256); ESY (1974, Table 183). Labour and the self-employed: see Table C.3

Notes to and sources for Table C.4 Columns 3 and 4: For sectors 1-30, the ratios of export to domestic prices are from a detailed price comparison survey by Nam and also one by Kim & Westphal who measured the 'nominal rate of protection' as the difference between the world price and the domestic price of a commodity. We have assumed that this world price, bearing in mind that these number-gatherers were in pursuit of differences between domestic and import prices, is the export price. These figures were reported at a 152-level of aggregation and apply to the years 1968 and 1978. We assume that the 1968 price differences applied also in 1966. The sources are Nam (1981, Annex Table 1) who took his 1968 figures from Westphal & Kim (1977, Annex Table 2B).

Aggregation into our sectoral distribution was carried out on the basis of subsectoral contributions to sectoral exports. For 1968 these are contained in Westphal & Kim (1977, Annex Table 1); for 1978 we used the 1978 I-O tables supplemented in one or two cases by KSY (1979, Table 132).

Sectors 31, 34-38 and 40-44 are service sectors which have zero or negligible exports and since there are no figures available we assume that the ratio of export to domestic prices is 1. The same reasoning is used to justify the setting of the export-domestic price ratio of Sector 39, which is a big export earner, equal to 1. In Sectors 32 and 33, domestic trade and transport and storage, are recorded the trade and transport margins of all other exports, and so the export-domestic price ratio of these is taken to be the weighted (by export value) average of export prices of Sectors 1-30.

Sectoral Characteristics

Notes to Tables C.5 and C.6

a.   Non-competitive imports are classified differently from competitive imports and in fewer sectors. We have allocated them to the sectors where the bulk of the imported product would be produced if it were produced domestically. In the case of non-competitive imports in the undifferentiated 'machinery' sector we have allocated them to nonelectrical machinery, electrical machinery and transport

Table C-5: Sectoral characteristics, 1966

		prop. of total supply imported[a]	prop. of inputs imported	share of total exports	prop. of product exported	total domestic product(mw)
1	Grain	4.88	3.76	1.52	0.69	250866.5
2	Otherag	9.23	2.13	1.65	1.02	184349.0
3	Forest	2.32	1.17	0.01	0.06	27400.0
4	Fishery	0	6.39	2.14	9.92	24516.8
5	Coal	.03	1.25	0.25	1.84	15412.5
6	Othmin	10.75	2.10	5.36	40.13	15149.5
7	Profood	6.63	9.32	6.18	7.07	99161.2
8	Bevstob	.23	1.18	1.96	3.89	57019.4
9	Fibresp	6.18	43.30	3.47	9.71	40593.2
10	Textfab	6.32	10.67	5.61	14.90	42766.1
11	Fintext	1.24	4.88	10.02	18.46	61606.9
12	Lumply	33.37	51.67	6.98	34.99	22636.6
13	Woodpro	2.58	5.31	0.22	3.60	6825.4
14	Pulpap	17.99	19.63	0.27	1.61	18861.1
15	Print	1.77	4.91	0.14	1.00	15295.5
16	Leather	2.61	4.91	0.34	4.53	8529.8
17	Rubber	1.16	31.42	2.25	17.38	14675.0
18	Baschem	57.51	21.51	0.20	3.16	7046.3
19	Othchem	28.22	20.58	0.05	0.21	24708.9
20	Chfert	73.58	9.68	0.00	0.00	4889.7
21	Petcopr	26.08	24.50	1.49	4.64	36348.8
22	Nonmet	6.74	5.77	1.14	5.73	22633.7
23	Irost	22.57	34.20	0.02	0.31	7728.2
24	Steelpr	37.30	24.38	1.87	13.41	15864.2
25	Nonferm	34.55	17.27	0.57	11.99	5433.8
26	Fabrmet	33.98	24.91	1.08	10.17	12094.6
27	Nonelm	76.30	15.19	0.87	8.82	11230.1
28	Elmach	39.39	15.79	1.38	10.34	15178.4
29	Transeq	43.06	16.40	0.35	1.60	24989.4
30	Miscman	8.12	18.15	4.47	24.36	20828.5
31	Build	0	7.78	3.09	2.69	130474.5
32	Trade	0	0.78	6.12	4.00	173569.2
33	Transto	1.38	4.82	9.15	13.38[b]	77655.7
34	Fininre	.10	0.20	0.11	0.19	62012.3
35	Electr	0	0.78	0.70	4.05	19501.3
36	Water	0	1.36	0.09	2.96	3337.1
37	Commun	.56	0.81	0.05	0.52	11065.3
38	Socserv	1.59	2.30	2.41	2.26	120860.4
39	Other	11.78	2.09	16.43	30.34	61464.0
40	Foreign	0	0.00	0	0.00	208925.4
41	Labour	0	1.56	0	0.00	321357.4
42	Selfem	0	1.41	0	0.00	412496.4
43	Capscon	0	1.15	0	0.00	126188.4
44	Govern	0	4.87	0	21.67	152584.1

Source: I-O Tables 1966

equipment so that total (competitive and non-competitive) imports of machinery are in the proportions contained in the trade data (ESY, 1967, p287). Imports in both 1966 and 1978 are taken at c.i.f. value and thus exclude customs duties and import commodity taxes.

b. This is only an export sector by accounting procedure since the transport margins on all other exports are recorded in this sector. The same comment will apply to this sector and to the domestic trade sector (32) in Table C.6, for 1978.

Sectoral Breakdowns

The sectoral breakdowns appear below and are presented first as category 1 against 2, then as 1 against 3 (for definitions of categories see Chapter 4, Section 1). Note that although transport and storage (Sector 33) appears to fall into the 'export-oriented' category it only does so in an accounting sense since the transport margins of all exports are recorded here. The same comment will apply to this and the domestic trade sector (32) for 1978.

Table C-6: Sectoral characteristics, 1978

		prop. of total supply imported[a]	prop. of inputs imported	share of total exports	prop. of product exported	total domestic product(mw)
1	Grain	8.51	0.21	0.13	0.32	2861789.0
2	Otherag	10.40	0.64	1.29	3.38	2717335.5
3	Forest	53.31	0.39	0.32	6.86	329401.1
4	Fishery	1.78	10.24	2.84	27.20	742640.5
5	Coal	4.39	7.26	0.00	0.01	214609.0
6	Othmin	80.10	1.40	0.56	13.77	288537.1
7	Profood	12.14	15.61	2.56	7.90	2306979.0
8	Bevstob	0.86	4.87	0.21	1.03	1460891.6
9	Fibresp	2.95	24.95	2.48	15.02	1175676.3
10	Textfab	8.50	5.20	5.58	32.93	1204371.6
11	Fintext	1.70	7.38	16.37	60.18	1934583.5
12	Lumply	0.76	50.45	2.96	37.51	561576.9
13	Woodpro	2.57	5.80	0.40	26.91	106527.8
14	Pulpap	19.09	21.56	0.31	4.80	466926.5
15	Print	4.05	2.40	0.11	3.39	228102.2
16	Leather	15.13	31.04	3.85	52.79	518510.9
17	Rubber	1.58	23.19	3.79	49.23	548289.7
18	Baschem	42.28	13.56	0.59	8.47	498196.8
19	Othchem	17.35	22.48	1.40	5.50	1805418.6
20	Chfert	4.33	8.99	1.08	25.16	304515.8
21	Petcopr	13.03	55.08	1.22	4.61	1889953.5
22	Nonmet	6.25	4.63	1.65	14.84	790456.2
23	Irost	17.93	28.18	0.07	0.77	666048.1
24	Steelpr	26.61	19.83	3.85	22.06	1241142.6
25	Nonferm	44.06	27.26	0.39	11.90	231001.6
26	Fabrmet	8.16	19.19	3.71	41.51	636264.6
27	Nonelm	65.11	17.42	0.91	9.97	650042.1
28	Elmach	26.14	23.91	9.23	33.30	1971918.8
29	Transeq	28.22	21.41	6.67	35.10	1350889.4
30	Miscman	19.02	13.11	6.35	57.47	786209.7
31	Build	0.08	6.04	0.15	0.26	4005945.0
32	Trade	0.60	1.30	6.18	10.47[b]	4199602.5
33	Transto	4.59	9.39	9.59	27.93[b]	2441356.8
34	Fininre	1.75	1.94	0.61	2.14	2025948.8
35	Electr	0.27	4.96	0.05	0.47	694892.4
36	Water	0.52	1.61	0.00	0.12	54028.9
37	Commun	5.51	0.68	0.35	7.72	318779.2
38	Socserv	0.57	2.01	0.93	1.83	3617585.8
39	Other	11.44	6.35	1.27	8.73	1033034.7
40	Foreign	0	0.00	0	0.00	7792632.5
41	Labour	0	1.68	0	0.00	8257198.7
42	Selfem	0	1.61	0	0.00	6165907.2
43	Capscon	0	1.41	0	0.00	4306117.5
44	Govern	0	3.99	0	0.00	4244308.5

Source: I-O Table 1978

Table C-7: Breakdown of sectors into categories, 1966

	Export oriented	Domestically oriented
Domestic inputs	6,11,39	5,7,8,13,15,16,20,22 31,32,33,34,35,36,37,38
Imported inputs	10,12,17,24 25,26,28,30	9,14,18,19,21 23,27,29

	Export oriented	Domestically oriented
Domestic supply	10,11,17,30	5,7,8,9,13,15,16,22 31,32,33,34,35,36,37,38
Imported supply	6,12,24,25, 26,28,39	14,18,19,20, 21,23,27,29

Table C-8: Breakdown of sectors into categories, 1978

	Export oriented	Domestically oriented
Domestic inputs	6,10,11,13 20,22	5,8,15,31,32,33,34 35,36,37,38,39
Imported inputs	9,12,16,17,24,25 26,28,29,30	7,14,18,19,21 23,27

	Export oriented	Domestically oriented
Domestic supply	9,10,11,12,13,17 20,22,26	5,8,15,31,32,33,34 35,36,37,38
Imported supply	6,16,24,25,28 29,30	7,14,18,19,21 23,27,39

Appendix D
Treatment of Fixed Capital

To be theoretically correct, we should treat fixed capital as a joint product of the production process, after Sraffa (1960, Chapter X). In addition to its annual product, each yearly production process finishes up with its capital stock one year older.

Combining the price and output equations 2 and 4 of Chapter 3 we obtain

$$P\hat{X} = PA\hat{X} + rPB\hat{X}$$

where the hat ($\hat{}$) indicates a matrix formed by diagonalizing a vector, and the matrices A and B and the vectors P and X have been augmented to include labour (ignoring the other value-added sectors). For a particular industry j

(1) $\quad P_j X_j = \Sigma P_i a_{ij} X_j + r \Sigma P_i b_{ij} X_j.$

If M_a is the quantity of machines of a certain type and of a certain age a, where $0 \le a \le n$ and n is the life-span of M, then the value of the capital stock of a production process which begins with new machines only can be written $P_{mo} M_o$ where P_{mo} is the new price of the machine. For simplicity it is assumed that there is only one type of machine. Each process produces fixed capital one year older. In the first year in industry j, we can write

$$\Sigma P_i a_{ij} X_j + (1+r) P_{mo} M_o = P_j X_j + P_{m1} M_1.$$

In the second year

$$\Sigma P_i a_{ij} X_j + (1+r) P_{m1} M_1 = P_j X_j + P_{m2} M_2$$

and so on, until in the last year

$$\Sigma P_i a_{ij} X_j + (1+r) P_{m,n-1} M_{n-1} = P_j X_j$$

and the machines are scrapped.

Multiplying these n equations respectively by $(1+r)^{n-1}$, $(1+r)^{n-2}$, ..., $(1+r)$, 1 and adding them we obtain:

$$[1/r][(1+r)^n - 1](\Sigma P_i a_{ij} X_j) + (1+r)^n P_{mo} M_o$$

$$= [1/r][(1+r)^n - 1] P_j X_j$$

since

$$[1/r][(1 + r)^n - 1] = 1 + (1+r) + (1+r)^2 + ... + (1+r)^n.$$

Multiplying through by $r/[(1+r)^n - 1]$ we obtain

(2) $\quad P_jX_j = \Sigma P_i a_{ij} X_j + \{r(1+r)^n/[(1+r)^n - 1]\} P_{mo}M_o.$

Comparing equation 2 with 1 in which the replacement cost of capital goods is $\Sigma P_i b_{ij} X_j$, we can see that the difference between the joint product and no-joint-product treatments of fixed capital lies in the factor s, where s is defined in:

$$r(1+r)^n/[(1+r)^n - 1] = r\{1/[1 - (1+r)^{-n}]\} = r.s.$$

The factor s is large for small n (short life-spans of machinery) and for small r (low profit rates), but small for large n and large r. Thus empirically the treatment of fixed capital as a joint product, although always infeasible, becomes unnecessary if the profit rate is high or the average life-span of capital goods is long. For example, if r is 10 percent and n is 16 years (buildings, with an average life-span of around 50 years, usually make up the largest part of capital stocks) then s is 1.3.

Note that Sraffa assumes that machines operate at constant efficiency - they do not gradually deteriorate over their working lives. If it were otherwise, the price of the product would change each year with the efficiency of the machine. This is a 'one-horse shay' deterioration function. Financial depreciation, on the other hand, is assumed to be of straight-line form, with equal quantum parts of the value of the machine passed on to the product each year.

Appendix E
Deriving the Reduced Form from the More General Model

The first model below, equations 1 to 12, is a general equilibrium model involving many nonlinearities. Having written it down, the next step is to show how it can be modified so that it can be solved for prices of production, balanced growth outputs and maximal growth and profit rates in the manner specified in Chapter 3. This involves, in addition to the assumption of uniform growth and profit rates, closing the model by turning several nonlinear relationships into linear ones. Nonlinearities remain only in the determination of profit and investment.

There are n domestic sectors, a foreign sector (producing a single, composite imported good), a labour sector, a self-employed sector, a capitalists' consumption sector and an investment activity. We have the following set of relationships:

(1) $\quad X = AX + E + C_w + C_v + C_c + C_g + gB_dX$

(2) $\quad M^T = mX + C_{wm} + C_{vm} + C_{cm} + C_{gm} + gb_mX$

(3) $\quad L = a_LX + L_g$

(4) $\quad N = a_NX$

(5) $\quad Y_c = (1 - s_c)\pi = (1 - s_c)r_c(PB_dX + \bar{\epsilon}P_mb_mX)$

(6) $\quad Y_g = T_x + T_f + T_w + T_v + T_c + T_g$

(7) $\quad P = PA + \bar{\epsilon}P_mm + wa_L + va_N + t_x + r_c(PB_d + \bar{\epsilon}P_mb_m)$

(8) $\quad \bar{\epsilon}P_mM^T = PE + T_f + S_f$

(9) $\quad Y_w = PC_w + \bar{\epsilon}P_mC_{wm} + T_w + S_w$

(10) $\quad Y_v = PC_v + \bar{\epsilon}P_mC_{vm} + T_v + S_v$

(11) $\quad Y_c = PC_c + \bar{\epsilon}P_mC_{cm} + T_c$

(12) $\quad Y_g = PC_g + \bar{\epsilon}P_mC_{gm} + T_g + S_g$

where		dimension
A	coefficient matrix of domestic intermediate inputs into domestic industries	$n \times n$
a_c	input coefficients for capitalists' consumption	$n \times 1$
a_L	input coefficients for labour in productive sectors	$n \times 1$
a_{Lg}	input coefficient for labour in the government sector	1
a_N	input coefficient for self-employed labour	$n \times 1$
B_d	matrix of capital coefficients for domestically produced capital goods in productive sectors	$n \times n$
b_f	vector of capital coefficients for producing a basket of imports	$1 \times n$
b_m	vector of capital coefficients for imported capital goods used in productive sectors	$n \times 1$
b_{mf}	capital coefficient for imported capital goods used in producing the import basket	1
c	price of capitalists' consumption services	1
C_c, C_{cm}	vector of capitalists' consumption of domestic/imported goods	$1 \times n+1$
C_g, C_{gm}	vector of government consumption of domestic/imported goods	$1 \times n+1$
C_v, C_{vm}	vector of self-employed consumption of domestic/imported goods	$1 \times n+1$
C_w, C_{wm}	vector of workers' consumption of domestic/imported goods	$1 \times n+1$
E	vector of sectoral export volumes	$1 \times n$
e^m	sectoral export volumes per basket of imports	$1 \times n$
e^x	share of exports in sectoral outputs	$n \times 1$
G	total demand for government services (measured in units of government consumption)	1
g	uniform growth rate of output	1
I_d	gross investment in domestic capital goods	$1 \times n$

I_m	gross investment in imported capital goods	1
K	total 'demand' for capitalists-as-consumers (measured in units of capitalists' consumption fund)	1
L	total demand for labour (measured in units of workers' consumption fund) in productive sectors	1
L_g	demand for labour in the government sector	1
M^T	total import volume (a composite commodity)	1
m	vector of imported intermediate input coefficients	n x 1
N	total demand for self-employed workers (measured in units of the self-employed consumption fund)	1
P	average (over domestically sold and exported goods) unit producer prices of domestic goods	n x 1
P_d	domestic unit producer prices of domestic goods	n x 1
$\bar{P}_e$	unit producer prices of domestically produced exports in domestic currency	n x 1
$\bar{P}_m$	c.i.f. price of the import basket in foreign currency	1
r_c	profit rate net of taxes on profits but including depreciation and the part of profits payable to the capitalists' consumption fund (& including returns to the capital ownership of workers & the self-employed)	1
r	rate of profit when profit excludes the capitalists' consumption fund but is otherwise the same as r_c	1
s_c	capitalists' saving rate out of profits net of taxes	1
S_f	foreign savings in domestic currency	1
S_g	government savings	1
S_v	savings of the self-employed less returns to their capital-ownership (i.e. on past savings)	1
S_w	workers' savings less returns to capital-ownership (i.e. on past savings)	1
T_c	taxes on capitalists' consumption	1
T_f	foreign aid in domestic currency	1

T_g	taxes on government spending	1
T_v	taxes on the self-employed less government transfer payments	1
T_w	taxes on workers less government transfer payments	1
T_x	taxes on production (indirect taxes less subsidies, customs duties on intermediate and capital goods imports, taxes on profits)	1
t_c	taxes on capitalists' consumption per unit of capitalists' consumption	1
t_f	foreign aid per unit of import value	1
t_g	taxes on government per unit of government consumption	1
t_v	taxes on the self-employed per unit of their consumption expenditure	1
t_w	taxes on workers per unit of their consumption expenditure	1
t_x	taxes on production per unit value of output	1
u	price of government services	1
v	'wage rate' of the self-employed	1
w	wage rate of wage-workers	1
X	vector of sectoral outputs	1 x n
Y_c	total capitalists' consumption income	1
Y_g	total government income	1
Y_v	total income of self-employed	1
Y_w	total income of wage-workers	1
ϵ	exchange rate	1
π	total profits net of taxes	1
ϕ_c, ϕ_{cm}	capitalists' consumption of domestic/imported goods per unit of capitalists' consumption	1 x n+1
ϕ_g, ϕ_{gm}	government consumption of domestic/imported goods per unit of government consumption	1 x n+1

ϕ_v, ϕ_{vm} self-employed consumption of domestic/imported goods   1 x n+1
per unit of self-employed consumption

ϕ_w, ϕ_{wm} workers' consumption of domestic/imported goods   1 x n+1
per unit of workers' consumption

In this model, prices P are average prices, averages of domestic and export prices, i.e.

$$P = P_d(I - \hat{e}^x) + P_e\hat{e}^x$$

where the hat (^) indicates a diagonal matrix formed from the vector e^x. In the more-linear model below we preserve this and do not disaggregate into domestic and export prices.

Starting with the commodity balance, equation 1. Here investment I_d has been expressed as an increment to domestically produced capital stocks at the uniform growth rate g, so that

$$I_d = gB_d X.$$

Sectoral exports of each domestic product per unit of the basket of imports M^T can be written as $e^m = E/M^T$, and

$$E = e^m M^T.$$

Domestic consumption of workers, C_w, can be similarly written in terms of consumption per worker

$$C_w = \phi_w L$$

and the same for self-employed and capitalists' consumption

$$C_v = \phi_v N$$

$$C_c = \phi_c K.$$

The government sector is not quite so straightforward. It will be argued below that the output of the government sector can be interpreted as a 'physical' index of services provided to other sectors in exchange for taxes, G, with a corresponding price, so that government consumption can be written

$$C_g = \phi_g G.$$

Putting these together, equation 1 can be rewritten as

(1') $X = AX + e^m M^T + \phi_w L + \phi_v N + \phi_c K + \phi_g G + gB_d X.$

The procedure is much the same for reinterpreting equation 2. Here, investment in imported goods has been written as an increment to the stocks of imported capital goods at the unifrom growth rate g, i.e.

$$I_m = gb_m X.$$

By the definitions of ϕ_{wm}, ϕ_{vm}, ϕ'_{cm} and ϕ_{gm} we get

$$(2') \quad M^T = mX + \phi_{wm}L + \phi_{vm}N + \phi_{cm}K + \phi_{gm}G + gb_mX.$$

In equation 3 we can use our 'physical' index of government services G to define a labour input coefficient in the government sector, a_{Lg}, so that it becomes

$$(3') \quad L = a_LX + a_{Lg}G.$$

Equation 4 is unchanged,

$$(4') \quad N = a_NX.$$

In equation 5, the fund for capitalists' consumption is a fixed proportion $(1 - s_c)$ of total profits, where the latter depends on the rate of profit, relative prices and output proportions (the last two affecting the total value of the fixed capital stock on which the profit rate is calculated). First of all, capitalists' consumption is thought of as depending on the 'physical inputs' of capitalists-as-consumers (i.e. some 'service' provided by capitalists in the production process) and the 'price' at which these services are provided. Formally, then, capitalists' consumption is treated analogously to labour income derived from the production process. The physical inputs are provided by a certain 'number' of capitalists K, measured in units of the consumption fund, and this number is assumed to stand in fixed proportion, a_c, to the output of the sector in which it forms an input, in exactly the same way that labour does. Symbolically, $a_c = K/X$.

The price of this 'productive activity', c, is discussed below. In order to linearize equation 5, we interpret the capitalists' consumption fund not as a proportion of total profits but as the product of the 'number' of capitalists and the price of their services (which is fixed in the base years), i.e.

$$Y_c = cK.$$

Here we are interested in the output side - in the determination of the number of capitalists-as-consumers K (the number of units of the capitalists' consumption fund) - so that equation 5 becomes

$$(5') \quad K = a_cX.$$

In equation 6, government income Y_g depends on taxes levied on each of the productive, foreign and value-added sectors. In practice, as in equation 6, these taxes are value magnitudes and the tax rates (eg. t_x) are the values of taxes on the relevant sector per unit of output. If we think of these taxes as payments for government services then their values will depend on the amount (volume) of these services provided to each sector and the price of the service, u. In the case of taxes on production we have for the value measure $T_x = u.\bar{T}_x$ where a bar indicates a physical measure and no bar a value measure. Alternatively, one can think of $\underline{t}_x$ as the tax rate in base year prices and $u.\bar{t}_x$ as the tax rate at the new price u. T_x is then a specific tax whose value depends on relative prices. Our physical tax rate now becomes

$$\bar{t}_x = \bar{T}_x/X.$$

Similarly the value of taxes on labour T_w can be thought of as a volume of government services $\bar{T}_w$ supplied to workers at a price u, $T_w = u.\bar{T}_w$, and we can write

$$\bar{t}_w = \bar{T}_w/L.$$

Exactly the same applies to the self-employed, government and foreign sectors.

Government income is considered to be a product of the volume of government services provided to all sectors and the price at which they are provided:

$$Y_g = u.G .$$

Here we are interested in the determination of the volume of government services; this depends on the 'physical tax rates' defined above, and on sectoral outputs. In place of equation 6 we have

$$(6') \quad G = \bar{t}_x X + \bar{t}_f M^T + \bar{t}_w L + \bar{t}_v N + \bar{t}_c K + \bar{t}_g G.$$

Now for the price equations. In equation 7 the valuations of the first four types of input (domestic intermediate, imported intermediate, wage-labour and self-employed labour) are clear. From the definitions of t_x and $\bar{t}_x$ above we can write

$$t_x = u.\bar{t}_x .$$

Unit profit in equation 7, $r_c(PB_d + \bar{\epsilon P}_m b_m)$, is earned at the uniform rate r_c on the unit value of fixed capital in each sector. This (after-tax) profit rate is the rate before the deduction of the capitalists' consumption fund from total profits. This fund we have interpreted as a fixed proportion of sectoral physical outputs evaluated at the price of 'inputs' of capitalists' consumption. If we write the profit rate on fixed capital after deduction of capitalists' consumption as r, then we have

$$r_c(PB_d + \bar{\epsilon P}_m b_m) = r(PB_d + \bar{\epsilon P}_m b_m) + ca_c$$

and equation 7 can be written as

$$(7') \quad P = PA + \bar{\epsilon P}_m + wa_L + va_N + ca_c + u\bar{t}_x + r(PB_d + \bar{\epsilon P}_m b_m) .$$

The foreign exchange balance, equation 8, must also be linearized. The value of foreign aid, T_f, is written as the product of a volume of services $(T_f = t_f M^T)$ and the (domestic) price of these services u, i.e.

$$T_f = u\bar{t}_f M^T .$$

Foreign savings, S_f, are considered to be a surplus which, like investible profits in the productive sectors, is allocated in the price solution among all sectors on the basis of fixed capital stocks at the uniform rate of profit r. This is due to the nature of the solution process. If we write the vector of fixed capital stocks employed in producing each unit of the output of the foreign sector (a composite imported commodity) as (b_f, b_{mf}) then equation 8 can be written equivalently to equation 7':

$$\bar{\epsilon P}_m M^T = PE + u\bar{t}_f M^T + r(Pb_f + \bar{\epsilon P}_m b_{mf}).$$

It will soon become clear why this step is made. In practice $(b_f, b_{mf}) = 0$ since the model can deal only with inputs 'produced' domestically, so that, dividing through by M^T, we obtain

(8') $\quad \epsilon \bar{P}_m = Pe^m + u\bar{t}_f$.

In the case of the labour income equation 9, note first that $Y_w = wL$; also $C_w = \phi_w L$, $C_{wm} = \phi_{wm}L$ and $T_w = u\bar{t}_w L$. If we were to write the vector of fixed capital stocks in the labour sector per worker as b_w and allow the model's solution process to interpret workers' savings (net of returns to previous savings), S_w, as 'profit' earned on this capital at the going rate then

$$S_w = rPb_w L .$$

Making these substitutions into equation 9 and dividing through by L we obtain

$$w = P\phi_w + \epsilon \bar{P}_m \phi_{wm} + u\bar{t}_w + rPb_w .$$

In practice, $b_w = 0$ and the model solves for

(9') $\quad w = P\phi_w + \epsilon \bar{P}_m \phi_{wm} + u\bar{t}_w$.

The implication of this is that net workers' savings are taken each year and allocated as investible surplus to the productive sectors.

Exactly analogous reasoning gives an expression for the 'wage' of self-employed labour from equation 10:

(10') $\quad v = P\phi_v + \epsilon \bar{P}_m \phi_{vm} + u\bar{t}_v$.

Similarly, the price equation of capitalists' consumption is derived as the sum of physical inputs into unit consumption evaluated at prices of production (the solution prices), although here there are by definition no savings in Y_c. From equation 11 then,

(11') $\quad c = P\phi_c + \epsilon \bar{P}_m \phi_{cm} + u\bar{t}_c$.

Finally, the same can be done for the price of government services as has been done for labour, observing that $Y_g = u.G$ and that there is no fixed capital used in the production of government services. From equation 12,

(12') $\quad u = P\phi_g + \epsilon \bar{P}_m \phi_{gm} + u\bar{t}_g$.

The implication of this is that government savings are allocated in the solution process to industry for investment with no return to the government; or, more likely, that the government deficit is financed by the surplus of productive sectors.

This completes the transformation of the more general model, equations 1-12, into the near-linear system of equations 1'-12'. The latter is still nonlinear because of the presence of terms like gB_dX and $r\epsilon\bar{P}_m b_m$. In the near-linear system there are $2n + 10$ equations (both equations 1' and 7' consist of n equations each, for the n domestic industries). The endogenous variables number $2n + 12$ and are:

P,X $\qquad$ n-element price and output vectors

M^T,L,N,K,G $\qquad$ output scalars

$\epsilon\bar{P}_m$,w,v,c,u $\qquad$ price scalars

g,r   growth and profit rates.

To complete the system two normalizations are required since the solution provides only relative prices and output proportions. To do this it is first necessary to write the augmented vector of outputs

$$X^* = (X, M^T, L, N, K, G)$$

and the augmented vector of relative prices

$$P^* = (P, \epsilon\bar{P}_m, w, v, c, u).$$

Our normalizations are, for outputs

$(13')$ $J.X^* = 100$

where J is the n + 5 element summing vector $J = (1,1,1 \ldots 1)$, and for prices

$(14')$ $P^*.X' = 1$

where X' is the vector of optimal output proportions such that $J.X' = 100$.

If we write the augmented matrix of input coefficients A^* and the augmented matrix of capital coefficients B^* as follows,

$$A^* = \begin{bmatrix} A & e_m & \phi_w & \phi_v & \phi_c & \phi_g \\ m & 0 & \phi_{wm} & \phi_{vm} & \phi_{cm} & \phi_{gm} \\ a_L & 0 & 0 & 0 & 0 & a_{Lg} \\ a_N & 0 & 0 & 0 & 0 & 0 \\ a_c & 0 & 0 & 0 & 0 & 0 \\ \mathfrak{k}_x & \mathfrak{k}_f & \mathfrak{k}_w & \mathfrak{k}_v & \mathfrak{k}_c & \mathfrak{k}_g \end{bmatrix}$$

$$B^* = \begin{bmatrix} B & b_f & 0 & 0 & 0 & 0 \\ b_m & b_{mf} & 0 & 0 & 0 & 0 \\ 0 & 0 & 0 & 0 & 0 & 0 \\ 0 & 0 & 0 & 0 & 0 & 0 \\ 0 & 0 & 0 & 0 & 0 & 0 \\ 0 & 0 & 0 & 0 & 0 & 0 \end{bmatrix}$$

then the system of equations $1'$-$12'$ can be written as

$$X^* = A^*X^* + gB^*X^*$$

and

$$P^* = P^*A^* + rP^*B^*$$

which, as explained in Chapter 3, can be solved as eigenequations for P^*, X^*, r and g with the normalizations $13'$ and $14'$.

This model has been used to solve for outputs and prices. One of the difficulties with it is that exports are valued at endogenously determined average prices. Not only is this incorrect so far as export and domestic prices are unequal, but export prices should be given exogenously and not determined within the domestic economy. If export prices are given and binding, then we can interpret the activities of the state in providing tax rebates and subsidies to exporters as interventions aimed at modifying the domestic economy to conform to the requirements of trade in the world economy.

In order to have the correct determination of the exchange rate, with exports valued at world prices rather than domestic prices, we can solve the model iteratively. The model above, equations $1'$-$12'$, then becomes a first approximation only. If export prices are regarded as being fixed in the base year at unity then the export proportions are in fact $\bar{P}_e e^m$ (and foreign aid is $\bar{u}t_f$), so that the first solution of the model gives an expression for the exchange rate of

$$\epsilon^1 \bar{P}_m = P^1(\bar{P}_e e^m) + u^1(\bar{u}t_f) .$$

(P^1, u^1) is normalized in the same way as $(\bar{P}_e, \bar{u})$, i.e.

$$\bar{P}_e e^m + \bar{u}t_f = 1 - s_f .$$

Dividing the export coefficients through by (P^1, u^1) and solving again gives

$$\epsilon^2 \bar{P}_m = P^2(\bar{P}_e e^m / P^1) + u^2(\bar{u}t_f / u^1).$$

The process is repeated until P^n converges and the final solution for ϵ is

$$\epsilon^n \bar{P}_m = \bar{P}_e e^m + \bar{u}t_f$$

as desired.

When this iterative procedure is applied to the 1966 Korean data then the exchange rate and growth rate converge to four decimal places in four iterations.

Iteration	1	2	3	4
Exchange rate	.7264	.7359	.7357	.7357
Growth rate	10.581	10.481	10.482	10.482

Bibliography

BOK   Bank of Korea
EPB   Economic Planning Board
ESY   Economic Statistics Yearbook (BOK)
FEER   Far Eastern Economic Review
FSA   Financial Statements Analysis
I-O   Input-Output Tables 1978/Interindustry Tables
       for 1966 (BOK)
KDI   Korea Development Institute (Seoul)
KSY   Korea Statistical Yearbook (ROK)
MMC   Report of the Mining and Manufacturing Census
       (Survey) (ROK, EPB)
NIK   National Income in Korea (BOK)
PSS   Price Statistics Summary (BOK)
RKE   Review of the Korean Economy (BOK)
ROK   Republic of Korea

Adelman, Irma et al. (1969), 'The Korean Sectoral Model' in Irma Adelman (ed.),
    *Practical Approaches to Development Planning: Korea's Second Five-Year
    Plan* (Johns Hopkins Press, Baltimore).
Adelman, Irma & Sherman Robinson (1978), *Income Distribution Policy in
    Developing Countries: A Case Study of Korea*, World Bank Research
    Publication (Oxford University Press).
Amin, S. (1976), *Unequal Development* (Harvester Press Ltd, Hassocks, UK).
Baker, James & Nam Yong Choi (1973), *The Unorganised Money Market in Korea*,
    Centre for Business and Economic Research, Kent State University,
    International Business Series No. 2 (Kent, Ohio).
Balassa, B. (1971), 'Industrial Policies in Taiwan and Korea', *Weltwirtschaftliches
    Archiv*, 106(1).
Ban, Sung Hwan, Pal Yong Moon & Dwight Perkins (1980), *Rural Development*,
    Council on East Asian Studies, Harvard University (Harvard University
    Press, Cambridge, Mass.).
BOK, *Annual Report* 1972 (Seoul, 1973).
BOK, *Chosen Economic Yearbook* 1948 (Seoul).
BOK, *Compilatory Report on the 1975 Input-Output Tables* (Seoul, 1978).
BOK, *Economic Statistics Yearbook*, various issues (Seoul).
BOK, *Financial Statements Analysis* 1979 (Seoul).
BOK, *Input-Output Tables 1978* (Seoul, 1980).
BOK, *Interindustry Tables for 1966* (Seoul, ?).
BOK, *National Income in Korea* 1982 (Seoul, 1982).
BOK, *Price Statistics Summary* 1977 & 1970, Research Department (Seoul).
BOK, *Review of the Korean Economy in 1965* (Seoul, 1966) and various other
    issues.

Brenner, R. (1977), 'The Origins of Capitalist Development: a Critique of Neo-Smithian Marxism', *New Left Review*, No. 104, July.

Bródy, András (1970), *Proportions, Prices and Planning: A Mathematical Restatement of the Labour Theory of Value* (North-Holland Publishing Co., Amsterdam).

Brown, Alan & Joseph Licari (1977), 'Price Formation Models and Economic Efficiency' in Alan Abouchar (ed.), *The Socialist Price Mechanism* (Duke University Press, Durham, North Carolina).

Brown, G. (1973), *Korean Pricing Policies and Economic Development in the 1960s* (Johns Hopkins University Press, Baltimore).

Brun, Ellen & Jacques Hersh (1976), *Socialist Korea: A Case Study in the Strategy of Economic Development* (Monthly Review Press, New York).

Byun, H.Y. & S.H. Kim (1978), 'Modernization of Private Enterprises in the Republic of Korea: A Study of the Fifty Groups' Development Pattern', Institute of Developing Economies, Joint Research Program Series No.7 (Tokyo).

Cardoso, F. & E. Faletto (1979), *Dependency and Development in Latin America* (University of California Press, Berkeley).

Carter, Anne (1970a), *Structural Change in the American Economy* (Harvard University Press, Cambridge, Massachusetts).

Carter, Anne (1970b), 'A linear programming system analyzing embodied technological change', in A. Carter & A. Brody, *Contributions to Input-Output Analysis* (North-Holland Publishing Co., Amsterdam).

Cole, David & Princeton Lyman (1971), *Korean Development: The Interplay of Politics and Economics* (Harvard University Press, Cambridge, Mass.).

Cole, David & Yung Chul Park (1979), 'Financial Development in Korea, 1945-78', KDI Working Paper 7904 (KDI, Seoul).

Cumings, B. (1974), 'American Policy and Korean Liberation' in Frank Baldwin (ed.), *Without Parallel: The American-Korean Relationship Since 1945* (Pantheon Books, New York).

Cumings, B. (1981), *The Origins of the Korean War* (Princeton University Press, Princeton, New Jersey).

Dervis, K., J. de Melo & S. Robinson (1982), *General Equilibrium Models for Development Policy*, World Bank Research Publication (Cambridge University Press).

Dos Santos, T. (1973), 'The Crisis of Development Theory and the Problem of Dependence in Latin America' in H. Bernstein, *Underdevelopment and Development* (Penguin, Harmondsworth).

EPB, *Economic Survey* (for 1968) (ROK, Seoul, 1969).

EPB, *Report of the Mining and Manufacturing Census (Survey)*, various years (ROK, Seoul).

EPB, *Social Indicators in Korea* 1981 (ROK, Seoul, 1981).

Evans, H.D. (1972), *A General Equilibrium Analysis of Protection: The Effects of Protection in Australia* (North-Holland Publishing Co., Amsterdam).

FEER, various issues (Hong Kong).

FEER Asia Yearbook, various issues (Hong Kong).

Frank, C., Kwang Suk Kim & L. Westphal (1975), *Foreign Trade Regimes and Economic Development* (National Bureau of Economic Research, New York).

Foster-Carter, A. (1977), 'North Korea. Development and Self-Reliance: A Critical Appraisal' in G. McCormack & J. Gittings (eds), *Crisis in Korea*, Korea Committee (Spokesman Books, London).

Ganczer, Sandor (1965), 'Price Calculations in Hungary on the Basis of Mathematical Methods', *Economics of Planning*, vol. 5, no. 3.

Gittings J. & G. McCormack (1977), *Crisis in Korea*, Korea Committee (Spokesman Books).

Grajdanzev, Andrew (1944), *Modern Korea* (Institute of Pacific Relations, New York).

Halliday, Jon (1977), 'The Political Background' in McCormack and Gittings, *ibid.*

Hamilton, C. (1983), 'Capitalist Industrialization in East Asia's Four Little Tigers', *Journal of Contemporary Asia*, Vol. 13, No. 1.

Hamilton, C. (1984), 'Class, state and industrialization in South Korea', *IDS Bulletin*, vol. 15, no. 2, April 1984.

Hamilton, C. (1985), 'Linkages with Fixed Capital', mimeo. (National Centre for Development Studies, Australian National University, Canberra)

Han, Kee Chun (1970), *Estimates of Korean Capital and Inventory Coefficients in 1968* (Yonsei University, Seoul).

Han, Woo-Keun (1970), *The History of Korea* (Eul-Yoo Publishing Co., Seoul).

Harcourt, G. (1972), *Some Cambridge Controversies in the Theory of Capital* (Cambridge University Press, London).

Harris, Donald (1982), 'Structural Change and Economic Growth: A Review Article', *Contributions to Political Economy*, Volume 1, March, Cambridge Political Economy Society.

Hatada, Takashi (1969), *A History of Korea* (ABC-CLIO Inc., Santa Barbara, California).

Henderson, Gregory (1968), *Korea: The Politics of the Vortex* (Harvard University Press, Cambridge, Mass.).

Hirshman, A.O. (1958), *The Strategy of Economic Growth* (Yale University Press, New Haven).

Hong, Wontack (1979), *Trade, Distortions and Employment Growth in Korea* (KDI, Seoul).

Hymer, S. (1975), 'The Multinational Corporation and the Law of Uneven Development' in H. Radice (ed.), *International Firms and Modern Imperialism* (Penguin, Harmondsworth).

International Management Institute (1972), *Study on Criteria for Foreign Direct Investment and Joint Ventures in Korea* (Korea University, Seoul), July.

Jacoby, N. (1966), *US Aid to Taiwan* (Praeger).

Japan Emergency Christian Conference on Korean Problems (1983), *Korea Communique* No. 46, February 15, 1983.

Jo, Sung-Hwan & Seong-yawng Park (eds) (1972), *Basic Documents and Selected Papers of Korea's Third Five-Year Economic Development Plan (1972-1976)* (Sogang University).

Johansen, L. (1960), *A Multi-Sectoral Study of Economic Growth* (North-Holland Publishing Co., Amsterdam).

Jones, Leroy & Il Sakong (1980), *Government, Business and Entrepreneurship in Economic Development: The Korean Case*, Council on East Asian Studies, Harvard University (Harvard University Press, Cambridge, Mass.).

Kahn, A. & A. MacEwan (1967), 'A Multi-sectoral analysis of capital requirements for development planning in Pakistan', *Pakistan Development Review*, Vol. VII, No. 4, Winter.

Keim, Willard (1979), *The Korean Peasant at the Crossroads*, Western Washington University, Center for East Asian Studies (Bellingham, Washington).

Kim, Dong-Hi & Yong-Jae Joo (1982), 'Reconsideration of Food Policies in Korea', *Journal of Rural Development*, vol. V, no. 1 (June).

Kim, Joungwon (1975), *Divided Korea: The Politics of Development 1945-1972*, East Asia Research Center, Harvard University (Harvard University Press, Cambridge, Mass.).

Kim, Kwang Suk (1974), 'Outward-looking Industrialization Strategy: The Case of Korea', KDI Working Paper 7407 (September).

Kim, Kwang Suk & Michael Roemer (1979), *Growth and Structural Transformation*, Council on East Asian Studies (Harvard University Press, Cambridge, Mass.).

Kim, Kyong-Dong (1976), 'Political Factors in the Formation of the Entrepreneural Elite in South Korea', *Asian Survey*, vol. XVI, no. 5 (May).

Kim, Seung Hee (1970), *Foreign Capital for Economic Development: A Korean Case Study* (Praeger, New York).

Kim, Sooyong (1982), 'Contract Migration in the Republic of Korea', International Labour Organization, International Migration for Employment Working Paper No. 4.

Kim, Yoon Hyung (1977), 'A 53-Sector Interindustry Projection Model, 1974-1981' in Chuk Kyo Kim (ed.), *Planning Model and Macroeconomic Policy Issues* (KDI, Seoul).

Koopmans, T. (1970), 'Maximal Rate of Growth' in A. Sen (ed.), *Growth Economics* (Penguin, Harmondsworth).

Korea Annual (Hapdong Newsagency, Seoul)

Korea Exchange Bank, *Monthly Review*, Vol 14, No 11, 1980 (Seoul, 1980).

Korea Housing Bank, *Twelfth Annual Report* 1978 (Seoul).

Kravis, I. (1970), 'Trade as a Handmaiden of Growth: Similarities between the Nineteenth and Twentieth Centuries', *Economic Journal*, Vol. LXXX, December.

Kuznets, Paul (1977), *Economic Growth and Structure in the Republic of Korea*, Economic Growth Center, Yale University (Yale University Press, New Haven).

Lee, Eddy (1979), 'Egalitarian Peasant Farming and Rural Development: The Case of South Korea', *World Development*, vol. 7, no. 4/5.

Levitt, Kari (1965), *Input-Output Study of the Atlantic Provinces*, Statistics Canada, Ottawa.

Lewis, A. (1954), 'Economic Development with Unlimited Supplies of Labour', *The Manchester School*, Vol. 22, No. 2.

Lim, Youngil (1981), *Government Policy and Private Enterprise: Korean Experience in Industrialization*, Institute of East Asian Studies, Korea Research Monograph No. 6 (University of California, Berkeley).

Little, I. (1979), 'The Experience and Causes of Rapid Labour-Intensive Development in Korea, Taiwan, Hong Kong and Singapore, and the Possibilities of Emulation', ILO-ARTEP, Asian Employment Programme Working Paper II-1 (February).

Long, Don (1977), 'Repression and Development in the Periphery: South Korea', *Bulletin of Concerned Asian Scholars*, vol. 9, no.2, (April-June).

Luedde-Neurath, Richard (1983), *Import Controls and Export-Oriented Development: A Reexamination of the South Korean Case, 1962-1982*, Institute of Development Studies, University of Sussex (mimeo.)

Lui, Tchin-Ching (1969), 'The Process of Industrialization in Taiwan', *The Developing Economies*, Volume VII, No. 1, March.

Marx, K. (1956), *Capital*, Volume 2 (Progress Publishers, Moscow).

Marx, K. (1973), *Grundrisse* (Penguin, Harmondsworth).

Marx, K. (1976), *Capital*, Volume 1 (Penguin, Harmondsworth).

McCormack, G. (1977), 'The South Korean Economy: GNP versus the People' in McCormack & Gittings, *ibid.*

McCune, George (1950), *Korea Today* (George Allen & Unwin Ltd, London).

Moon, Pal Yong (1974), 'A Brief Review of the Evolution of Rice Policy in Korea', KDI.

Moscowitz, K. (1974), 'The Creation of the Oriental Development Company: Japanese Illusions Meet Korean Reality', *Occasional Papers on Korea*, No. 2 (Joint Committee on Korean Studies of the American Council of Learned Societies and the Social Science Research Council).

Murakami, Y., K. Tokoyama & I. Tsukui (1970), 'Efficient paths of accumulation and the turnpike of the Japanese economy' in A. Carter & A. Brody, *Applications of Input-Output Analysis* (North-Holland Publishing Co., Amsterdam).

Murray, R. (1971), 'The internationalisation of capital and the nation state', *New Left Review*, No. 67.

Nam, Chong Hyun (1981a), 'An Analysis of Industry Incentive Policy and the Structure of Protection in Korea', KDI Research Paper 81-10, August (in Korean).

Nam, Chong Hyun (1981b), 'Trade and Industrial Policies, and the Structure of Protection in Korea' in W. Hong & L. Krause (eds), *Trade and Growth of the Advanced Developing Countries in the Pacific Basin* (KDI, Seoul).

OECD (1983), 'Service Lives of Fixed Assets', Economics and Statistics Department, Working Paper No. 4, March.

Pak Ki-Hyuk & Sidney Gamble (1975), *The Changing Korean Village*, Royal Asiatic Society (Shin-Hung Press, Seoul).

Park, Sung-Jo, Taiwhan Shin and Ki Zun Zo (eds) (1980), *Economic Development and Social Change in Korea* (Campus Verlag, Frankfurt).

Pasinetti, L. (1977), *Lectures on the Theory of Production* (Macmillan, London).

Pasinetti, L. (1981), *Structural Change and Economic Growth* (Cambridge University Press, Cambridge).

Payer, Cheryl (1975), 'Pushed into the Debt Trap: South Korea's Export "Miracle"', *Journal of Contemporary Asia*, vol. 5, no. 2.

Ranis, G. (1978), 'The NICs, the Near-NICs and the World Economy' (mimeo.).

ROK, *Korea Statistical Yearbook*, various issues (Seoul).

Rhee, Myung Jai (1981), *International Banks and Financial Markets in Korea*, Korea International Economic Institute (Seoul).

Roxborough, I. (1979), *Theories of Underdevelopment* (Macmillan, London).

Sakong, Il (1980), 'Economic growth and concentration of economic power', *Korea Development Study* (KDI).

Sedjo, Roger (1972), 'The Turning Point for the Korean Economy', in Sung-Hwan Jo & Seong-Yawng Park (eds), *Basic Documents and Selected Papers of Korea's Third Five-Year Economic Development Plan (1972-1976)* (Sogang University).

Sekerka, B., O. Kyn & L. Hejl (1970), 'Price systems computable from input-output coefficients' in Carter & Brody, *Contributions, ibid.*

Shin, Susan (1975), 'Some Aspects of Landlord-Tenant Relations in Yi Dynasty Korea', *Occasional Papers on Korea*, No. 3 (Joint Committee on Korean Studies of the American Council of Learned Societies and the Social Science Research Council).

Sohn Pow-Key, Kim Chol-choon & Hong Yi-sup (1970), *The History of Korea* (Korean National Commission for Unesco, Seoul).

Song, Byung-Nak (1975?), 'Observations on Korean Capital Coefficients', KDI Working Paper 7405 (KDI, Seoul).

Sraffa, P. (1960), *Production of Commodities by Means of Commodities* (Cambridge University Press, Cambridge).

Stone, Richard (1970), *Mathematical Models of the Economy and Other Essays* (Chapman & Hall Ltd, London)

Suh, Suk Tai (1975), *Import Substitution and Economic Development in Korea*, KDI Working Paper 7519 (KDI, Seoul).

Taylor, L. (1979), *Macro Models for Developing Countries* (McGraw-Hill Book Co., New York).

Taylor, L. & F. Lysy (1979), 'Vanishing Income Redistributions; Keynesian Clues about Model Surprises in the Short Run', *Journal of Development Economics*, vol. 16.

Walker, Douglas (1973), 'Socialist Price Formation Models and the Hungarian Economy', Studies in East European and Soviet Planning, Development and Trade, No. 19 (International Development Research Center, Indiana University, Bloomington, Indiana).

Warren, B. (1980), *Imperialism: Pioneer of Capitalism* (New Left Books and Verso, London).

Westphal, L. (1978), 'The Republic of Korea's Experience with Export-Led Industrial Development', *World Development*, Vol. 6, No. 3.

Westphal, L. & Kwang Suk Kim (1977), 'Industrial Policy and Development in Korea', World Bank Staff Working Paper No. 263 (IBRD, Washington D.C.), August.

Westphal, L.E., Y.W. Rhee and G. Pursell (1979), 'Foreign Influences on Korean Industrial Development', *Oxford Bulletin of Economics and Statistics*, vol. 41, no. 4, November 1979.

Wideman, B. (1974), 'The Plight of the South Korean Peasant' in Frank Baldwin (ed.), *ibid.*

Yotopoulos, P. & J. Nugent (1973), 'A Balanced-Growth Version of the Linkage Hypothesis: A Test', *Quarterly Journal of Economics*, Vol. LXXXVII, No. 2 (May).

Index

Accumulation
  constraints on, 52-54, 71, 119-120
  in industrial development, 51, 105,
    107, 110, 114, 119, 121
  primitive, 2, 29, 38, 50, 116
  See also Marx, K.
Adelman & Robinson model, 70, 83,
  108, 135, 149
Adelman, I., 145, 154
Agriculture
  effects of colonialism on, 9-13,
    19-20, 113 See also Colonialism,
    Japanese
  in industrialization process, 39,
    52, 82, 92, 98, 103, 108, 109,
    117
  terms of trade with industry, 39-41,
    73-74, 83, 85, 90, 107, 110
  See also Surplus
Aid, foreign, 3, 50, 111
  in model, 89-91 See also
    Savings, foreign
  See also United States, foreign
    aid; Public Law 480
Allende, S., 76
Army Military Government (AMG),
  22, 30, 32

Balassa, B., 124
Banks, 108, 111, 121
  nationalization of, 37, 46
  See also Curb market; Interest
    rates
Ban, Sung Hwan, 24-25, 31, 39
Bottlenecks (in model interpretation),
  61, 75, 82, 86, 103
Bródy, A. 57, 61-62, 66n17, 68, 77,
  78, 80n
Brown, G., 85, 110n5
Bureacracy, political role of, 23
Byun, H.Y. & S.H. Kim, 32

Capitalists' consumption sector (of
  model) 59, 62, 67, 92, 94,
  137-138, 157
Cardoso, F. & E. Faletto, 113n,
  118n14, See also Dependency theory
Carter, A., 94
Chaeból (family-based industrial
  conglomerates, 32, 35, 46, 49, 83
Collaborators, 21, 23-24
Colonialism
  in general, 1, 18, 52, 111-114, 116
  Japanese in Korea, 2, 3, 8-20, 50,
    52, 113-115
  US in Korea. See United States
  See also Dependency theory;
    Warren
Commercial capital. See Merchant
  capital
Communism, in colonial Korea, 18
Concentration of ownership. See
  Chaeból
Consumption, 51, 64, 66, 67, 92-93,
  110
  utility of, 65
Corporation Law, 13, 14, 15
Cumings, B., 16
Curb market, 37, 47-49, 76, 111
  See also Banks; Finance capital;
    Interest rates

Declaration of Independence (1919),
  18
Democratic Republican Party (DRP),
  28
Dependency theory of underdevelopment, 1, 2, 111-112, 114, 116
Dervis, de Melo & Robinson model, 70
Determinism (in explanation of development, 3
Development
  and dependency theory. See